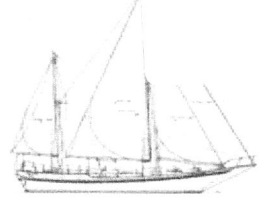

SHARE THE DREAM

Our adventure with family and friends aboard the Sailing Yacht Spectra

from August 2014 to July 2015

By Paul Russell

Welcome to our story, I do hope you enjoy the journey.

This is a memoir from our adventure with friends and family. Many years in the planning, and far too short in the execution, it was life changing for us in many ways.

I started writing this book as a blog a month before we set off. Initially I had great plans to top and tail our adventures with the back story of our lives and include sections specifically dealing with victualling, repairs, customs formalities et al.

After much thought I have decided to keep it as is.

I think it stands alone rather well and reflects the day to day joys, frustrations, and challenges of an Atlantic circuit, written as it happened, warts and all. Perhaps at some point in the future I may well decide to make this into a mini pilot or passport to adventures for the armchair sailor, but for now I am happy to leave it as our story divided up into bite sized chunks so that you can dip in and out as suits your busy lives. My sincerest hope is that you enjoy the read and that it may give you the inspiration to go and have an adventure yourself.

We will go again for sure, before we are too old to climb masts, stay awake half the night on watch, or we simply get too bogged down in the daily grind, but for now it's back to the commute into London every day.

Spectra Vagabond 47

Blue Water Yachts 1980 Hull number 227

SSR 66654   RTYC Ramsgate Kent United Kingdom

Type of Craft: Long keel, full displacement, aux Cutter Rigged Ketch.

Dimensions:	LOA	14.46m + Bowsprit	
	Beam	4.06m	
	LWL	10.97m	
	Draft	1.61m	
	Air Draft	17m	
	Displacement	18144Kg	
	Ballast	5447Kg	(Encapsulated Iron)
Sail Area:	Fore Sail	45.43 m2	(Yankee Furling)
	Stay Sail	16.48 m2	(double as Storm Jib)
	Main Sail	36.33 m2	(3 Reef points)
	Mizzen Sail	9.97 m2	(2 Reef points)
	White Sail area	108.21 m2	
	Cruising Chute	71.6 m2	

	Mizzen Stay Sail	33.2 m2
	Downwind sail	104.8 m2
Tankage:	Fuel	950 Litres (In 2 stainless steel tanks)
	Water	827 Litres (In 2 plastic tanks)
	Holding	90 Litres (Forward)
		90 Litres (Aft)
Engine:	Perkins Sabre	92b – 4 cylinder, 86hp
Anchor:	CQR, Bow	35 kg 80 meters 12mm chain
	Plough Bow	25 kg 20 meters 12mm chain
	Fisherman, Stern	15 kg 10 meters 10 mm chain
	70 meters anchor plait rode.	

CONTENTS

Share the Dream

Contents

Ramsgate to Guernsey

Guernsey to Muxia via Biscay

Muxia to Sines

Sines to Tenerife

Tenerife to the Cape Verde Islands

Cape Verde to Barbados

Barbados & Grenada - Christmas & new year

The Winward Islands Grenada to Dominica

The Leeward Islands, Ilse de Saintes to US Virgin Islands

USVI's to the Bahamas

George Town to Fort Lauderdale

Fort Lauderdale to Wilmington

Wilmington to Bermuda

Bermuda to Flores, Azores

Flores & Horta, Azores

Horta to Brixham

Brixham and Home

RAMSGATE TO GUERNSEY

AUGUST AND SEPTEMBER 2014

Getting ready to go:
16th Aug 2014 to 31st Aug 2014
Position: 46:21.49 N 14:05.38 E

Here we are finally, at the start line and ready to go and I have to say that it has been an absolutely manic couple of weeks. Gemma, my daughter and Duncan (now son-in-law) were married in Lake Bled, Slovenia on the 16th of August and what a wonderful wedding that was. I am sincerely grateful that they accepted not-a-single-one of my ideas and so had one of the best organised and beautiful weddings you could imagine. Having spent a fantastic few days in Slovenia, we bade a fond fare thee well to Gemma and Duncan as they headed off on their honeymoon. We drove back to Ramsgate, Norma, my better half, our son Tony, granddaughter Lily and myself arriving very late on Tuesday the 19th, having caught the ferry with 5 minutes to spare after a 14-hour mad dash across Europe!!

The next morning, we were up bright and early in order to take *Spectra* out with a group of corporate guests, this being our contribution to the Royal Temple Yacht Club (RTYC) Ramsgate Week coffers. Lily impressed the guests with her waitressing skills, before heading up to London with Tony to stay with him for a few days while the honeymoon ran its course. *Spectra* did not play fair and we had a nightmare getting sails up or, indeed, down again. At one point I did think the boat was trying to warn us not to go on our circuit but with Steve, our loyal crew helping and a lot of manual grinding we managed to get her sailing properly for the guests, not an auspicious beginning me thinks! Thursday and Friday were our last sails as a team on *Magnum*, club racing out of Ramsgate. On the Friday, the old crew formed up with Stu on the wheel, Steve on Main, Tommy on foredeck and my good self as navigator, tactician and general gobby bloke in the middle. A real end of an era day, and what a shame that Martin and Jo, *Magnum's* owners, could not be with us, hale, hearty, and full of joy just like the old days. Our thoughts were with them, as we parked *Magnum* up for the last time; how generous they have been over the years, letting us continue to sail their yacht while Jo has been so ill.

On Saturday night we had a farewell meal at Tommy and Sue's, good food, good company, and the drinks certainly flowed. Thanks to Andrew and Paula, I enjoyed a 30-year-old Port which was so good that I completely missed the Pavlova. I made it clear to Paula that she will have to bring one out to Grenada just for me, when we meet up for the New Year's Eve party at the Grenada Yacht Club. The rest of the week passed in a blur, with handing over my projects at NSC Global and O2 whilst finding time to buy all those last-minute things for *Spectra*.

Thursday night started with another excellent meal at Steve's house, followed by final drinks at the yacht club. We walked into the club to find balloons, banners and 30-40 people gathered to see us off. We are so incredibly lucky to have met such a nice bunch of people through our association with the RTYC. Finally, late on Friday, we managed to cram the last tin of beans into a corner and settle down to the worst night's sleep I have ever had as *Spectra* bounced about all night on Ramsgate's outer breakwater pontoon.

Ramsgate to Calais 30th August.
Position: 50:57.4 N 1:51.31 E

Six o'clock found us bleary eyed but up and about getting ready to go. Steve had spent the night aboard getting settled into his cabin and by 7:30 Andy, Sarah, Tommy and Sue had arrived all looking very smart and yachty after a good night's sleep in solid beds. After final goodbyes on the pontoon from Andy K and Mark we left 15 minutes late, which is nothing short of a miracle all things considered. As we turned around the breakwater Andrew, Paula, Bob and Bibi were waving from the harbour wall; the fresh wind explained the manly tear in my eye.

I was so busy waving at people and hugging Norma that only a sharp reminder from Port Control via the VHF kept me the on right side of the channel buoy and in the deep water; how embarrassing would that have been! We had a fairly incident free passage over to Calais, five hours with the wind gusting up to 28 knots for most of the way which certainly cleared the cobwebs.

Saturday night and the Calais Yacht Club opened its doors to seven Ramsgate yacht crews who had either cruised or raced over to see us off, or perhaps to make sure that we did actually leave this time. It was especially nice to see Frank Martin the RTYC Commodore make the journey over by car with Steph and Stan, my replacement as Rear Commodore Cruising, just to say good bye (in fluent French by Frank, the dark horse). Calais was holding a band tournament, with the main square hosting the big stage, whilst the Calais Yacht Club also had its own selection of musicians performing through to 2 am! After a hearty meal and plenty of lubrication three RTYC flag officers were observed burning off excess energy by running through the street fountains in central Calais, much to the amusement of the locals who joined in with those crazy English.

Sunday morning, nursing huge hangovers, we decided on a lazy day repacking and maintaining the boat. After saying good bye to Tommy and Sue, who will be re-joining us in Madeira, Tony Smythe (a friend and experienced theatre nurse) came down to

Spectra and gave Norma a lesson in sewing sutures on a piece of pork belly before he also had to head back to the UK. Neville and Stan also called around to say goodbye and firm up timings for when they are joining us again, Stan in Lisbon, Neville and Elizabeth in Dominica. That left us with Norma, Steve King, Andy and Sarah Beaumont-Hope, plus my good self for the Biscay crossing sometime next week. We plan to be up 'early doors' tomorrow for the trip down to St-Valery-sur-Somme and what feels like the real start of the adventure.

Calais to St Valery Sur Somme
2nd Sep 2014 21:04:34
Position: 50:10.82 N 1:38.72 E

Monday morning 02:00 and we were up and ready to go. The Calais lock gate opened at 02:37 and I watched on as Norma took *Spectra* out through the lock gates, before handing over to both Norma and Steve to complete the first shift and taking us down the French coast towards Cap Griz Nez. A very clear night with shooting stars a-plenty for the first watch, although they did spend a busy few hour dodging ferries and a multitude of fishing boats. All of which, I am happy to say, had gone away by the time I took over two hours later for the next 3-hour watch on my own, before handing over to Andy and Sarah at 08:00. My watch consisted of light fog, lots of clouds but no shipping came anywhere close, so not nearly as interesting as the first watch. I spent three hours willing Old Grey Nose lighthouse to get closer as we punched against nearly three knots of tide. When the sun came up so did Andy and Sarah who got up early for their shift and we had a good chat about life in general over a cup of tea, just about managing to put the world to rights before I went back to bed for a couple of hours. We reached the ATSO buoy outside Valery Sur Somme and had dropped anchor by 13:30. Out came the fishing rods as we had mackerel leaping out of the water all around us on the approach. Needless to say, the sight of our fishing gear scared them all off, but we did spend a nice hour chilling in the sun as we waited for the tide to rise high enough for us to get into the estuary. At 14:45 Norma called up the Capitainierie who confirmed that we had enough water to get in.

Only just! 1:30 hours later I moored *Spectra* with a few more grey hairs to call my own. The entrance channel doubled back on itself completely at one stage and has at least three 90 degree turns along the way. The channel could not have been more than 10 metres wide in parts and the depth sounder alarm beeped all the way in as an accompaniment to my jangling nerves. It actually showed zero on more than one occasion. Having said that, what a lovely port of call! The medieval town is immaculate, and the marina staff very friendly and helpful. We had a beer or three in the marina yacht club to celebrate our entry and a meal aboard. As the river seemed full of fish, Steve and I decided to try out our fish trap overnight, baited with the leftovers from dinner. We had great ideas for fried fish in the morning or maybe even a lobster or two, but all we got for our efforts, minimal that they were, was a trap stuffed to the brim with small hard-shell crabs and certainly nothing you would want to put in a cooking pot. Onwards and upwards! After a breakfast of more traditional fare, and a thorough clean down of *Spectra*, we all piled onto the tourist steam train for a 1-hour trip around the estuary to Le Crotoy. Nothing new here then, get up, have breakfast, and a one-hour commute on a train. It was however a Thomas the Tank Engine type of affair and you could stand out on the carriage foot plate and watch the world go by. Boyhood dreams of being a train driver fulfilled, we headed back to the boat on a boring old diesel train.

A meal, a few beers tonight and we are off at 05:00 in the morning for the 80-mile sail to Fe Camp. That is if we manage to find our way out of the estuary of course!

A Day on the Beach
4th Sep 2014 19:08:57
Position: 50:10.82 N 1:38.72 E

Today's adventure was to negotiate the route out of the Somme estuary and then a shortish hop down the coast to Fe Camp in time for a meal ashore. At 05:00 we were up and about. The plan was for an 05:30 departure, with me on the helm, supported by Andy and Steve with powerful torches, to spot the buoys as we went out. The tide had one hour to rise and the girls were blissfully asleep below full of confidence in the ancient mariners on deck. "What could possibly go wrong with such a cunning plan, I ask you? Especially as we had not one, but three Yacht Masters on deck, two of them Instructors to boot"? Thirty minutes later, directly between a red and green channel buoy, *Spectra* ran aground. No amount of reversing, tweaking the bow thruster or leaning the boat over could get her off. I tried to move her into the middle of the channel in the hope of finding some deep water but eventually the tide turned against us and it became apparent that we were stuck for the day. The predicted tide failed to rise any more, in fact it dropped away rapidly = hard aground.

All of the commotion, not to mention the large thump as we hit the bottom, brought Norma and Sarah on deck, and it was all hands to the pumps if you will excuse the pun. After plumbing the depth all round I decided to lean the boat on her port side if possible. Initially we hung Andy out on the end of the main boom, and later a flare box full of chain, plus our stern anchor, out on the mizzen boom to get *Spectra* leaning in the desired direction. The water dropped at an alarming rate, so Andy jumped in and stuffed all of our fenders as far under the hull as possible, we then dragged all of the spare chain out of the anchor locker and laid it along the side deck. Norma and Sarah pumped the boat's fresh water out which reduced our weight by about 1 tonne for the re-float later. We then shut all of the sea cocks as a precaution against back flooding, in case we got too much of a lean on during the lift off. We were all very active for half an hour or so and then it was the big wait. *Spectra* was completely high and dry within 1:30 hours and we were playing beach tennis within two.

Things to do when stranded on a sand bank,
1. Double check your navigation to see what went wrong. (Nothing, rising tide and smack bang in the middle of the channel??)
2. Look at the green buoy to one side and the red one to the other and convince yourself that you are indeed high and dry in the main channel.
3. Play beach tennis.
4. Write messages in the sand.
5. Phone family and friends.
6. Sleep
7. Collect samphire for dinner later.
8. Sleep some more.
9. Wade out into what water is left and drop the anchor for use later. The channel, by the way, consisted of a 10-metre-wide drain right up against the port hand mark, leaving the

remaining 100 metres over to the green buoy, as a desert.
10. Sleep even more.

Finally, after many hours, and many curious stares from passing kayakers, the tide started to come back in. We did not lift completely at any stage. This was despite using a combination of forcing the boat to lean right over, which included Steve working the windlass, Norma resetting the circuit breaker as it popped repeatedly, Andy swinging the booms from one side to the other and Sarah backing the staysail to keep the lean on, whilst I worked the wheel and throttle. We kept this up for nearly an hour before I made the management decision that foul language was required. "Will this @"$%&** boat ever !"£$%^& move I was heard to exclaim (in a calm and measured manner of course), at which point *Spectra*, good old girl that she is, took the hint and oh so very slowly bumped and dragged herself over the sand and into the deeper water.

Back to St Valery Sur Somme it was, and onto the berth we had left all bright eyed and hopeful 14 hours before.

The marina staff were, as always, very polite and helpful and assured us that we had enough water to get out "BUT YOU MUST STAY IN THE CHANNEL THEY SAID". "We ran aground smack bang in between the channel buoys at near on high water", Norma said. "OH, YOU MUST ALSO STAY IN THE

DEEP WATER IN THE CHANNEL", they said. I am off to the shops tomorrow to purchase some Gallic flair for the next attempt on Saturday morning.

As a footnote we gave the decks a quick scrub down in a vain attempt to remove the thick layer of sand that had accumulated and went to the yacht club for a beer or three.

As soon as we had all sat down with a cool beer on the yacht club balcony a Seagull did what Seagulls do best all over us.

Some days you should just stay in bed!!!

Maintenance, Changing Plans, Hitch-hikers and Fog:
4th -6th Sept 2014
49:45.97N 00:21.90E

The two days in St Valery Sur Somme have been well spent. Andy stripped the carburettor on my outboard umpteen times before we finally replaced all the fuel pipes and the beast burst into life. Steve managed to get the sat phone speaking to the computer and we can now download Grib (weather) files from anywhere on the planet, in theory at least. Sarah and Norma managed to get the boat sorted out from our day on the beach. I think we must have had about a tonne of sand on the decks. We are now all washed, re-victualled and raring to go. All we need now is some deep water so that we can get out of here. Oh, and we have finally eaten the last of Sue Fosters home-baked Biscotti biscuits so we will have to wait until Madeira for some more (hint, hint). St Valery is a very nice place but two days is pretty much it I think. If you are thinking of going, enter at half way between springs and neaps, and be sure to skedaddle the day before MHWS, it should then be all good news. If you have a deep keel (anything approaching 2 metres) I would go to Calais or Dieppe and get the bus.

Saturday morning and the tide was high enough for us to attempt exit plan number two. After questioning the locals, it would seem that the tide rushes in but does not get properly deep until it rebounds back from the sluice gates in the town. This meant that the ideal time to leave is as we had previously calculated one hour before high water but to go slower and ride the back wash. Armed with this knowledge we cast off our lines at 08:40 with all hands on deck. It was dead calm, with fog patches aplenty, and seals all around, popping their heads up to watch us pass by. I crept rather nervously past the 46 buoys marking the channel, out to the open sea. No problems at all, we never had less than 20 cm below the keel at any time, I just cannot see what all the fuss was about!!!!!

Now it was decision time, 145 miles to Cherbourg including punching the tide around Barfleur or the shorter hop of 75 miles down to Fe Camp spend the night and then on to Cherbourg tomorrow with the tide most of the way. The thick fog and light rain at the entrance to the Somme estuary made the decision for us. No wind, rain and fog, Fe-Camp it was then.

We stuck to the shift pattern to keep things regular and it turned into a bit of a plod along sort of day. Steve broke out the fishing gear and successfully deployed two lines of lures astern. The third line resulted in a knot of Gordian proportions which took Steve several hours to untangle, earning himself many a stab in the finger along the way. Andy and myself managed to take a brace of sun sights with the sextant that Steve Stokes gave me a year or so ago for the princely sum of a beer in the club. All very Nelsonian. Andy went through the plotting process with me; I must admit it has been five years since my Ocean course and I had forgotten most of it. Anyway, Andy managed a plot within three miles of our position which is rather good in my books. I cheated and bunged the figures into an app on my i-phone and likewise managed to plot a position in the blue stuff, so happy with that. No chance of a noon site as we did not see the sun again all day.

About lunchtime a hitch hiker landed on the mizzen boom and spent about 20 minutes hopping around the boat steadfastly refusing Norma's offer to share her cheese and onion crisps, before flying off to France for finer fare I am sure.

Arrived Fe-Camp at 1800. Next hop Fe-Camp to Cherbourg, unless we change our minds of course. That's it, all going well, and life is sweet.

Cherbourg
7th Sep 2014 22:03:17
49:38.7N 01:37.2W

Arrived late in Cherbourg, all safe but cold wet and tired. On the way in an intense discussion ensued between Andy and Steve accompanied by much finger pointing and chart analysis regarding various leading lights and channel markers. All of this was carried out whilst standing right in front of me blocking my view while I tried to actually steer the boat. With the benefit of my wonderful chart plotter, we managed to miss everything and finally moored up in a vacant slot on a pontoon without shore access. Not really an issue, as we were all very tired and the light rain certainly did not encourage a trip ashore. Up early for the trip to Guernsey tomorrow. Time to break out another flag :)

Guernsey and the Alderney Race
8th Sep 2014 19:15:13
49:27.31N 02:32.09W

Here we are, just over a week into the trip, and I have just filled in my first Customs form. We came into St Peter Port, in the Bailiwick of Guernsey, at 15:30 after a quick down-wind sail from Cherbourg. For the first time on the trip the wind was good with 15-25 knots from astern all day. *Spectra* lifted her skirts and fairly flew along. Well, 7 knots, which isn't bad for a fat bottomed girl. The Alderney Race was reached spot on slack water giving us a clear run down the Little Russel to the finish line. Andy was on Mother Watch today and kept us supplied with good fare as we sat around watching the world go by, oh and I missed filling in the Log much to Steve's delight, who has been crowing about attention to routines ever since. I, of course, have risen above the criticism like a phoenix from the flames. It seemed like good progress until the Condor Ferry came past doing 34 knots which rather put us in our place.

No problems today, we are tucked up safe in the marina and ready for a meal ashore along with a small drink to celebrate.

By the way, I have been chastised for not mentioning our first dolphin sighting yesterday on the way to Cherbourg. So here we go; "we sighted three dolphins yesterday on the way to Cherbourg"! They swam about and smiled a lot, which dolphins tend to do. I just don't trust them by the way, I think anyone, or any species that smiles all the time is definitely up to something.

Tomorrow we leave for La Coruna at 18:00. The weather looks good and the swell is light so fingers crossed Biscay will be kind to us.

Next report from La Coruna, 400 miles south of here, on Friday or Saturday.

GUERNSEY TO MUXIA VIA BISCAY

SEPTEMBER 2014

Position Report
10th Sep 2014 14:25:02
48:30.925N 05:09.654W

All going well, on target for 130-140 mile run over the first 24 hours approaching Ushant TSS.

Guernsey-Biscay-La Coruna days 2-3
12th Sep 2014 12:49:41
45:02.285N 07:37.111W

A very busy couple of days. We managed 135 miles over the ground on day one, 148 on day two resulting in a current estimated time of arrival (ETA) for La Coruna of sometime around lunch on Saturday. Andy's sun sights with the sextant are still in and around our GPS course so it proves the old ways still have validity. I am still cheating by doing the sight with the sextant, and then letting my phone app do the number crunching, best of both worlds I think. We initially shaped a course inside the TSS and outside of

Ushant. I have since moved us eastward from our rhumb line into the bay by 20 miles or so which has kept all of the shipping safely over the horizon on our starboard side. What has been amazing is the amount of wildlife. The first nightshift for Andy and Steve had a pod of dolphins playing around the boat for several hours keeping them company, and little birds kept landing on the deck for a breather, before heading off to who knows where. They are very tame and last evening one was even hopping over our laps in the cockpit while we had dinner. Yesterday afternoon I spotted our first whale. I think it was a pilot whale or something similar. For you whale watchers out there, it was brown with a blunt nose and about three to four times the size of the dolphins we have seen so far. Later that afternoon a pod of 5 – 10 of them cruised past going the other way which caused a stir aboard. Again, this morning a hawk pursued a little bird onto the boat in a real life or death chase. We ended up with a hawk sitting on top of the mast eyeing up the little bird which had found a spot under our spray hood and was having a snooze. The stand-off went on for an hour or two with the little bird making several escape attempts and being chased back aboard by the hawk until eventually he managed to slip away undetected. That was three hours ago, and the hawk is still sitting on our upper spreaders keeping an eye on things. Raising the spinnaker didn't even phase him for long, and all that more than 80 miles from the nearest land.

Last night we were having trouble trimming the sails and the boat needed 20-30 degrees of rudder on just to maintain course. I tried every combination of sails I could think of. but she still persistently kept rounding up. As daylight approached we had a concerted effort to get the boat balanced but she just would not trim correctly. The realisation finally came that we had rudder problems. I checked the hydraulics, no leaks, and so I woke Norma up as she was sleeping after doing the 3am to 6am watch, to get at the rudder post under the rear berth. The first thing I saw was a loose nut lying next to the rudder post upper bearing. The yoke had vibrated free, even with double locking nuts, and was twisting on the post as the retaining key had slipped half out of its slot. We had managed to trim her onto course right through the night at 6- 8 knots in 15-20 knots of wind for most of the time with little or no rudder! With Andy turning the wheel gently under instructions passed up on deck by Norma and Sarah in a Chinese whisper chain, Steve and I managed to get it all lined up again. The sea state didn't help much, as the rudder swung about in the seaway, as did we, with a steady one-metre swell passing under the keel, Steve and I were sliding all over the place in the aft cabin. I did note that very hard, moving metal and very soft squishy fingers really are not a match made in heaven. All tightened up well however, with an absolute minimal amount of well-directed swearing and after a quick count to make sure we had the requisite 20 digits still in place between the two of us, *Spectra* set off again.

Here we are, 120 miles from La Coruna, weather gods still smiling, one night to go and the chocolate bar sweep stake has been set for predicted arrival times.

Sarah won the choccie bar for the predicted 24-hour mileage run over the first night out, and Norma won it for the second 24-hour run. Must be my turn soon, I am the blooming navigator!

+ New flag number three up the mast ;-)

Arrived La Coruna
13th Sep 2014 11:04:54
43:22.059N 08:23.792W

Arrived at 10:30 local time this morning. Very tired, lightning and heavy rain last night. Full report later but all safe and showered, now we're off out for breakfast somewhere.

La Coruna the Day After the Night Before
14th Sep 2014 23:33:38
43:22.059N 08:23.792W

Saturday (13th) 10:30 local time *Spectra* delivered five bedraggled, tired and wet sailors onto the Club Marina Real La Coruna pontoon. What a last night Biscay saved for us. All went well up to my shift handover to the girls at 21:00. The wind had been steady all day and the coast of Spain was creeping ever closer. Thirty minutes later I was on deck again helping Norma and Sarah drop a reef in the main and roll up some of the foresail as the wind was up to 18+ knots. A few flashes of lightning could be seen way out to the West, no problems. Thirty minutes later I was up again as we furled up the rest of the foresail, winds now 20 knots and lightning regular but still way off to starboard. Andy came on watch and it all died down so out came the foresail again. My next watch was 03:00 to 06:00 and again all good, but now it was the weather witches on deck again at 6 am. Thirty minutes later, wind up, foresail reefed. One hour later big bang and a flash as lightning hit the sea close to port with sheet lightning crackling across the sky above. The AIS antenna began to glow with a reddish blue light which flickered up the antenna across the metal boom crutch and up the rigging until eventually all of the rigging shrouds on the main were glowing with the same flickering blueish light. I missed it, but we had a bad dose of St Elmo's fire aboard. Then the inevitable, too much static electricity in the air, the plotter and all instruments shut down and we lost steering as the auto pilot had also joined in the fun and shut down in auto mode. After the earlier incidents, I had decided to sleep in the saloon so when the shout came from on deck that we have lost the steering, I was fast asleep on the saloon seat. Andy rushed through from the forward berth busily trying to pull his boots on which involved sitting down. I was awoken by Andy sitting on my head!!! That is going to take one hell of a lot of counselling to get over I can tell you. Up again for me, this time with Andy. We switched all of the electrics down and isolated the batteries, counted to ten, crossed our fingers then brought it all back up again one system at a time. Amazingly, everything popped back into life, *Spectra* shrugged it off and carried on, all in a day's work for the good old girl. At this point the heavens opened and it poured with rain, proper monsoon stuff and that was it for the rest of the night.

Around 9am Steve popped out, bright as a button, and asked if we wanted breakfast. It was his turn on Mummy Watch but, even so, there was no need for that level of chirpiness in the morning.

When we moored up in La Coruna we found our single casualty of the trip. One of the little birds that have accompanied us had taken shelter on the aft deck and had died in the night, probably from the torrential rain or shock from the lightning. We buried him at sea as we approached the harbour. It was a simple ceremony with few words, but his mother would have liked it.

> Distance run from Guernsey: 483 miles.
> Time taken: 76.5 hours.
> Average speed 6.3 Knots
> About half of it under sail.

Lures set by Steve dragged behind for 38 hours x 2 lures.

Fish caught 0

Great crew, great company and a great achievement!

Here we are; it is now Sunday, we have had a good night's sleep, a great meal out and drank a lot of the local fire water. Today we walked out to the oldest working lighthouse in the world. Steve enjoyed the walk, Norma thought it was too far and Sarah played with the hunky joggers along the way. Andy and I just got on with it, as good husbands do.

Tomorrow the plan is to leave after breakfast for a 40 mile hop down the coast to Camarinas where we will spend a couple of days. But tonight, it is tapas and more wine for *Spectra's* motley crew.

17th Sep 2014 15:17:23
La Coruna to Muxia, Dancing in the Streets and Weather Bound
43:06.29N 09:12.835W
La Coruna to Muxia. 15th September 2014

The last night in La Coruna was intended to be a simple affair with tapas ashore. Norma had fired up the washing machine in the afternoon, leaving the boat looking and smelling like a Chinese laundry leaving no room to eat aboard so off into town for us.

The tapas bar was a mixture of traditional tapas but the portions were huge. It was excellent and we gorged like gods on Olympus and all for 20 Euros a head including beer and a couple of bottles of wine. A very hearty goodbye to La Coruna.

We planned to leave at 08:30 but a downpour delayed us for 30 minutes as we sat below and had just the one more cup of coffee, (after all any damn fool can get wet). The 44-mile trip down the coast was pretty uneventful with the wind dead on the nose all of the way so the opportunities for sailing and actually getting anywhere were limited. Norma did manage to produce her first painting of the trip and I spliced some shackles to keep myself busy. Over the last two hours the wind gusted up to force 7 at times from the SE which was a bit lumpy. The weather reports are for gale force 8 over the next few days so we changed plans and went into a new marina in Muxia, on the opposite shore from Camaranis, which promised more shelter.

It was one of those approaches where you creep around the harbour wall watching the depth sounder like a hawk as none of the pilot books mentioned the place, and we only knew that it existed because a passing sailor recommended it to us while we were in La Coruna. What opened up in front of us were lots of brand new and very empty pontoons with, what looked like, a wooden hut for an office. Oh well, in we went.

No sign of any life at the Capitainaire or any answer on the VHF but a telephone number was taped to the window. Andy called him up and 10 minutes later a very tired looking young man came down and did the necessary formalities. He explained that it was the last night of a three-day fiesta, by the look of him, he hadn't missed a minute of it. He opened a little bar (another wooden hut) next to his office and we sat down for one of the coldest beers I have ever had. Pretty soon thoroughly jollivated we noticed a ukulele hanging on the wall behind the bar. The barman was learning to play, ten minutes later, Norma was strumming a tune of sorts (Jingle Bells, it's the only tune she has learnt so far) and we were trying to get the barman/Capitainaire to join in. Andy finally managed an excellent rendition of a 'Horse With No Name' before we headed into town.

Today was Sarah and Andy's 15th wedding anniversary and I must admit that I was feeling a little guilty re the venue. Muxia turned out to be a rather bland little town but what made it worse was the few locals that were actually walking about all looked very tired this being the tail end of its fiesta weekend. The market stalls were closing down as we walked along the front and most of the restaurants were shut. We did however spot three tables in the middle of a side street and, while investigating further, we were accosted by a very enthusiastic Australian girl with an American accent (go figure) and her Spanish boyfriend. The couple were on a walking pilgrimage and Muxia was the last stop of their Camino de Santiago 500 Kilometre odyssey. They (she) waxed lyrical about the food at this restaurant/someone's front room so we pulled up some chairs and joined them. What a meal! The lamb stew was similar to Kleftico from Cyprus and the seafood was piled up high on the plates. The owners spoke not a word of English but enjoyed waving their arms around and so did we, therefore we managed to communicate enough to get by. After the meal we went down to the sea front to see the little fair we had noticed earlier and thought that would be it for the night.

Now remember I mentioned a small town with a sleepy population. At least 500 of them were in the square looking at a big stage. The curtains came up and a 10-piece Latina/salsa band sprang into life. Dancing girls, flashing lights, smoke and a stage set that would not have looked out of place at Glastonbury, all in this little fishing village. This went on for about an hour and then the curtain came down. Five minutes later, the curtain went up on another, equally large, stage set at 90 degrees to the first. Another similar 10-piece Latino band struck up and carried on at a frenetic pace through to 3 o'clock in the morning. We danced in the streets with the locals until the early hours and finally made our way back to the empty marina again, eating street food along the way. Sometimes great nights out have the most inauspicious beginnings, and this was definitely a great night out!

The weather report is for force 8s for the next three days and as I write this on Tuesday afternoon the wind is a steady 7 gusting to lots more than that so we are going nowhere for a day or so.

PS: Steve still hasn't caught any fish, three lines out this morning!

"Give a Steve a fish and he will feed the crew for a day, give him £300 pounds worth of state-of-the-art fishing gear and we will probably starve to death"

19th September 2014
Weather, more weather and Fare-thee-Wells,

Muxia has finally beaten the crew and their time has run out. What a shame that after such a great trip it kind of fizzled at the end. The initial weather system has run its course and has, unfortunately, immediately been followed by another. We have been bounced about by force 9 gusts and driving rain for three days now. The weather is not due to change until Sunday at the earliest and then it will take a day at least for the swell to die down. The only bit of excitement over the last couple days was when the bow thruster battery decided to cook itself. Lots of sulphur smells on board which we finally traced to the battery hidden up forward under Sarah's bunk. Unfortunately, after an exhaustive search, Muxia could not provide us with a new battery. I have therefore moved the generator start battery up front and we will have to live without a generator until we get into a bigger port. That's not really a problem in the short term as we only plan to hop down the coast in 30-mile jumps for the next week or so.

Sadly, due to the continuing bad weather Andy, Sarah and Steve have had to say goodbye and will be catching a taxi to Santiago today at 14:00. Last night we decided to go ashore for a final meal together and so out came the crew T Shirts and off we set. After a few beers in the WIFI café we went into the first restaurant we came to. First impressions were not good to be honest, but just as we were about to leave the waiter turned up and saved the day. He was a bit like Uncle Fester from the Addams Family and amazingly for Muxia could not only speak pretty good English but had a really dry sense of humour. The meal was excellent and towards the end we were joined at the table by a retired Dutch commercial skipper and the Port Capitainaire (the sleepy young man mentioned in an earlier blog). As I have already mentioned, Muxia is a small place and the Port Capitianaire's girlfriend was also the waitress in the restaurant. Anyway, good food, good wine and good company; a fitting last night for a great trip.

Today we have the retired Dutch commercial skipper on board as he is planning a trip next year across the Indian Ocean and is interested in the ketch rig, our navigation and weather instruments plus anything else yachty. He has not spent much time on yachts but is planning his retirement. Unfortunately, as it turned out he was far too interested in our navigation equipment, the sun cover from our plotter went ashore with him never to be seen again. In the meantime, he has just completed the Camino de Santiago, a pilgrims' walk that ends in Muxia, so "mucho respecto" to him for that.

Andy, Sarah and Steve have been an absolutely brilliant crew, we have all managed to get along and above all kept laughing as we handled all of the little niggly problems that you would expect at the start of a trip. What more could you ask for? We are now even laughing about the day on the beach, the rudder coming loose, being weather bound for four days and St Elmo's fire, although Sarah and Norma do have a nervous twitch or two when you mention the lightning. Steve will be re-joining us in November at Tenerife for the Atlantic crossing and Andy and Sarah are certainly welcome back anytime they want.

So that's it, for the first time on the trip *Spectra* only has Norma and myself for company. Let the next stage begin, but first we still need to get of Muxia!!!

MUXIA TO SINES

SEPTEMBER AND OCTOBER 2014

21st Sep 2014 17:15:45
All alone and the great escape
42:45.821 N 08:56.771 W

It has been a bit surreal over the last couple of days with just Norma and myself aboard. We have had to re-adjust to all of the extra room, now that the crew have departed for good old Blighty. At a fast lick I can now run from one end of our little world to the other in 2.5 seconds flat, impressive eh! It was at least 3 seconds before I got all fit on this trip. Life is normalising again, our normal life cycle is; potter about the boat putting a line through a few items on the to-do list, whilst adding twice as many to the bottom of it. Norma meanwhile sets forth to find interesting people and bring them back with her as prizes like a trusty cat would do with a dead mouse. We had the Dutch commercial skipper aboard as mentioned in an earlier blog and an ex-electricity linesman/Navy rating from Norway popped over for a chat. The skipper from the rather swish Swan next door came aboard and said nice things about *Spectra*, so he's a keeper and the Swedish lads from the little red yacht came over to say goodbye as they were braving the high winds to cross the bay for a festival that was just starting in another village. Finally, the German chap and his wife from the yacht that has been anchored outside the harbour all week had a catch up with us on weather, Muxia and all things nautical.

Meanwhile the wind and rain continued to batter poor old *Spectra* right up to midnight on Saturday and then it went dead calm (spooky). I reset the alarm for 7am and when I got up it was still calm (amazing). With the weather window looking good on the latest Grib file we virtually cut our lines in our hurry to get out of Dodge. Muxia is a great little place, but 48 hours is about it, after a week I was beginning to think I must have been a really naughty boy in a previous life, (shame I couldn't remember any of the details though). Anyway, I digress, we pushed the start button all full of hope and joy. Nothing! Flicked several switches and tried again. Nothing! At this stage a very large and ominously dark cloud was beginning to form, it was exactly 53 feet long and 12 feet wide with its epicentre directly above *Spectra's* mainmast. A quick prayer to Neptune and a very liberal spray of WD40 behind the cockpit electrical panel and everything burst into life, including Norma and myself. What a relief. As Muxia could not provide a spare battery, an engine repair man was probably going to be a stretch. Navigation lights ablaze, we motor-sailed due West out into the Atlantic with no land between us and the Americas, in order to test our mettle and see what all of that ocean had in store for us. What it actually had in store was a flat calm and a rather sea-sick inducing 2 metre swell; ho hum at least Muxia was behind us. Our little patch of the Atlantic was a bit like the start line of an RTYC Sunday race, we had nine yachts in sight all scurrying on to their next ports of call after being holed up for a week. The main difference from a Sunday morning race was that with 90 horses throbbing away in the engine room and not a single IRC handicapper in sight, this was one race *Spectra* and I could win. Norma then told me it was breakfast time and I had to slow down, so I let the other yachts win, just this once.

With the problems starting the engine a re-plan was in order. The original idea was to anchor up in the Ria de Muros for a couple of nights and then move on. I really didn't fancy risking an overnight anchor until I was confident in the engine starting up the following morning. Having said that, I am pretty sure it was damp in the circuit, as we had been exposed to some pretty monsoon-like conditions over the last week. Anyway, we decided to go to Portosin marina instead as it has repair facilities should we need them.

A notable point of the 46-mile trip was that we passed by Cabo Finisterre, the most westerly point of mainland Europe, along the way. The approach to the Ria de Muros was pretty spectacular, it being a very picturesque location with Portosin tucked into the bottom right hand corner about five miles in. We moored up after motor sailing for 8.5 hours and typically the engine restarted five times on the trot. I shall however test again in the morning and reseal the panel edges.

I am now sitting on the aft deck in glorious sunshine with a cold beer at my elbow updating my travails for you good people.

That's it for now. Norma has just invited the grizzly-looking Frenchman from the yacht at the end of the pontoon over for a beer or three. I wonder why she never meets any nice young ladies on her travels? Just bad luck I suppose.

23rd Sep 2014 22:22:29
Portosin and Muros, or plan left, go right.
42:46.575N 9:03.364W 905 Miles from Ramsgate by Log

The aforementioned grizzly-looking Frenchman turned out to be great company. He was just finishing his summer cruise and was leaving his yacht in Portosin for the next seven months and returning to France. He had crossed the Atlantic several times and the Pacific twice so he had a tale or two to tell. On top of all that his English was first rate so we had a good natter on board *Spectra* and later over a beer on the Club Nautico balcony. The sun went down giving us a spectacular show as it highlighted all of the features of the Ria de Muros.

Now onto Portosin as a town; essentially it was closed. Quaint, clean, with lots of restaurants, but oh so very closed. The friendly girl running the yacht club was very apologetic on the town's behalf but she did have to admit that, apart from the fish dock, it closes down for the winter. Now a few comments on the fish dock. This had a wailing siren, not unlike a nuclear attack warning, which was set off every time a fishing boat came in for unloading. Startling the first time, curiously fascinating the second, it got very old, very quickly and by the tenth time it jangled every nerve ending as the siren went on right through the night! Portosin had to go! Out with the charts and pilot books. With Norma chipping in we came up with a mutually agreeable and cunning plan. It was perfect, get up at 07:00, be underway by 08:00 for a 45-mile trip down to Bayona in order to mix it up with the super yachts for a few days. The wind was fair and in the right direction for a change, so we went to bed listening to the nuclear attack warning from across the harbour confident in our escape plan.

The next morning my alarm went off at 7 o'clock, I gave it a long hard stare and decided Portosin was ok for another hour. 8 o'clock and I was up, we could still do this! Norma gave the alarm clock and me a very hard stare and we both unanimously decided Portosin was good for another hour. 9 o'clock and another cup of coffee would not make any difference as we were late anyway. 10 o'clock and a very relaxed breakfast was being followed up by another cup of coffee. 11:30 and bang on time according to the revised schedule we slipped our lines and turned Spectra's nose towards the sea.

It was around about the third cup of coffee that the delightful port of Muros seemed like an excellent alternative choice. It had the entire Ria named after it and so it would be positively rude not to visit. It was directly under that glorious sunset from the previous evening and so the streets were probably paved with gold. But it's most appealing attribute was that it was only five miles away across the Ria and if I stood on tiptoes on the cabin top, I could just see it over Portosin's harbour wall.

We motored out of the harbour pointed our nose at Muros and switched the engine off. With just the foresail up we managed 7.3 knots through the water, yes it was blowing a bit. Dropping the foresail 30 minutes later we motored into Muros. Another cunning project successfully delivered on time and to budget if I say so myself. You just have to keep an eye on the big picture and be flexible.

Muros is great by the way. On arrival Norma radioed ahead giving *Spectra's* vital statistics. Pedro, the Port Capitainaire, came down to the pontoon and waved us into a spare berth next to a British flagged yacht. The couple on the yacht jumped up and rushed to assist as there was a wicked 20 knot wind whipping across the harbour. We were also chased in by a large trawler and I had to be a bit nippy as I turned the final corner. All went well until Pedro noticed that half of

Spectra was still hanging out from the end of the pontoon. "How long are you?" he asked in very good English. "14.5 metres", I answered with my best poker face. "Does that include the bowsprit?" he asked. "Of course not" I said "a yacht's bowsprit is for the enjoyment of all", "Ok" he said with a smile and directed me onto a 20-metre berth. This new berth involved a long reverse across the wind with a tight right-hand turn at the end which, served me right for being cheeky. Anyway, by the time I had got *Spectra* going backwards at least 10 people had gathered to watch the impending chaos. Ya boo sucks to them, I nailed it, perfect first time, if I do say so myself. As they walked away one was heard to mutter, "well he did have a bow thruster". Like all good artists, I suffer for my art.

Later in Pedro's office he admitted that *Spectra* was a beautiful boat and reduced our fees to 14 metres, just like another Pedro that I know would have done.

We will be staying here for the rest of today and tomorrow at least, so more on the town later. First impressions though are very good as there appears to be a large boating community here all heading South either for the Med, the Canaries or the Caribbean, just like our good selves.

That's it for now. For all of you old enough to remember, it's just like Saturday morning pictures, you will just have to wait for the next exciting episode.

26th Sep 2014 12:35:09

Muros to Caraminal, or high winds and fish hooks

42:36.263N 08:56.046W 945 Miles from Ramsgate by log

We spent a very relaxed couple of nights in Muros which is a great port of call if you happen to pass this way. We explored the town in the mornings and caught up with some maintenance in the afternoons. I finally managed to track down a new battery for the generator and at only 90 Euros from a hardware/sell everything store in town, that was recommended by Pedro the Capitinaire, it was a real bargain. We also had a bit of stitching to do where ropes had chafed the sails and covers, and so we set forth with the sail repair kit. Norma managed a first-rate patch on the stay sail sacrificial strip, while I bodged a mend on the mainsail cover's first reef point. A point to note: spray-on carpet adhesive from Wickes holds everything in place brilliantly while you stitch it all together.

The weather looked good, force 3-4 from the North as we slipped our moorings and headed for the next Ria to the South. At the harbour entrance we experienced a steady 15 knots of wind from the North and up went all of the sails and off went the engine. Thirty minutes later found us steadily overhauling a similar sized ketch that was two miles or so ahead of us. Thirty minutes later again and *Spectra* was showing

9.3 knots through the water. A quick flick onto true wind showed that we now had 30 knots plus from astern. Time to reduce sail, methinks. Norma depowered the boat while I put three reefs in the fore sail, then up to windward and I dropped a single reef in the main. Back on course, 8 knots, all comfortable and still catching the ketch. We passed the ketch with a friendly wave about an hour later. I had debated calling for water at the mark (Cape St Vincent) but as it was over 200 miles away, I guess that would have been slightly unnecessary.

Thirty minutes later the wind died to nothing, engine on and motor sailing for a couple of hours while dodging the fishing boats. As per standard practise the fishing boats were changing direction seemingly randomly as we approached. They did all give us a friendly wave as we sailed or motored past, depending on what the wind was doing at that moment. It is churlish to complain about fishing boats changing direction, after all they are earning a living while we are just messing about on the water, kudos to them I say.

At 2pm we were romping along in 20 knots of wind and just about to begin our entry into Ria de Arosa which has a large National Park and Fishery Protection Area across its entrance. Due to this, and not knowing the local rules in any detail, I thought it best to pull in the fishing gear before we entered. Not that we have ever actually caught a fish, you understand.

The next bit is a bit icky so if you are squeamish stop here!

As I reeled in the fishing line it seemed to momentarily catch on something, the rod bent and then pinged upright. I sensed, rather than saw, something approaching and instinctively put my hand up in front of my face. I felt a thump and I had a fishing lure hanging from my hand. The barbed treble hook had buried itself in my finger. "Ooh" I exclaimed in a calm and even tone, "that smarts a bit. Norma could you help me"? Norma sprang into first aid mode and with a set of wire cutters managed to cut the hook from the lure which left me free to sit down at least. We then assessed the situation, the hook had buried itself straight in, so pushing it out the other side right through my nail was not an option that I was willing to consider. We needed to tack soon, and I couldn't handle any ropes with a hook in my hand meaning it had to come out. I asked Norma to get me a razor blade from the sail repair kit and tried to cut down to the hook. Lots of blood and bad aiming on my part (I was using my left hand) and I couldn't find the little blighter. That left us with just the one option. Norma pushed the head of the hook flat down against my finger and lined it up with the way it went in and I reached for the pliers. One, two, three, PULL, "Ooh!" I exclaimed again, "that also smarted a bit"!!!! But it was out. Norma then quickly did the necessary with Savlon and finger bandages, before we tacked *Spectra* round. This time though, I did the wheel and Norma pulled the sheets.

> Extract from the ships log compiled by Norma:
> 2PM Paul fish hook in finger
> 3PM Paul feeling better after a cup of tea

> Narrative Log: 2PM First aid administered to Paul after removal of hook, slap of Savlon, finger dressing, cuddle and kiss followed by a telling off for not taking more care (anything to get out of washing up).

Icky bit over.

Again, within 10 minutes of us tacking, the wind died to nothing and it was a motor for the eight miles up the Ria to Port Caraminal, past numerous mussel barges and rocky islets. One high point was that as we were putting the sails to bed I looked back and a pod of 20+ dolphins crossed our stern lazily drifting along. We are now safely tucked up in Caraminal for the night.

As an aside, we were given a marina passport by Pedro at Muros that entitles us to 15% off from nine marinas in the area, Caraminal being one of these. The fee for the night was 14 Euros including WiFi and electric for a 14-16 metre yacht. Not bad at all. Ramsgate Marina please take note.

29th Sep 2014 18:46:42

Caraminal -Eugenia (Uxia) - Isla Salvora - Vigo or a lot of 'firsts'
42:13.951N 08:44.581W 975 Miles from Ramsgate by Log.

We had missed the fiesta in Caraminal by one day, and found the town was in recovery mode with not much going on. As the town was busily sleeping off its collective hangover, we had another maintenance morning, polishing the portholes on the starboard side, to make *Spectra* look all shiny again. The harbour was very exposed to swell and we were overhanging our rather spindly pontoon by about a third of the boat's length. Even though the weather is set to be fair for the next week, I was rather keen to move on before we got caught out. We slipped away at lunchtime on the 26th with the plan to anchor somewhere, which would be a first for this trip. The first anchorage we looked at was an open exposed beach with an onshore breeze, it was voted down by the entire crew (Norma). The second anchorage looked more promising. It was in a little bay, protected on three sides by wooded hills and with the entrance channel flanked on both sides by mussel barges. Unfortunately, as we turned the last corner we were met by a small fleet of fishing boats all on fixed moorings. We did however manage to find a likely spot and dropped our anchor several times to no good effect. It refused to dig in and hold, slipping each time, and bringing a huge bundle of seaweed up with it as well. By the time we had gone through this manoeuvre several times it was beginning to get dark, Choosing caution over valour we crossed the Ria again in order to go into the marina at Eugenia (Uxia) for the night.

Here comes 'first' number one: our first bad harbour in Spain. Eugenia (Uxia) could not fit us in as all of the visitor's pontoons (there were supposed to be 40 of them) were taken up with small fishing boats. We were therefore instructed to moor alongside the outer breakwater which was a rickety affair. Having moored up we surveyed our surroundings. Eugenia is a commercial fishing port with all of the attractive features of Grimsby on a wet Friday night. The fishing harbour, 100 metres south, was extremely busy with the associated wailing sirens, and the fish smell was, how shall we say, pungent, which is being exceedingly kind! Anyway, we went into the Club Nautica to pay; shock number two, 47 Euros the most expensive yet. Apparently, they have decided here to do away with the winter rate. What more can I say? The showers were dirty and cold, the facilities shabby, and the WiFi did not reach as far as *Spectra*. Oh, and the locals used the outer breakwater as a fishing platform all night as it had no security gate. We left the following morning.

Again, as the plan was to anchor somewhere we headed out towards the mouth of the Ria. On the approach to the Isla Salvora we noticed a group of yachts moored along a small inlet beach inshore. "That will do" we thought, and headed in. A great place. As it was Saturday, the local yachts were out in force enjoying the sun. We dropped the hook and it bit first time, 2000 revs in reverse and *Spectra* stayed put, still all good.

Number two 'first'. We have anchored for the night. This was shortly followed by number three 'first'; I went for a swim which was very refreshing. This being the Atlantic after all. Number four 'first' was the deployment of our hammock which Gemma, my daughter, had bought for my birthday. Twenty minutes later, Norma was reclining comfortably suspended below the main boom surveying all that passed. Later Norma set herself up to do a painting of the bay while I tried the fishing gear again, (no fifth 'first' I'm afraid, the fish still scoff at my efforts). As evening approached the local yachts headed back home leaving us alone with the lighthouse beaming out from atop the island. With the sun going down, I pulled in the bathing ladder and switched on the anchor light. At this point there was a loud bang from across the Ria. About four miles away a town was having a firework display which we sat and watched while drinking a sundowner. Some days just end right, don't they?

On the 28th, and after a disturbed night's sleep (I guess being anchored takes a bit of getting used to) I was up and about getting ready to go. Norma wanted to finish her painting and so it was a reminder of my military days; a big rush, a frantic run around followed by the big wait, or as we used to say, "hurry up to stop"! Finally, we set off for Vigo in a dead calm chugging along under the motor for the 15 or so mile leg. Just around the corner three adult dolphins and a baby joined us for a short while and that was really the highlight of the day.

Vigo is looking good so far. The marina Davila Sport is very modern and efficient although it is in the middle of an industrial estate. Anyway, sightseeing tomorrow, and we have just come back from a meal ashore............more later.

30 Sep 2014 14:24:00
Viana do Castelo

02 Oct 2014 10:26:00
Vigo to Viana do Castelo and on to Porto…First 1000 miles logged
41:.08.585N 08:39.049W 1036 Miles from Ramsgate by Log

We had a day away from the boat, sightseeing in Vigo, and I even managed to get Norma to climb another big hill. The view over the Ria Vigo was worth it though and so were the ice cream drinks in the castle café. Later in the day, Norma found an Irish couple walking around the marina who obviously needed a new friend. They were leaving their yacht in

Vigo for the winter months and travelling back to Ireland the following day. The blarney was good for an hour or two. She also found a lonely Dutchman who was instantly co-opted into the conversation (resistance is futile). He was also leaving his yacht in Vigo for the winter but had another couple of weeks sailing around the Rias before he finally departed. Who can blame him, the Rias are an amazing cruising ground which are so often missed as yachts push on South. We have been very lucky in that our timely weather window in Biscay allowed us to get across well ahead of schedule, and this has gifted us the last few weeks to visit the lovely bays and marinas in this part of the world. To be honest though we have barely scratched the surface, but it is now time to move on.

Up early the next day, we headed *Spectra* south again for the long-awaited entry into Portugal. At exactly 12:00 Spanish time we crossed the line and ran up our Portuguese courtesy flag. The good thing about heading south from Spain to Portugal is that the local clocks go back which means that we had 12 o'clock twice, obviously resulting in two lunches for Paul. Another high point for the trip was that we have now completed our first 1000 miles by log which certainly deserved a beer when we hit port. It was another day of light winds, meaning again we motor sailed along the coast dodging the fishing buoys and relaxing in the sun. The hardest working member of the crew is our poor old auto pilot and I certainly don't begrudge it the amp or three it uses to keep us on track. We pulled into Viana do Castelo and were moored up on the waiting pontoon in the river by 14:00. It would have been earlier, but I made a complete hash of the mooring. On the approach I had asked Norma to rig the lines and fenders to starboard, for no other reason than I thought I would varnish the starboard rubbing strake that afternoon. As we approached the marina I noticed a large swing bridge firmly shut over the entrance which left us the only option of the waiting pontoon in the river. I wasn't brave enough to ask Norma to swap everything over to the other side of the boat, (although to her credit she did offer) so I elected to try and moor starboard side to which meant a downstream approach. A stupid decision! With two knots of stream from behind and a boat that doesn't like going backwards at the best of times it wasn't pretty. After two attempts the poor Swiss guy who was moored on the end of the pontoon was looking quite shaken as near-on 20 tonnes of fully loaded *Spectra* repeatedly shot towards him at a rate of knots, only to pull away again at the last moment. Anyway, Norma called a halt to proceedings and the third attempt, by announcing that she was moving the fenders to port. Port side to, upstream, and we fairly glided in first time to general relief and smiles all round. Once again Norma knows best.

The marina is situated a mile upstream from the harbour and close to a road/rail bridge built by Monsieur Eiffel of the Tower fame. We entered the marina office loaded down with every document we could think to bring, having been warned of Portuguese officialdom in dire tones by our pilot book. Two minutes later all paper work completed we were having a friendly chat about likely restaurants with the Port Captain (Antonius). I actually felt a little cheated when he showed not the slightest interest in our Bill of Sale, OffCom radio licences, sailing certificates or even proof of VAT paid certification.

Needless to say, this is a very friendly little marina. There was no room inside for us but as we wanted to push on the next morning that was a moot point and we stayed on the visitors' pontoon in the river. The town itself is quite small, but it does have a well-preserved old quarter with the usual clutch of restaurants and bars, some of which we visited in order to sample their wares. Viana do Castelo was only ever meant to be a stopover and again it was up early (well, about 8 o'clock) and nose pointing south again for the 40 mile hop down to Porto.

It was a bit of a 'Groundhog Day'. light winds from dead astern meant motor sailing for half the day and a final sail as the wind got up in the afternoon. I did make good use of the time by servicing the two foresail halyard winches, while Norma practised on her ukulele, as we rolled along in the 2-metre swell. Even with *Spectra* doing a rhythmic roll, I still managed to get the winches back together without any spare parts being left over, which is always nice. We also passed a single windmill, which wasn't on my charts, looking very lonely all by itself in the middle of the sea.

A new marina has opened in Porto on the River Douro, much closer to the town centre, for which we had been given a voucher for a 20% discount by Antonius, thereby making it our destination of choice. When I radioed up the marina responded first time, sending a launch out to meet us and guide us in. This was probably fortunate as you have to stay in midstream until the entrance is at 90 degrees to your stern before turning sharply in. Without the guide I suspect that I might have cut the corner a bit and fallen foul of a shoal that runs the full length of the marina's outer breakwater extending out into the river for 30 metres or so.

Now this is a really friendly and well-run marina. We are moored up with an 86ft 'Gin Palace' on one side and another 65ft one on the other. I knew *Spectra* would shrink as we approached the Caribbean but I didn't expect it so soon; I feel like I'm living on a Topper dinghy. To our front there is another railway/road bridge connecting Gaia with Porto which we plan to cross today or tomorrow. Oh, and the marina staff informed, me rather proudly, that it was also built by Monsieur Eiffel. He was a busy boy, I wonder if he had as big a hat as our very own Mr Brunel? The marina maintenance team came down to the dock and introduced themselves, as did the marina manager. They are organising a gas refill for our UK bottles, which is handy, and we have got courtesy tickets to Churchill's port warehouse which is even handier. They also run a courtesy bus to the supermarket and generally can't do enough for you, we are very happy bunnies tonight. That's it for now, we will be in Porto for three days having a look around and visiting the sights (Churchill's).

This morning we awoke to a bit of excitement. Poking my head up through the hatch, a steaming cup of Rosie Lee in hand, I noticed a paramilitary group complete with guns, big boots and dogs searching boats on the other side of the marina. "Looks like there's a drugs raid going on", I called down the hatch to Norma. She joined me on the steps in an instant. Both with cups of tea in hand, we became proper nosy neighbours. It was at this point that we noticed that a sealed white plastic bag had been dropped into our cockpit overnight. Instant paranoia reigned as we looked from the package, to the now approaching Customs man with his dog. I grimaced a, "Bon dia" to him as he walked past and allowed his dog to relieve itself against the post at the end of the pontoon. Norma, by the way, had shot back down the hatch like a rabbit down a hole. Once his dog had done its business and he had walked back past, nodding another good morning to me, I tentatively reached out of the hatch and pulled the bag towards me. I prodded and smelt it then ripped it open at the corner; two freshly-baked bread rolls, courtesy of the marina, fell out onto the cabin floor. Phew, blimey that was a relief! As an extra bonus, in what is an excellent marina, the staff deliver a complementary bag of bread rolls every morning, one for each crew member. Great idea, but I kind of wish they had told me before I had the heart attack. I really can't imagine Ramsgate Harbour copying this idea any time soon.

Porto is a great place to visit and, as I am sure I saw a few Ryanair/Easyjet planes flying into Porto Airport, it would make for a super choice for a bargain weekend break. The city is actually two, Oporto on the north bank of the Douro river and Gaia on the south. Interestingly enough, all of the fortified wine (Port) warehouses are situated on the south bank, so why we don't finish a nice meal with some cheese and a glass of Gaia, I do not know. Andrew and Paula take note, a nice bottle of Gaia to bring in the New Year in Grenada would go down rather well especially after some pavlova. Well, we wandered around and took pictures of the sights as all good tourists do and tried a few samples of the local wares which were very tasty. Norma announced that my deckies had reached their sell by date and so I was taken shoe shopping!!!! Personally, I think they had a few miles in them yet; one even still had all of the sole attached and the smell was only really noticeable if you stood down wind. Once she had beaten me into a virtually catatonic state, (Norma can shop for Britain by the way) I relented and bought two new pairs, an action which apparently has saved me a considerable amount of money. Finally, in an attempt to bring the proceedings to an end and with a rush of blood to my head I bought her a new ukulele, which is much better than the old one she has been strumming for weeks. You may wonder how shoe shopping ended up in a ukulele shop, well I refer you to the statement above "Norma can shop for Britain!" We never did make it to the port warehouse tour, I know not why, but it just didn't happen.

5th Oct 2014 11:24:58
Porto to Figuiera da Foz with lots of dolphins!
40:08.858N 08:51.435W 1138 Miles from Ramsgate by Log

We left Porto early on Saturday morning just as the sun was coming up. Motoring along toward the river's seaward entrance, a small fishing boat came over with one old man on board waving his arms. I slowed the engine as he pulled up alongside and with a big thumbs up said, "Lovely boat, good bye, come back soon", and then headed back to continue his fishing. Wow, what a send-off! Sixty-five miles down to Figueira da Foz and, as is normal now, no more than 10 knots of wind from directly behind. The engine stayed on at low revs and we played with different combinations of sails. Unfortunately, there was a fairly large swell running which kept us rocking and rolling, with the result that the cruising chute just would not stay full. In the end we had the foresail, mizzen and mizzen stay sail out which gave us a knot or two above the engine revs. This allowed us to maintain about 7 knots all day. Even so, it was quite uncomfortable at times as *Spectra* almost rolled her rails under in the swell.

At about 13:00 the cooker decided it had had enough of the swell and with a crash it launched itself out of its mounting brackets. Twenty minutes later I persuaded it back into place and tightened everything down again. Luckily enough we had lunch earlier in the day so no food ended up on the floor. That was it really until 16:00 when we were lazily watching a group of Cormorants dive bombing for fish about 100 metres to port. Suddenly we noticed a few dolphin fins in the area meaning that this was a combined attack on the poor fish. Cormorants from above, dolphins from below - a classic maritime pincer movement. The water was fairly boiling with activity as they all enjoyed a fish supper. I think it only fair to mention at this point that I have dragged a lure behind us for the last 35 miles with not the slightest bit of interest shown by anything living. A group of three dolphins split from the pack and came our way, shortly followed by about six others. They were really going for it, leaping clear of the water as they approached to play on our bow wave. A mad scramble for phones to take pictures ensued which resulted in Norma hanging over the side taking loads of pictures as the dolphins played and leapt around us for the next 30 minutes. Not wanting to be left out, I eventually found my phone and decided to take some photos. Norma, unbelievably, took 147 pictures mainly by pointing and pressing the button on the phone as quickly as possible. Out of that lot she managed a few really good shots. In the excitement, and because I couldn't find my phone, I only managed a total of seven pictures. Six of these were of my own face and the last one was of a Dolphins tail (well nearly), I will let you be the judge of who is the budding David Bailey here.

Finally, we arrived in Figueira da Foz at 17:30 and tried to find a mooring under the rather helpful suggestion from the harbour master of, "Put her anywhere you can fit". Not easy. We tried to thread *Spectra* through the eye of a needle and managed to get alongside one berth but over half of the boat was extended beyond the pontoon and we blocked most of the other yachts in, so no good. Eventually, we managed to get alongside an inside berth amongst the small boats at the other end of the harbour, much to the amazement of the locals, as I reversed past a line of 20-25 footers to berth *Spectra* on the inside of them all.

That's it for now, we are all safe and sound in Figueira da Foz; sightseeing tomorrow and a good night's sleep tonight, if the mosquitoes will allow!

Position update
7th Oct 2014 09:10:03
39:35.5N 9:04.5W Position update

9th Oct 2014 11:15:56

Figueira da Foz to Nazare to Peniche………… and a fish at last!

39:21.119N 9:22.598W

We planned to leave Figueria da Foz at 8am, after paying our harbour dues of course, but unfortunately that plan didn't survive first contact. The harbour office was due to open at 8 o'clock and Norma was sitting outside the café next door at 07:50 waiting, whilst I got *Spectra* ready for sea. At 09:30 a rather sleepy security guard turned up and opened the office, so there went that plan. At 10am we set sail for Nazare and, as is the norm, had 15 knots of wind smack on the nose all the way. On went the engine again! About two hours later, wonder of wonders, the fishing gear started streaming out line which caused a bit of a flap on board I can tell you; this definitely being new territory. Norma slowed the boat while I, rather nervously, began to wind in the line, still half expecting to see a large clump of seaweed attached to the hook. But no, Paul the hunter gatherer extraordinaire had provided for his clan of one by capturing a beast from the deep. Well not exactly a beast, it was a 1.5lb Mackerel-type fish which had taken a snap at my lure as it shot by at 6.5 knots. All I can say is that 30 minutes from catch to plate it tasted great, and, no Steve, there is not a shopping bag or fishmongers in sight, oh ye of little faith.

Nazare is billed as an all-weather port which is pretty rare on this coast; even more so when you consider that this is also the town that registered the largest wave ever surfed. There are pictures of it all over the place, even in the harbour office, which is a bit disconcerting. The monster waves are created by deep seabed canyons just off shore, and boy are they deep! One on the chart drops to over 700 metres from a surrounding depth of 50 metres, within a matter of 100 metres or so, and it is only a mile across. The monster wave in question was 30 metres high and the photographs show a tiny surfer flying down the face of it, as it towers over the lighthouse on the cliff top at the headland. Needless to say, we encountered none of that nonsense as we entered harbour on a manageable, if uncomfortable, three-metre swell.

Norma did what Norma does best, and we were soon chatting to Dave who was single-handing a 36-foot yacht, *Wild Beast II* down to the Med for the winter. He had more or less been one step ahead of us for the whole trip, with the exception that he went around the coast of Biscay rather than across it as we had ('thrupenny bit-ing' the bay, Johnny Foster called it). The weather was due to change and, to prove the point, a 30ft British yacht staggered in that night with a very wet and bedraggled bunch of twenty some-things on board, who had been caught out in a squall coming down from Figueira Da Foz. The next day we headed into town for breakfast and to get internet access somewhere. Nazare is very much a holiday town with all of the restaurants selling off the same menu and lots of camper vans around. I think it must be included on the bucket list of the European Caravan Club's '100 Places to Visit Before You Die'. Anyway, the weather showed a window of opportunity that afternoon and then it was closing in for 2-3 days so we made the decision to move onto Peniche, 25 miles further south.

A rush back to Spectra was followed by a quick move onto the fuel pontoon, whilst Norma walked over to the petrol station on the road outside the marina, which bizarrely controlled the pumps. After much confusion about which pump was actually diesel, I put 400 litres of fuel into the tanks and gave my bank balance a good kick in the pants to be sure. The dash down to Peniche was pretty horrible; 20 knots of wind dead on the nose (where else would it come from with the other 359 degrees being out of bounds at the moment?). We also had 1.5 knots of tide against us, a three-metre swell bizarrely coming from the North against the tidal flow and rain showers to boot, it was head down and get the journey over with.

'No Room at the Inn' at Peniche leaving us rafted up outside of a French yacht and in front of a very worried Halberg Rassey owner who gave plenty of unrequested or needed advice, but not a lot of actual help in the mooring procedure. Anyway, I got *Spectra* alongside on the second attempt without any bumps or scrapes which is always nice. As I went ashore to fasten the shore lines a friendly English voice shouted, "long time no see". It was Vicky, who had completed her Day Skipper course at the RTYC Nav School and subsequently gone on the first RTYC Spanish Cruise with Nigel Collingwood and crew a couple of years ago (small world). She was helping to crew a large trawler yacht *Western Star* down to the Med. As it was raining, we organised a meet up for the following day because, lo and behold, Dave on *Wild Beast II* from Nazare had also come down to Peniche and was rafted up alongside *Western Star* (even smaller world).

      The rain then began to really fall from the heavens and we dashed below, Norma to get dinner on the go and me to put the boat to bed. After dinner, whilst I was back on deck sorting out a clanging halyard, I heard a shout and very unladylike language from below. With 31 years of marriage under my belt I thought it best to stay on deck until the dust had settled and it was a good ten minutes later that I felt brave enough to go below. Norma had walked into the galley at full pelt forgetting that she had opened the drop-down, oven door. This door, being at knee height, had cut deeply into her leg. When I came below, she was lying flat on her back, her right leg in the air with a four-inch gash oozing blood onto the carpet. It did look pretty nasty, under repeated and prolonged advice from the ship's Medical Officer, I cleaned it up and applied a dressing. Luckily it was not too deep, so Tony Smythe's suturing lesson did not have to be put to the test, but it was a stinger, that's for sure. I settled Norma down with a cup of coffee, elevated her leg and then did the washing up, as all good husbands should do in an emergency.

The next day we went into town on a very rainy and windy Wednesday in October in order to experience the hot spots of Peniche. We did the usual rounds of harbour office and Port Capitinaire to book ourselves in and then had an absolutely ginormous pancake for breakfast. The weather report was strong winds for Wednesday, large residual swell on Thursday and it will be Friday before we can sensibly head of down to Cascais to meet up with our new crew. We met up with the *Western Star* crew again in a coffee shop with WiFi (you always find the yachties huddled where they can get internet access) and we were invited aboard for a look around. After we had done the rounds of the shops in Peniche and restocked *Spectra's* larder, Norman from Belfast (go figure), one of the long-term crew and Chief Engineer, gave us a guided tour of the *Western Star*. Tony, the owner and ex fireman, had spent five years refitting the trawler for the trip down to the Med and she was very nicely done, if I say so myself. After that it was a reciprocal visit and obligatory beer aboard *Spectra* before going out for a group meal in Peniche.

On the way back to the boat we helped moor up a small yacht staggering in with a very wet and bedraggled crew of twenty some-things. It was the same crew from Nazare who had again left late and battled the weather that we had made the dash to avoid the previous day. (Even smaller world). I think they are either gluttons for punishment or just don't check the weather very well, because they are certainly making hard work of it. Still they all very keen and seemed happy enough the next morning as they hung out all of their sailing gear including mattresses, to dry------- again!!

We are off to Cascais weather permitting..........................

Position update
11th Oct 2014 09:17:01
38:41.30N 9:25.11W

15th Oct 2014 21:22:54
37:57.014N 8:51.963W
Peniche, Cascais, Sines and new Crew
1311 Miles from Ramsgate by Log

Well, the weather was 'permitting' and we decided to leave early on Friday morning for the 45 mile leg down to Cascais. The Capatinaire in Peniche was extremely helpful and did not charge us for the last night which is always nice. Norma and I had a last day in the town walking around the castle and out to the headland before early to bed and ready for a 7am start in the morning.

We left Peniche in company with Dave on *Wild Beast II* as he was also heading down to Cascais and had rafted up alongside us so he had to move anyway. This is the way on this coast with long day sails and the majority of yachts heading in the same direction, Mediterranean or Canaries. One down side of staying near a fishing fleet was the greasy layer of fish detritus that we had to motor through to get out of the harbour; *Spectra's* fenders, sides and side decks were coated with a fine layer of the slimy stuff which was a devil to get off (yuk).

We enjoyed the company of a group of dolphins for a while as we gradually pulled ahead of Dave. The day progressed in a dead calm and we finally arrived at Cascais by 15:30, having gone through a couple of rain showers along the way. Rain was not on the project plan at all when we planned this trip but we had a lot more to come. That night we had all of *Spectra's* winter covers on as a huge weather front came through with plenty of thunder and lightning to keep us up, as the rain pounded the decks. The next day, when the sun finally broke through, we had a good walk around Cascais and, if I say so myself, it is a bit posh. There are lots of really large villas belonging to the rich and famous along the waterfront and, of course, we felt right at home amongst the glitterati and beautiful people.

The marina is very nice but at a cost which meant a host of yachts were anchored outside keeping their budgets down. As the wind picked up and a second night of thunderstorms passed through, the anchorage slowly emptied and the marina slowly filled making for quite a nice community by the second morning. We met the usual clutch of sailors heading mainly South, with a few going North, from many different countries and spent the morning swapping stories of our adventures. At lunchtime Peter Duke arrived to help us crew across to Madeira and ultimately the Caribbean.

It's great to have Peter aboard and I can catch up on all of the O2 gossip, but he could have left the British weather behind, it is miserable at the moment. Due to the large swell and yet another front coming through, we decided to take the train into Lisbon on Monday and do a bit of sightseeing. The day started fine but by lunchtime it was raining hard and we settled in under a big umbrella at a café in a park, to wait for it to pass. It rained and rained and rained some more, at one point you could hardly see 20 metres in front of you, the rain was so heavy. Many coffees, a cherry brandy or two and several hours later we were huddling ever closer to the umbrella's central pole, trying to keep dry while debating how long it would be before *Spectra* floated past and we could just step aboard. Needless to say, Lisbon was a washout; I haven't seen rain like that since we last visited Norma's Mother in Lisburn just outside of Belfast.

Back in Cascais we paid for our stay, (Ouch! The quoted price did not include tax so that was a stinger). and got ready to set off the next morning. It was a glorious departure and after lots of talking and lengthy instructions in order to acclimatise Peter with the boat and how we do things, we finally managed to leave in style. Ten minutes later we returned in style to pick up the mooring line we had left behind, which a nice Dutchman coiled up and passed to Norma as we came alongside. I have booked the crew in for a ritualised flogging later in the week.

The 55-mile trip to Sines was very lumpy with a 3+ metre swell coming in from starboard all the way, making *Spectra* roll all over the place and us rattle around inside her like peas in a pod. Oh, and of course the predicted westerly wind moved south leaving it dead on our nose all day. Dare I say, yet again! On a brighter note, we did see two large pods of dolphins, but they didn't come over to play, so no pictures I'm afraid and, of course, my fishing lure was completely ignored. I am beginning to think that the one fish I have managed to catch was a bit depressed and probably suicidal. I did make good use of the time by getting the sail repair kit out and repairing my old deckies. Much to Norma's disgust, with the soles sewn back on, they now have at least another thousand sea miles in them. The new deckies that we bought in Porto are far too good for padding around the deck and besides they hurt my feet.

We are now moored in Sines which is the last port before Cape St Vincent and will hopefully be our hopping off point for the 500-mile(ish) trip across to Madeira. I say hopefully, because the weather is very unsettled and the swell is pretty huge. I am keen, but there is no way I am going head into wind for four days with a 4-5 metre swell running. We will just have to wait it out. Annoyingly, the weather in Madeira looks fine, it's the bit in between that is just horrible. We are planning to meet up with Tommy and Sue in Madeira and they have a hotel booked up to the 23rd, leaving us a few days yet before the timeline becomes critical. Until the weather breaks the gallant crew of *Spectra* will just have to be content with the hot spots and highlights of Sines to keep them amused.

As an aside, Dave on *Wild Beast II* came into Sines a couple of hours after us and the trawler *Western Star* is still here awaiting spare parts and a new crew member, having leap-frogged us while we were in Cascais. I am pretty sure that like all good honest travelling folk we will be gathering around a campfire (saloon table) soon for storytelling, dancing and liquid refreshment (one dry sherry for Norma I think).

16th Oct 2014 08:46:06
We are stuck for the moment,

Weather report issued this morning by the Met office so another couple of days stay in Sines methinks.

Updated: 0452 UTC Thu 16 Oct 2014
Shipping forecasts and gale warnings Gale warnings Shipping forecasts

Trafalgar
Gale warnings - Issued: 2125 UTC Wed 15 Oct
South-westerly gale force 8 expected soon
Trafalgar forecast - Issued: 2315 UTC Wed 15 Oct
Wind
South or south-west 5 to 7, occasionally gale 8 until later, decreasing 4 at times.
Sea state
Moderate or rough in south-east, otherwise very rough or high.
Weather
Thundery showers.
Visibility
Moderate or good.

18th Oct 2014 15:47:38
Stir crazy in Sines

We have now been in Sines (pronounced Singe) for five days and we should be good to go at 7am tomorrow morning. We did plan to leave this morning and were all up and about at 6 am, dressing in the dark and generally getting in each other's way. Peter headed up to the marina office complex to have a shower and return the marina access cards (and get the 60 Euro deposit back), whilst I jumped on the laptop to get a final weather report. At that point the front wheels fell off our wagon; a large low has settled to the west of Madeira. From yesterday's report this should have shifted further west but basically hasn't, which leaves us with 15-20 knot headwinds for the first 24 hours. A quick chat with Norma, and I decided to postpone until tomorrow morning. I dashed, well walked quickly, as I refuse to run in public, to catch Peter before he returned the cards. At that point the rest of the wheels fell of our wagon because I met Peter returning along the pontoon. Ho hum, book the boat in again for another day at 10 O'clock when the Marina day staff turn up for work.

What have we been up to in Sines for the last week? As I mentioned earlier, the trawler *Western Star* was in harbour, as was Dave on *Wild Beast II.* We have also chummed-up with a couple from Northern Ireland, Eilish and Richard aboard the yacht *Granuaiile*, which means that Norma has been in her element making new friends all around. We all went out for a meal on Wednesday (10 at the table) which was a great craic, as they say in Ireland. We found out that Richard used to be a fireman in Ireland, as was Norma's father and brothers. It took about 20 seconds to trace the known associates back and discover that Richard is a friend of Norma's cousin, John Belshaw, also a fireman in Ireland; small world. Richard and Eilish are on their second Atlantic odyssey, this time for two years and so we have thoroughly picked their brains, gaining a wealth of top tips and good advice on all things cruising. Richard actually built their yacht, a steel gaffer, in his back garden, teaching himself to weld along the way, and she is a real credit to his workmanship.

While we are on the subject of workmanship, Peter and myself have been using our time productively by replacing the nasty cork material on the flat areas either side of the companionway with teak planking. We have also pulled out all 80 metres of the main anchor chain, and marked it up as the old paint had faded, put chaffing tubes on the bowsprit stays, fixed the VHF as it was playing up, put a new clip on the mizzen boom crutch and generally been all round workaholics. *Spectra* is now gleaming again and ready to go.

Today we walked up to the castle overlooking the town and visited the museum inside. The castle has a great view of the harbour from its battlements, which is not really surprising I suppose, it being a castle and all, but it did provide a photo opportunity. On the way back we played a tune or two on a pair of xylophones that are set up in a children's park below the castle. I just know the locals were impressed but to their credit, they kept their cool and didn't let it show.

Western Star picked up their replacement engine bits yesterday and with a new crew member aboard set of for Lagos at 18:00 last night. From there they plan to go to Gibraltar (cheapest fuel apparently) and into the Med. We plan to leave at 7am tomorrow morning for Madeira and Dave plans to head out on Monday for Portimao and then the Med. Richard and Eilish will be heading down to the Algarve in the next few days and then onto the Canaries and the Caribbean. They plan to start at the top of the Caribbean and work their way down which is the opposite to us so I am sure our paths will cross again. Our little troop of travellers are splitting up and going their own ways, which is really the nature of the beast.

If I write again tomorrow it will mean we haven't been able to leave and I will be narked to say the least, I will probably be writing in BOLD CAPS. If I don't write, it is four days to Madeira so watch this space. I will update ASAIP.......(As Soon As In Port).

SINES TO TENERIFE

OCTOBER AND NOVEMBER 2014

20th Oct 2014 15:08:00
Sines to Madeira update
30:19.085N 11:25.019W

One night out and all going well, roughly one-third of the way over. We have managed to sail about half of it so far and motored or motor sailed the rest. Should be within sight of Madeira by Wednesday night or Thursday morning.

Our auto pilot has broken! I have spares but not willing to open up the steering hydraulics at sea unless I really have to and so we are hand-steering two hours on and four hours off. A bit tiring but definitely do-able. Lots of dolphins, one whale, a small bird and a bat; no sharks.

More later when I have decent Wi-Fi.

22nd Oct 2014 16:36:47
Sines to Madeira-------------Or Tyranny of the Tiller!!!
33:20.4N 15:50.09W

We are still on passage and sending updates by Sat phone. We left Sines at 7am on Sunday 19th October for the 490-mile trip across to Madeira, estimated time 3-4 nights. It was a lovely send off with Richard getting up to pass us our lines and wish us bon-voyage; hopefully we will meet again in the Caribbean. All went well and we were soon scooting along under all plain sail at a very respectable 6 knots average and were joined by a party of bottle nosed dolphins (the real 'Flipper' type not the other smaller imitations we've been getting up until now). They were slower than the dolphins we have been used to but jumped a lot more which kept us fascinated for 30 minutes or so.

Around lunch time Norma said there was a funny noise coming from our cabin and, on investigation, I realised that it was the steering gear. Peter and I stripped the mattress off the bed, no small feat in a three-metre swell which had us rolling all over the place, to check things out. We quickly realised that the gears on the hydraulic pump for the self-steering motor were grinding. This was potentially a major problem so I called all three of us together for a Steering Committee Meeting (sorry couldn't resist that one) and we looked at our options:

1. Turn back
2. Carry on using the self-steering until it fails
3. Replace the hydraulic pump at sea (I carry a spare)
4. Hand steer and keep going.

1. We agreed not to turn back as we carried a spare and we had emergency steering gear as an extra backup should everything go wrong.
2. That was just silly and could have caused irreparable damage.
3. I vetoed that as I was not willing to crack open the hydraulic steering system unless we really had to, due to the risk of losing the manual steering.
4. Hand-steer and keep going; this is what we agreed to do.

In order to make hand-steering for long periods a practical option, I changed the shift pattern around to two hours on and four hours off. Going into night number four this has worked pretty well, we are tired but still functioning as a unit.

Onto more normal things - we had a cracking sail for the first 24 hours and clocked up 140 miles all under sail. During the second night the wind dropped and we have been engine on and off ever since as the wind keeps falling away. Dolphins have been regular visitors plus we also sighted a whale and a turtle. On board it has been a complete menagerie with two little brown birds dropping in on a regular basis resting for an hour or so. Norma has named them Christina and Christopher; I have no idea why? One unusual visitor has been a bat. He flew in on the morning of day two about 100 miles from the nearest land and immediately went to sleep with his head tucked under a strap on deck. That night he disappeared, and we thought that was that, until I found him hanging upside down from the foresail halyard winch about lunchtime the next day, again fast asleep. After night three he came back again, and he is still there sleeping upside down as we approach Porto Santo. It would seem that he made a wise decision by joining the crew. Norma has named him Batty, which is pretty unoriginal, I wanted to call him Vlad but was outvoted.

Last night the engine failed and so did my sense of humour. I fervently wished Tony, my son, had been on board as he likes smelly diesel engines and understands them. It took a while, I checked the fuel level - all good, 400 litres still in the tank. The primary fuel filter was a bit loose so I tightened that and the engine started. Big smiles all round and then after an hour it died again. Bugger! I then remembered a conversation I had with the previous owner about a set of relays under the exhaust manifold. I stripped them out and found one had worked itself loose with the constant vibration. I pushed it back in with a click and then I could hear the fuel pump buzzing. After a bit of cranking she fired up and has been running sweet as a nut for the last eight hours, so big smiles all round.

That's it for now. We have just cut our hair and had showers on deck, sprucing ourselves up for

Tommy and Sue in Madeira. We should be in there by midnight tonight. One cold beer and straight to bed; steering gear to fix tomorrow.

26th Oct 2014 11:18:29
Madeira at last
32:38.696N 16:54.63W
Madeira at last. .... 1842 Miles from Ramsgate by Log

I have been a bit remiss in my blogging of late, and I also noticed that one of my position reports put us about 400 miles further south than we should be. By the time you read this it should have been corrected. On to my excuses for not writing – well, we are in Madeira and have met up with Tommy and Sue. When you add to that mix restaurants and bars aplenty, what chance did I stand? I have now resurfaced and so here we go.

The last night of the sail over was not pleasant at all, again no wind, so we were motoring the last 50 miles as the sun went down. Batty bat woke up again as was his routine and did a couple of circuits of the boat before noticing that the island of Porto Santo was only a couple of miles away. Without a backwards glance, he was off heading straight for shore, the blooming freeloader. Anyway, it was strangely sad to see him finally go as, to be honest, I didn't rate his chances much when he first crash landed onto our decks. We carried on chugging along and all was fine with the world until around midnight, when we were abeam of the last light before turning right for Marina Quinta do Lorde and the engine decided to die again. Serious sense of humour failure now, but a wiggle of the wires, the fuel pump started to buzz and the engine fired up. The entry to the marina was pretty fraught, as I was waiting for the engine to die all the way in. I shot through the marina entrance doing 6.5 knots, slammed the old girl in reverse and she settled alongside the arrivals berth, leaving Norma a bit of a jump to get the lines ashore. Not my best manoeuvre, especially as Norma fell onto her cut knee and bruised it again. But, all in all, we were just glad to be tied up and able to go to bed. I must say Norma and Peter have been brilliant on this leg; it has not been easy hand steering for over 500 miles, especially when added to the stress of gear failure, but they have both been cheerful and supportive, whilst I quietly went doolally. Norma typified it, by responding, when told we would have to hand steer all the way with, "Oh well, that will be good for keeping the 'bingo wings' away then".

The next day we booked into the marina and had a look around; not very impressed. To be honest, it is a bit of a toy town and a very expensive one at that. The marina also had a swell running through it (in a force 1??) which was uncomfortable as we tied onto our allocated pontoon, a rather spindly affair that *Spectra* could have pulled to pieces in short order if the wind and swell really got up. On top of that, the bus service to Funchal stops at 6 o'clock and a taxi ride was 50 Euros one way. Peter and I pulled all of the engine electrical connections apart and made sure they were secure, corrosion-free and dry. One of the connector plugs was not gripping as tightly as it should, and I suspect this was intermittently cutting the power to the fuel pump. With this now replaced hopefully we have solved the fuel pump problem. Thus, with our faith in all things mechanical restored, we decided to move the 15 miles down to Funchal that afternoon.

Finally, a pleasant sail, we even had the cruising chute up for a while arriving in Funchal at 18:30 to be met by Tommy and Sue on the quayside. We had the obligatory beer on board and a right good natter to catch up on all of the doings in London and Ramsgate. Unfortunately, I don't think Norma, Peter or I added much to the conversation as we only had about one functioning brain cell left between us. A good night's sleep and crew de-stress was in order. The good night's sleep was duly provided by a calm Funchal harbour and de-stress provided by copious quantities of well applied alcohol. The next day dawned bright and sunny, if a little hazy round the edges. Unfortunately, we have missed Roger and Davena by a couple of days, as they had to fly back to the UK, but that is the vagaries of a life dictated by wind and tide. Maybe they will turn up in another port on our travels? During our second night in Funchal we had a mini karaoke session in the cockpit after sundowners and treated the Polish yacht next door to a spirited rendition of Superman complete with all actions. I could tell they were impressed by their wide-eyed stares and open mouths. We also lent our marina shower keys to a passing British military crew that had arrived late aboard the 67ft training yacht *Discoverer*. This was the same yacht that Steve, our crew on the Biscay crossing, had sailed back across the Atlantic in 2012, small world yet again. The military boys and girls returned the key all smelling much nicer and even refused a beer!! I don't know what the UK military is coming to, in my day we would have sold the shower key to a local for beer tokens and probably raided *Spectra's* drinks locker whilst we were still singing Superman.

We spent a day on maintenance and have replaced the auto pilot pump (subject to sea trials). We also bled the hydraulic steering system as I suspect air might have been causing the grinding noise in the first place. We then re-checked the engine and compiled a list of spare parts required. The list will shortly be sent to my son Tony and our sterling crew mate Steve, along with a begging letter, asking them to bring the goodies out with them to Tenerife. I must mention that Norma, not being one to miss an opportunity, took herself up to Tommy and Sue's hotel before they booked out and had a really long and bubbly soak in the bath.

Here we are again, almost ready to set off for Tenerife. The plan at the moment is to leave on Monday 27th and head straight down to Tenerife passing close by the Ilhas Desertas and the Ilhas Selvagens. Both of these islands are Portuguese nature reserves inhabited by lonesome wardens so perhaps we will get the chance to give them a wave as we sail by.

I forgot to mention that during the trip over to Madeira, Norma finally perfected the art of bread making on board. We are now definitely ready to go.

29th Oct 2014 12:24:56
Madeira to the Salvage Islands -------- Ilhas Selvagens
30:08.963N 15:57.

Here we are happily bobbing along on the second afternoon of our trip to Tenerife. Having picked up and safely stowed our new crew, Tommy and Sue, we departed Funchal at 08:00 and motored out of the marina past *Discoverer*, the 67-foot UK military yacht which had come in the night before. Nine very grateful, and certainly cleaner-looking, squaddies came on deck to wave us off as we raised sails and headed out. Wind at last; we had a steady 12-15 knots on our beam all morning and *Spectra* lifted her skirts slightly and, like the dignified lady she is, positively skipped along at 6-7 knots for over eight hours. We passed the Deserted Islands (Ilhas Desertas) to port about 10 miles off, along with several of the huge catamarans the locals use as trip boats that were busily looking for dolphins, and we continued to head south. They had no chance with the dolphin-spotting, we didn't see any all day.

Nothing much happened as we settled into our routines, the steering gear was behaving itself and enjoying life with its new pump humming away and the fishing gear was out tempting the big one that I just know is out there somewhere. We drew lots for the shift pattern, 2 on 6 off, as that had worked really well on the way over and Sue prepared a feast for the first night at sea, Chorizo Chicken mmmmm! At 13:30 Norma, who was sunbathing on deck, let out a squeal of alarm when, with a bang, the spinnaker halyard broke and dumped 1,436 square feet of nylon into the sea. Everyone leapt into action and we managed to pull it all back on deck before it wrapped itself around the rudder or did itself any irreparable damage. On inspection the line had frayed at the point it comes through the mast and so my splicing skills remain irreproachable. Two hours and various attempts later we had managed to untangle the chute from its snuffer and successfully re-launched the spinnaker on a spare halyard.

As the sun dropped, the wind went with it, and so it was a motor sail through the night. The only memorable point of the night shift was when, on my handover to Peter, he made the coffee and put orange juice in mine instead of milk; definitely a taste sensation at 2 o'clock in the morning. The next morning our first group of dolphins gave us a visit. I wasn't sure whether the crew would appreciate being woken up so I settled for just saying down the hatch in a conversational tone, "there are dolphins up here". I heard a thump from below as Sue jumped out of bed and come scurrying on deck to see the dolphins, shortly followed by Tommy to see where Sue was going so early. There were about 12 of them jumping about, grinning in that dolphin kind of way (I still think they are up to something) and they were a new breed to add to our list; quite small and spotted, maybe they were teenagers? What a great way to start a day, especially as this spectacle was shortly followed by the call "land ho" - we are traditionalists aboard *Spectra* - as the Salvage Islands (Ilhas Selvagens) came up over the horizon. We have been sailing very slowly all morning and are now directly in between the two main Salvage Islands, having sighted a big whale venting as we approached.

That's it for this one, we expect to arrive in Tenerife tomorrow afternoon/early evening all being well, at which point I will send this in and update on the last night and day.

30th Oct 2014 23:05:08

Salvage Islands (Ilhas Selvagens) to Tennerife

28:01.166N   16:36.............   2137 miles from Ramsgate by Log.

We arrived in Tenerife at 16:10 Wednesday afternoon all safe and sound with no further dramas. Wow, that's a change! Tommy won the prize for closest arrival time and wouldn't share his Lion Bar with anyone. Going into the last night I seriously expected to be writing a tale of heavy rain and strong winds as a huge bank of ominous black clouds built up in front of us. We changed course by 20 degrees to see if we could dodge them, but we had no chance as they slowly spread right across our path. It was a case of batten down the hatches, get back on course and let what happens happen. What did happen? Nothing, that's what. As we got closer the clouds thinned rose and faded away - all very strange but also very pleasing to say the least.

Soon we were motoring along in a crystal-clear night with phosphorescence all around and a million stars lighting the way. Note the motoring again: as the clouds disappeared so did the wind and on went the 'donkey' for the remainder of the night. One notable incident in the early hours was Norma setting her clock wrong (not for the first time) and arriving on deck at 5 o'clock instead of 6, much to Peters delight and everyone else's amusement in the morning. We also had a couple of dolphins shooting past in a shower of sparks like torpedoes in an old war film as they set off the phosphorescence with their dorsal fins.

By morning Tenerife was clearly in sight and shortly after breakfast up came the wind. A steady 10-15 knots on our aft starboard quarter, this was a rarity not to be missed. Pretty soon I was playing with sails: full main, full mizzen and the spinnaker; down with the spinnaker; poled out foresail and stay sail; put away the staysail; goose wing the mizzen and main, great fun, I was loving it. I was just commenting that, with the last ½ a degree wind shift, how nice the mizzen staysail would look and it would probably fly well and give us a tenth of a knot if we just got it out from below the forward bunk, when my motley crew mutinied and told me to bugger off. So that was the end of that. In all honesty though, the cruising chute was still playing up and was a major pain to launch and recover.

Needless to say, and despite the motley crew's tardiness, we all agreed that it was a great sail along the full length of the coast down to San Miguel Marina. We are now safely booked in and stern-to, which is another first for the trip. Yet another milestone was the 2,000-mile mark crossed in the early hours; pat on the back for each other there, I think. We are moored next to where a tourist submarine is operating and alongside the waiting pontoon for the tourists. This provides an ever-changing audience as we potter about the decks. This morning, before Tommy and Sue headed off to their shore-side apartment with bath and pool, (sounds horrible to me but Norma is twitching), we decided to lay out the spinnaker on the pontoon and sort out the furling sock problems. As we began to pull the beast down the boarding ramp, or passarelle if you are very posh, I met up with a Turkish guy who was walking past *Spectra* with a handful of shiny, new, metal boat parts. Upon investigating, I discovered he was on his way back to a local manufacturer to get some adjustments made to his wind vane. What a bit of luck, as I needed to get a part made for the bowsprit in order to extend the cruising chute's tack line out further beyond the pulpit and stop another source of chaffing. I dropped Peter and Tommy like a shot and went off with my new friend to visit the steel makers. On my return I found the spinnaker all neatly laid-out and in its bag, but I did get told off by Sue for getting into a car with a strange man. Anyway, the workshop was fine and the price quoted even better, plus we are now booked to get lifted out next Friday to check the old girl's bottom before we set sail for the Cape Verde Islands and the Atlantic crossing.

Peter has now drawn up a design for our bowsprit extension which we will drop off tomorrow on our way over to visit Tommy and Sue in their hotel with swimming pool. I think I will take my trunks just in case the swimming pool is being under used, I hate waste.

Is it still raining in the UK by the way?

5th Nov 2014 17:11:46
Tenerife San Miguel Marina
28:01.166N 16:36.798W
still 2137 miles from Ramsgate by Log.

We have been here for four days now and, although Peter keeps mentioning that this isn't a holiday it is an adventure, I must admit we haven't been very adventurous. Tommy and Sue moved ashore for the second night and we have taken full advantage of the facilities at their apartment. We went out for a meal with Nikki, Sue's friend from yesteryear, along with her husband José and son Alex at a local restaurant of their choosing. What a great night; the food was superb, the wine better, and the company better still. It certainly pays to know a local!

We have hired a car between the three of us and took a trip up to Mount Teide, Tenerife's resident volcano and also spent a day at the beach.

It has not been all play though, I spent a morning at the top of the mast running new halyards down and trying to find ways of reducing chafe so that we don't have any more failures on the next leg. Dangling in the bosons chair, searching for the mouse line with a bit of hooked wire, I was beginning to lose all feeling in my legs as the chair was cutting into parts that you don't talk about in polite company, when Norma with her usual confidence said it must be at the back of the mast to port, so search there. Of course, first attempt, out came the mouse line and on went Norma's smuggest expression, 20 minutes I had been hanging there fishing for that damn line.

This morning we moved *Spectra* over, as our berth was a nightmare in the swell and the passarelle was getting caught on dockside obstacles all of the time which had caused some damage to our stern rail. We have now swapped neighbours, from a very uncommunicative eastern European group to a family from the Cook Islands. They have three young children all under five years old who are blond haired, and as brown as berries. The children run around like little monkeys all day, having an absolute whale of a time helping Mum and Dad to travel the world in a 30ft boat. The wind has picked up over the last two days and is now a steady 15-20 knots from the North, which is refreshing as it has been pretty humid here, so all fairs well for the next leg, if that keeps up. The surge in the harbour has caused us a few problems and the passarelle has managed to break one of its upright posts and scrape a chunk of paint and gel coat from two patches on the stern, so that's another job to add to the list. The hunt for anti-foul goes on with limited success but we have until the lift out on Friday to find some, so no panic yet.

Tommy and Sue flew off this morning and we had a meal out wearing our crew shirts last night to celebrate another successful trip. I am sure the locals thought we were a new tour operator, as we did seem to generate a lot of interest. Again, a really good meal but it was sad to say goodbye to Tommy and Sue.

Anyway, we will meet up again in Barbados for Christmas and we have already done the secret Santa draw so I have to find a suitable gift for under £10 somewhere mid Atlantic. Who knows I might catch a really big Tuna, that must be worth a tenner if I can only keep it fresh..............

10th Nov 2014 19:05:00
Lift out and a room with a bath
28:01.166N 16:36.
Tennerife San Miguel Marina......still 2137 miles from Ramsgate by Log.

Well we are still in Tenerife but we have moved ashore for a few days into a lovely apartment sourced by Tommy and Sue's friend Nikki. Norma is in her element, bath, shower, swimming pool, high ceilings and none of it moves when the wind blows, all very decadent. *Spectra* has been lifted out and is now safely ashore drying out and getting her bottom painted by Peter and myself, whilst Norma has stripped the marital suite and is busy re-varnishing an acre or two of woodwork. I have had a bit of a traumatic time this week as we have been getting a snap, crackle and pop noise from the hull, which was disturbing to say the least. I reassured Norma that all was well, and then found a darkened corner to research on the internet. Of course, my first thought was terminal osmosis or a new species of fibre weevil, my second thought was thermal expansion as it is now getting pretty warm. The internet gurus nearly all agreed that it is marine life, mussels or shrimps, although one chap did seem to be suggesting that it was something to do with the Russians in cahoots with Al Qaeda but one conspiracy theorist is about standard for every internet forum. I was still pretty sceptical until I talked to my new marina buddies and they all complained of the same noises, phew! I have now had a bowsprit extension made (don't tell Ramsgate marina or they will up my mooring fees when I get back) which should stop the spinnaker tack line from rubbing on the pulpit. If it doesn't bend on first use that is, as now that I have it fitted, I think I have had it made too long and too thin; time will tell. (Time didn't tell on that one as I then decided to take it back to the machine shop and have it cut in half and doubled the thickness so now it will never bend but will probably rip the bowsprit out; time will tell again.)

Peter has been busy stitching up all of our chaff damage from the last few months and a very good job he has done too. If I cut myself, I think he will find himself upgraded to emergency suture nurse. I have also given the outboard and dinghy another test run, all went perfectly. Well done Andy B-H for the service in France. Norma has finalised the meal plans: 3 meals a day x 5 people x 6 weeks plus snacks, and the shopping list keeps growing. Because we are not sure of what we will be able to get in the Cape Verdes, if anything, we have decided to stock up here and do the big shop after we are back in the water. I think the weight of all that shopping could break the crane if we do it before we are re-launched.

Three days later:

Spectra went back into the water this morning proudly flying her RAF ensign in respect of Remembrance Day. We now have a German yacht moored on one side of us and a French military training yacht on the other side of him, who were both very interested in the ensign so I had a bit of explaining to do. At least I wasn't flying a UKIP flag so I think we are all still all friends.

I finally sourced a good supplier of anti-fouling at the local fishermen's co-operative. It was a quarter of the price of anything that has a yacht on the label and, as it wasn't purchased from a yacht chandler who knows, it might actually work. If it is not impolite to speak of a lady's bottom on a public forum, I must say that *Spectra* is now very smooth and ship shape below the waterline. In fact, our fat bottomed, smiley girl is ready to set off again. To that end Norma took us shopping. She then took us shopping again and apparently one more shopping trip should do it. I think I should have painted the waterline a few inches higher as we are getting lower in the water by the day with all of the food that is coming aboard. In preparation for this trip I have spent many years learning to sail and my little Log Book is full of sailing certificates. Now, having now been at it in earnest for a few months, I think the most useful certificate I have is Prince 2; this is just one big project management task. I hope all the guys at O2 and NSC appreciate the fact that I am keeping my hand in. Having said that, I am over budget, behind schedule and under manned at the moment so perhaps I shouldn't brag. Anyhow Tony, my son and Steve, our intrepid fisherman, fly out on Tuesday evening, we should then be good to go on Thursday, next stop the Cape Verdes. All I need to do first is one more, or possibly two more, shopping trips, fill up with diesel, clear Customs, clean the boat, find out exactly where the Cape Verdes are (pretty sure it's south and west a bit from here). Oh, and then I have to pay for the lift out, food, fuel and marina. All contributions gratefully accepted in a plain brown envelope addressed to:

> The Yacht that is Bulging at the Seams
> End of the pontoon,
> San   Miguel,   Tenerife.

TENERIFE TO THE CAPE VERDE ISLANDS

NOVEMBER 2014

13th Nov 2014 09:32:46
Goodbye Tenerife
Tenerife San Miguel Marina to Sal Cape Verdes
28:01.166N 16:36…………..Still 2137 miles from Ramsgate by Log.

Tony and Steve arrived via Easyjet on Tuesday evening and we took them straight down to Santa Cruz to get our clearance paperwork all signed up. They managed to bring a bit of the English weather with them as it was raining when they arrived and the wind went into the South!! Anyway, things have settled now, a bit too settled to be honest. The wind has gone light, but we are ready to go. Steve is doing last-minute checks on the water maker, Tony is finding his way around the boat and the last food mountain has been stacked away. All we have to do now is fuel up and were off.

Last night we had our final meal out in Tenerife so it was out with the crew T shirts again and into town. Rather fittingly, we ate in the same restaurant that we had our first meal in. It is goodbye to Tenerife and onwards and downwards to the Cape Verde Islands. Seven hundred and sixty-two miles to go so it should take about 5 days… I will update every couple of days when I link up for our weather report downloads…talk to you soon.

15th Nov 2014 11:25:55
Clear Skies and Steady Winds 150 Miles West of Morocco
23:57……………2400 miles from Ramsgate by Log.

Day three and all is going well, 8 am and 250 miles logged. We finally managed to leave San Miguel at 13:00 on Thursday, having topped up the fuel tanks and a couple of extra containers that we managed to buy from the operators of the tourist submarine with 600 litres of diesel (at 98 cents a litre pretty damn good). Lucky for us we did, as it turned out, because we had a dead calm for the first 18 hours as we motored southwards trying to catch the winds, while Norma created another masterpiece from the aft deck. When we pulled away from Tenerife a pod of 12 pilot whales crossed our path which added a bit of excitement to the departure.

The first night came in with the most spectacular sunset of the trip so far and was followed by a clear and starry night, with shooting stars passing at regular intervals; just what the doctor ordered.

We are now settled into our routine of two hours on and six off and one crew member on Mummy watch which seems to be working well. With a steady force 3-4 from the North East pushing us along at 6 knots we are eating up the miles. Wildlife has been interesting so far, as usual we had a few isolated dolphins on the first night which were very impressive as the bio luminance was very active and then, as the night came in on day two, a group of 'white' whales appeared to port that were actually breaching. I think white whales are Belugas but without Wikipedia we can't settle any arguments aboard. The steering has been a bit "spongy" again and the auto pilot has been working hard, so we bled the system this morning which has improved the feel of the steering no end. We also have a fully working aft heads now that I have released the airlock that was blocking it. Oh! a life on the ocean waves, it's all glamour, you know. We now have two first-rate fishermen aboard, (Tony and Steve) and the talk has been non-stop of lures, ideal boat speed, wire traces and optimum depths for trolling. Result so far = Cottage Pie for dinner. Need I say more?

I will blog again in a couple of days by which time we should be getting close to the Cape Verdes.

16th Nov 2014 10:11:19

Bad news from home

Spectra Crew 21:42.84N 19:59.93W

Messages from the crew,

It was with great sadness that we learned today that Jo has lost her battle with cancer. I cannot think of a single instance where someone has put up such a determined and valiant fight only to finally be beaten by this nasty disease.

We first met Jo and Martin when they welcomed Norma and myself aboard their yacht *Magnum* for a delivery trip from Brighton to Ramsgate on a bitterly cold winter's day in 2006. That was our first meeting with Jo and our first trip to Ramsgate. Without Jo and Martin, and of course Magnum, we would probably never have come to Ramsgate, joined the yacht club and met such a great bunch of people, some of whom have become true friends and confidants. I would like to count Jo amongst those and I will miss her terribly. For Martin I can only express my deepest sorrow, offer my support and say that my door is always open, my shoulder available and my ear ready to listen.

A light has gone out in the world and tonight as I sail across this ocean I will look up at the billions of stars spread across the firmament and hope that one belongs to Jo, she deserves it.

Paul Russell

A friend.

Following on from Paul's words above, these alone cannot express the loss and sorrow we feel for

Jo, our dear friend who fought so vigorously to defeat this horrible disease that took her from us. We will miss you Jo and for Martin, whom you leave behind, we will do our utmost to support and comfort him at this very difficult time.

Life was so short for you Jo but you crammed it full of love, happiness and laughter. Your journey in life is done but the memories you leave behind will always remain.

Norma Russell

A friend

Jo,

Today is a sad day to hear that you have finally been defeated in your battle, let's hope that your experiences and how you eloquently described them in your blog will give comfort and hope to others. My lasting memory will be how stunning you looked when we thought you had won the first battle. Life is cruel. I have only known you for such a small part of your life but we had some wonderful times on *Magnum* and, needless to say, in the yacht club afterwards; our gang has lost a shining star. Martin, so sorry for your loss, I hope you look back on all the happy times you shared with Jo and that they will comfort you as you move forward. Sadly, unable to be around for you now but I know you have lots of people to support you in this difficult time.

Steve

18th Nov 2014 12:21:10

Nearly There...230 miles west of Mauritania (Western Sahara)

19:39.38N21:37.27W......2704 miles from Ramsgate by Log.

Apart from the bad news from home this has been a wonderful sail. The wildlife has been abundant and our fishermen have failed to capture any of it. The flying fish have shown up and at the moment there are regular groups of 10-20 of them flying away from our bow as we plough on through the waves. We have sighted whales at least once every day and the dolphins pop up every now and then to check on our progress. Apart from that, human life forms have been a rarity. We have seen four aeroplanes and two ships in the last four days, all way off except for one. That one showed up on AIS 15 miles behind us last night and closing. On investigation all it said was that it was a sailing yacht and it was doing 9 knots. We were doing 6.5 at the time and so a few surreptitious twitches started to be applied to lines, and sail trim became a topic of discussion. Not that we were racing you understand, but we managed to tweak her up to 7 knots. On checking, the other boat was still closing, now doing 9.4 knots. An hour later the AIS signal was strong enough to get more details; the other boat was called *Constance* and she was 97ft long and 24ft on the beam (obviously they couldn't afford a 100-footer), so honour saved, we let her sail past. She slowed down as it got dark, but inexorably closed us down finally passing still doing 8 knots 2 miles to starboard at 02:00 in the morning. And that is about as exciting as it gets. The generator has decided not to generate and it will have to be fixed in Cape Verde. I am pretty sure it is a relay or loose connection as the motor is running fine and it will provide power on occasion. We are running the main engine for three hours a day to keep everything topped up and cooled down which seems to be working so expensive on fuel but no dramas yet.

Thanks to everyone who has replied to my request for comments on the blog, it is much appreciated that you are enjoying the read out there. One blogateer commented that it was good to hear about the mundane trials of cruising life rather than just fast sails, glorious sunsets, storms and baggy wrinkles, etc, so here goes: An example of life on passage:

How to make posh coffee downwind in a force 6 and 3 metre swell

1. Someone who shall remain nameless (Steve) says that "a posh coffee would be nice, wouldn't it"?
2. Paul, who is on Mummy watch, decides to meet the challenge.

3. Get packet of filter coffee from cupboard and put on work surface.
4. Boat lurches; pick packet up from floor and lay flat on work surface.
5. Get coffee pot out of cupboard and put on work surface.
6. Boat lurches; pick up coffee pot from floor and place bottom part on gimballed cooker, fill top part with water by mistake and screw onto the bottom part unknowingly making it top heavy.
7. Cut top from filter coffee packet place on work surface and return scissors to drawer for safety.
8. Boat lurches; turn around and in slow motion watch filter coffee packet spill contents on galley floor.
9. Begin to pick up coffee granules from floor.
10. Boat lurches; watch in slow motion as coffee pot succumbs to gravity and spills water onto galley floor.
11. Try to catch it, slip and end up sitting in now wet coffee granules.
12. Scrape mess into top part of coffee pot and while hanging on to the sink with one leg braced across the galley, fill the bottom part with water, use both arms, both legs, chin and elbows to assemble the thing and clamp it down onto the cooker.

13. Start to mop up the layer of cold coffee coagulating on the floor, slip twice more.
14. Receive acerbic comment from a passing Norma about state of the galley, while on my knees mopping up.
15. Walk backwards into aft cabin as I mop, spread even finer layer of cold coffee on that floor.
16. Receive acerbic comment from a passing Norma about state of aft cabin floor while on my knees mopping up.
17. Finish cleaning, realise my feet are brown with coffee so crawl on my knees into aft toilet (heads) to wash feet.
18. Balance on one leg with foot in sink.
19. Boat lurches; Spread coffee from feet down the shower curtain, hit the (luckily closed) toilet seat face first while foot is still in sink (trust me – it is painful but possible).
20. Untangle my various body parts, strip off because I am now covered in coffee sludge and get myself wedged into a corner and return foot to sink.
21. Receive acerbic comment from a passing Norma about performing unnatural acts in the aft toilet (heads) when I should be making coffee.
22. Clean feet, clean me, clean toilet, clean shower curtains, clean wall, clean a coffee smudge from ceiling (not sure how that got

there but it hurt), put clothes in laundry basket, dress and then clean entire route back to the galley.
23. Check on coffee's progress and realise I haven't lit the gas!!!!
24. Light gas.
25. Watch coffee pot like a hawk. Note: a watched pot does boil, it just takes a very long time.
26. Coffee percolates, place three cups in sink to avoid spillage (getting clever now), pour coffee.
27. Boat lurches; Waste half of coffee down sink,
28. Boil water and top up filter coffee with that – they will never notice if I don't tell them!
29. Open fridge to get milk.
30. Boat lurches; half of the fridge's contents eject onto my lap.
31. Shove it all back into fridge except milk which has skidded under the chart table.
32. Retrieve milk on knees and crawl back to galley.
33. Receive acerbic look, but no comment, from Norma who is looking down the hatch from the cockpit with an expression of "I should have listened to my Mother" on her face.
34. Begin to pour milk into coffee cups (remember those -they have been going cold in the sink)

35. Boat lurches; Waste half of the milk down sink,
36. Open fridge and shove in the milk while boat is relatively stable.
37. Serve coffee to a delighted and grateful crew.
38. Total time: 1 hour 15 mins. Who said ocean sailing was tedious and boring? Sometimes there are just not enough hours in the day.

Now to wash up the dishes, but that's another story ....

20th Nov 2014 13:30:57
Sal Cape Verdes and our fishermen break their duck
16:45.255N 22:58.772W
2941 miles from Ramsgate by Log.

We have arrived!!! Longest passage yet and it all went really well. The wind was a steady force 4-6 from the North for most of the trip and we averaged a respectable 6.3 knots over the five days. The top news must be that the boys have broken their duck and we have caught some fish!!!! Ironically, the success came when they were playing with homemade lures instead of using the array of glitzy specialist ones that they have in their bag of tricks. But it would be churlish of me not to give credit where credit is due. Steve struck first with a dorada which he had filleted and on ice in record time; that one fish fed us all to capacity and very good it was too. That night, when Steve was on watch, he heard a thump on deck followed by another four bumps. Rather nervously he shone a light on deck, lo and behold! we had five flying fish flapping around which were soon bagged up and in the fridge. Peter made potato cakes with fried flying fish for breakfast, and we felt like proper blue water sailors. All we need to do now is grow decent pony tails and we will be there. The next day Tony struck, snatching a small tuna out of a school of them that had been swimming alongside of us, snapping up any flying fish that we scared up. Not to be beaten, I got the next one by dropping a lure right in front of one of the tuna, it just grabbed it and we had him. This went on for 15 minutes or so and then the fish got wise and disappeared.

The pilot books recommended against entering Palmeria on Sal by night and so with a dropping wind we motored the last 20 or so miles in a bid to beat the sunset. Failed that one miserably, but to be honest the entrance was pretty easy anyway. The only confusing thing was a large structure in the harbour entrance which turned out to be the 97ft yacht *Constance* that had passed us on the way down and was now anchored in the harbour mouth. Once we had steered around that obstacle we dropped our hook and were soon snugly anchored, listening to the gospel music coming out of a small chapel on the dark shore.

The next morning and it was all up and about early getting ready to go ashore. Norma and I went first to clear customs at the police station, whilst Peter and Tony stripped the Karcher jet washer unsuccessfully looking for a capacitor to fix our generator. The next step was for all of us to travel to the airport to get our passports stamped; we would then be all legal and the yellow quarantine flag could come down from our spreaders. The trip to the airport was by local minibus for 50 cents each and an exciting ride it was, dodging potholes and sleeping dogs in the road, in equal proportion. Everyone has been really friendly and helpful so far, which is great. I am really enjoying this place, it is definitely more Africa than Europe, and the area we are in has, so far, only had very limited impact from tourism. We had lunch in Espargos, the next largest town, at a restaurant that we found down a side road. The owner spoke good English and recommended a local dish of bean and meat stew which, I suspect, was all he had. We said "yes" and it was excellent. I asked him where we could buy a capacitor which stretched his English but he got the idea and phoned a friend. That friend phoned another one who recommended an Italian guy in Santa Maria and so the owner phoned him. All was sorted and he had a capacitor so it was back on the minibus and off we went. The mini bus driver took us right to the door of the shop which was, of course, closed. As we were peering through the window wondering what to do next, a quad bike pulled up with a smiling Italian on board and via Google translator on his IPad we managed to ask for a 25 uf capacitor. Oddly enough, in a shop that was pretty bare of anything else, he had a drawer full of them and so 13 Euros lighter we were in business. The Cape Verdean Escudos is 100 to 1 Euro by the way and the two are completely interchangeable. You pay in Euros and get change in Escudo and vice versa which is pretty easy once you get used to it.

The rest of the day was spent looking around Santa Maria and eating cold ice creams on the beach so it was a pretty full on affair and I was exhausted at the end of it. We jumped in a minibus with a couple of businessmen and a soldier for the trip back to the boat, picking up several other passengers along the way. Curiously, there are no bus stops. Instead, the driver sees someone he thinks needs a lift, slows down and turns his music down just enough so that he can shout out of the window and negotiate a price for any destination roughly along his route. If all agree everyone shifts over and they squeeze in, the music goes back up and off we go. It cost us a Euro each and we travelled nearly the length of the island; I loved every minute of it.

To top off a very successful day, when we got back to the harbour the local fishermen had caught four huge tuna and were filleting them on the dockside with the whole village looking on. One weighed in at 77 kg, without head or innards, which put our fishing exploits sharply into perspective.

Upon our return to *Spectra*, Tony and Peter replaced the capacitor and our generator burst into life along with the fridge, water maker, battery charger, electric kettle and washing machine; all of the modern conveniences restored. We celebrated with a meal aboard and several cool beers, the last one of which I am drinking now. The plan is to head for Mindello in a couple of days which is 113 miles to the west. That will be our last stop before the big crossing............. Good night. I will blog again soon.

22nd Nov 2014

Day two and we were on the busy minibus again heading to the airport to clear Customs a day early. This is a bit of a cheat but, as most of the boats in the harbour hadn't even cleared in, we decided to bend the rules a bit and clear out the day before we actually leave. The Customs process was quite easy apart from the slight problem that the Customs man had lost his ink pad, so we had to stand and watch while he coloured in the rubber stamp with his pen and then pushed it onto our passports. Five times!! Later, we were taken to the gas works by a local chap who knocked on a side gate and gave one of our gas cylinders to the security guard. Thirty minutes later we picked up a full gas cylinder for 5 Euro plus 1 Euro to our negotiator, which was all very legal and above-board, I am sure. The final stop-off was at the machine shop to pick up a bracket for one of our mast fittings, which had broken along one of the weld lines. All nicely welded, we now have a working kicking strap again which should be useful on the downwind legs to come. Back to *Spectra* with our stamped passports and bag of goodies, we are all ready to go .... Mindelo here we come!

23rd Nov 2014 10:53:40
Mindelo Cape Verdes and 3000 milestone reached
16:53.208N   24:59.480W…3075   miles   from Ramsgate by Log.

After a great last night out in Palemeria we have arrived at Mindelo and a very strange trip it was. We departed Palmeria Sal at 11:30 for the 118-mile trip over to Mindelo, expecting to arrive in time for breakfast the following morning.

Unfortunately, the wind went light leaving us limping along at 2 knots at times. Norma grabbed the slow sailing record by managing 0.3 knots for 30 minutes. I eventually gave up and we ran the engine for about six hours in total which pushed our average up to 5.1 knots for the trip and got us in at 13:00. Overnight, we were surrounded by strange flashes in the water as whatever fishy battles were going on under the seas lit up the bio luminance in great splodges of green light. When we shone the large spotlight out over the water we were surrounded by little red fish eyes glowing in the dark, literally hundreds of them, all very strange and quite spooky. Several flying fish landed on deck but we threw them back in this time, apart from one unlucky chap that we found in front of the forward hatch the next day. We had two new species to add to the list though; as we approached Mindelo harbour a shark measuring about 6 foot swam towards the boat before lazily turning and moving away. So, that was swimming in the harbour definitely off the agenda. As we came onto our mooring a very large turtle surfaced right next to us chewing away on some delicacy he had found, before diving back under not to be seen again.

The harbour is very hot and sticky with an atmosphere that is not as friendly as Palmeria, which is a shame. When you walk out of the marina you are immediately accosted by well dressed, well fed kids, begging for money, which is obviously their main job in life, and not a very savoury gauntlet to have to run. Also, the marina is very commercial with prices to match, and water is charged by the litre as an extra, even in the showers! Even though the marina comes with a glitzy office building it still has not got working internet, which is something we have become used to. Eventually, the marina staff, with bad grace, accepted that it wasn't our five devices at fault and that their internet wasn't working and directed us to a café over the road which has good internet. Unfortunately, Norma picked up a bug and had to take to her bed for the day. By the following morning, instructions were being issued out of the rear cabin at a fast and furious rate and poor old Peter and Steve were jumping to attention, the general consensus is that she is on the mend. In fact, as I sit here, she is poking Tony with a fishing rod through the forward hatch, in a vain attempt to get him out of bed.

We have a few maintenance tasks to try and complete before the big off, the first being to get out of Norma's way, the second to buy some rivets for our kicking strap plate that we managed to pull off in a gybe on the way over. The third is our secondary battery charger that has given up the ghost, so I will try to get that fixed on Monday. Apart from that it will be last-minute shopping, a whistle-stop sightseeing tour and then, hopefully, set sail for Barbados on Tuesday or Wednesday; all very exciting.

As always, I will update on progress and do a blog before we sail. No doubt from the cafe across the road with the free internet.

25th Nov 2014 09:17:47
The big off
16:53.208N 24:59.480W

Today is the day and we are all ready to set off for the Atlantic crossing. We spent a day on maintenance yesterday and have fixed many of the niggling little things that have sprung up over the weeks. Tony has replaced the blown mini bulbs in the engine instrument panel with LEDs and Peter and Steve fixed the loose bow roller for the main anchor. Norma and I managed to track down a couple of extra fuel containers, so that will be 100 litres we carry on deck and 1000 below decks. All of that meant a trip to the fuel pump is due before we head off, 83 cents per litre here by the way. We also did the Customs arrival and departure in one sitting at the commercial port which, if unusual, was at least an easy process. We joined the short queue to check in and then went to the back of the queue and booked out again. Rather surreal but we need the clearance forms to avoid any hassle in Barbados. Observation: Why are customs officers all so serious looking? Is there an international school of stern looks out there somewhere that they all must attend?

Tony, Peter and Steve had a day out on the beach and at the old military fort on the headland on Saturday and took a few really good photos. They also met up with some of the crew from the 97ft yacht *Constance*. Yes, the same one that passed us on the way down from Tenerife. The Skipper remembered passing us in the night and the fact that they had a discussion on their bridge about our red over green masthead lights and what size of yacht we might be, small world. Whilst all of this was happening, I was nursing a sick Norma who had relapsed. On the bright side, she has bounced back again and is now back in the land of the living and enjoying large pints of lager in the local hostelries whilst we, of course, drink water.

We have also managed to fill our last two blue gas bottles which have been empty since Spain. The marina's only advice on filling the bottles was, "this will be difficult" followed by a blank stare; great help that was. Norma and I went on a mission into town with gas bottles in hand asked around. "No problem, no stress" was the response from the lady at the petrol station and four hours later they were returned all filled up and for less than half the UK price. I am still awaiting a verdict on our secondary battery charger from the marina electrician, but we have sourced a simple car battery charger that will work if needed, just in case they don't come through.

Last night all five of us went out in the crew T shirts for the last meal ashore and a good one it was too. I am sending this from the café with internet, across the street from the marina, as the free marina Wi-Fi is still not working. As I have said before, 14-21 days for the crossing and then Barbados. I will try to update every couple of days or so it may be longer as I have to save my minutes and conserve the limited bandwidth on my satellite phone.

Until next time ....

CAPE VERDE TO BARBADOS

NOVEMBER AND DECEMBER 2014

27th Nov 2014 12:48:42
Heading West first blog
16:34.001N 29:46.448W

Before I blog I must say that we have finally been given permission to tell the world that we are going to be grandparents again. It has been killing me, keeping this quiet, but it is Gemma's and Duncan's baby so Gemma's and Duncan's rules. It will, of course be the best looking, cleverest, happiest and most loved baby in the world and I can say that without a hint of bias. Congratulations Gemma, Duncan and of course Lily, or as you will soon be known, big Sis.

Here we are, second night at sea just completed, and all is well. Peter's grandchildren will be pleased to hear that he has, so far, avoided being eaten by a shark. Having said that, he is on mummy watch after lunch today and it is sausage casserole for dinner. Depending on the final result he may well be thrown to the sharks yet. Steve is running around like the proverbial Duracell bunny, finishing off his mummy watch and cleaning all the onion skins from the saloon floor; more of that later. Tony is on watch and has just seen a flying fish land on deck, Norma is writing a piece for the next blog on night watches from the female perspective and I, apart from being the full time Master and Commander, am avoiding all work and writing this blog. So, life at sea and how has it has treating us:

We finally got away from the fuel berth in Mindelo at 14:30 and headed straight out to sea. It was strange but we didn't realise just how much Mindelo had got us down, the whole atmosphere on *Spectra* noticeably lifted when we motored out. I think Peter summed it up perfectly when he said that he had found the place oppressive. It was hard to put your finger on, but you felt as if you were being watched all of the time. We never did manage to get the battery charger fixed; every time I went back to the workshop it was "come back in two hours". After three days, you give-up, don't you? Even when I asked for the charger back it took them three hours and I only got it then after I saw one of the marina staff walking onto another boat with it under his arm and chased him down.

Anyway, enough of the moaning, we have left, are on our way and all is well with the world. We had a cracking sail down between the islands and by early evening we were clear of land and heading due west. The wind stayed at a steady force 4-5 until midnight when it all went wrong. Within 10 minutes it dropped away and left us wallowing in the swell and that's the way it carried on all night. I thought the mast was going to shake out of her at one point as we rolled and slammed in the swell. A hugely frustrating night and I was on deck at some point during every shift as we gybed the pole, reduced sails, raised them again, etc, etc, etc. No one had much sleep and it was a bedraggled crew that gathered for breakfast as we limped along at 1.5 knots the following morning. But then along came the wind; it has now been blowing a steady force 6 for over 30 hours and we have been flying along. The last 24-hour run was 173 miles which is pretty damn good. Being twitchy about any unusual noises on board, and there were a lot of them on the first night what with all of the rolling, I went into the second night pretty tired and praying for a peaceful sleep. I sleep in the saloon quite often at night when we are sea as it is easier for the guys to call me without disturbing Norma (and they are all scared of waking her, but that's another story). No sooner had I closed my eyes than I heard a crackling sound. I lay awake listening to this sound convincing myself it was one of the bulkheads cracking. So, up I got and with a torch in hand stuck my head in every locker in the saloon, no solution. I next thought it was a deck fitting so on deck I went, life jacket and harness on, to check the fittings – none loose. The galley next: all cupboards checked, lots of rattles but no creaks or crackles. I then decided to check the deck beams and shroud plates from inside, as every time we leant over and pressure came on the rigging the cracking sound would happen. As I passed through the saloon for the umpteenth time I bumped my head on the vegetable net that we have hung from the saloon ceiling. Four dry onions rolled across the hanging net. Two hours wasted and back to bed for me, lulled asleep by the gentle crackle of dry onion skins falling on the saloon floor. I eventually had a good night's sleep.

On the first night a deck wash tap was knocked open at some point, probably hooked on someone's lifeline, and we lost a lot of fresh water before it was noticed. Today we are having a bit of a marathon generator and water maker run to get the tanks back full again. All is well with us, we have all showered this morning leaving a lovely soapy smell down below and we are still averaging 6-7 knots, Barbados is getting closer all the time. I can almost smell the Mount Gay Rum Distillery from 1700 miles up wind.

I will blog again in a couple of days....................

29th Nov 2014 13:13:57
Heading West Second Blog, Norma's bit
15:59.218N 35:12.993W

Before we dive straight into Norma's contribution, here is the boring bit for all the accountants out there. Day five and all going well, the winds are due to drop in a day or two and so we are pushing on while the going is good. The watch system is working well, we are all eating together at each meal bar breakfast and getting at least some sleep as we roll along. The water tanks are full, and the generator is starting every time I push the button so big smiles from me.

Here are the stats so far:

Day 1	17.5 hours	84 miles	Average 4.8 knots
Day 2	24 hours	173 miles	Average 7.2 knots
Day 3	24 hours	187 miles	Average 7.8 knots
Day 4	24 hours	168 miles	Average 7.0 knots

That's it from me over to Norma.

Norma's bit

Well here I am thinking, "why let Paul have all the fame of writing to amuse, when I am sure I can add a little girly twist".

Sailing at Night from the female perspective or should I say mine as not all girlies are big whoosies like me. Sailing during the day is fun, I can read, paint, sew, practice my ukulele, watch films and generally make myself busy and, of course, I also have to make sure the boys are kept on their toes. Sometimes, however, things can get a little boring especially when all you can do is try to keep two feet on the floor/deck while using both hands to hang by your finger nails, just to stay in a safe position. Yes, all fingers nails are gone, broken off on the first day, but Paul has promised me a manicure when on land, something to look forward to along with a hot soak in Sue and Tommy's bath tub at their hotel in Barbados. At night though things change, you still have to balance and hang on while swinging around the cockpit like a monkey trying to keep all of your wits about you. So, this is where my on-watch time differs from the boys or is it that they simply lie?

I feel totally at the mercy of the darkness and all that lurks below, beside, behind and in front. If it's got lights and or AIS I am good, as I have the control to move if needed, the rest is just imagination. How do I survive as it really doesn't take much for my imagination to run riot? I do spook easily.

Now for all those things that make me jump and want to dive below leaving the boat to fend for herself while I run and hide:

Dark shapes lurch out of the sea beside me. "What is it"?

Dolphins, whales, turtles or something more sinister? Not to worry, it's only another large wave.

The boat is surrounded by lights flashing in the sea. "What's that"?

Aliens from the abyss coming to swallow us whole! Not to worry, only large fish swimming through the luminescence.

Lights directly ahead, and I mean, right on the bow. "What is it"?

A boat that I am now going to flatten. Not to worry, it's only our bow lights reflecting off the waves as we roll in the swell.

Something white flashes below in the saloon. "What is it"?

A ghostly presence now haunting the boat. Not to worry, only Steve getting ready for the watch change.

I've lost my boy, Tony. Where is he?

Has he been taken away by a giant squid? Not to worry he's in his bed fast asleep.

Something grinding and grumbling below my feet. "What is it"?

Is the rudder rattling free? Not to worry only Paul, snoring. (I don't snore -Paul)

Lights directly behind us. "What is it"?

Pirates getting ready to climb onboard. Not to worry, it's only our stern light as we surf down another large wave.

Something is on the deck next to me and still coming my way. "What is it"?

Torch in hand ready to strike anything that gets too near, but not to worry, the flash of light reveals another flying fish flapping around on deck.

I have survived another night! I thought Paul told me that he was taking me on an extended holiday. By the time this is ended I will have arms like Popeye, a head of grey locks like Steve and Peter and will probably be on some form of happy pills. As Peter always says "it's not a holiday, it's an adventure" and I am having a wonderful time and even though the night sailing makes me jump, it also keeps me awake. It is enjoyable during those periods of darkness when I am alone, I dream of our adventures and where the seas will take us next.

1st Dec 2014 12:32:51
Heading West Third Blog, A View from the Bosun's Chair
15:30.046N 39:58.358W

Before we dive straight into Steve's contribution, once again here is the boring bit for all the accountants out there. Day seven and all is going well, the winds have dropped and with them our daily averages but we are very close to the half way point now and way ahead of even our most optimistic schedule. We are keeping ahead of the maintenance and *Spectra* is in better shape now than when we left Mindello which can't be bad. So, without further ado here are the stats so far:

Day 1	17.5 hours	84 miles	Average 4.8 knots
Day 2	24 hours	173 miles	Average 7.2 knots
Day 3	24 hours	187 miles	Average 7.8 knots
Day 4	24 hours	168 miles	Average 7.0 knots
Day 5	24 hours	159 miles	Average 6.6 knots

Day 6   24 hours   149 miles   Average 6.2 knots

That's it from me, over to Steve.

A view from the Bosun's chair.

Today our thoughts are with Martin and his family; Rest in Peace Joanne.

Our life is a 15-mile circle within which everything concerns us and outside there could be nothing else. As our first week comes to an end, life on board has settled into a series of routines. Watch keeping which entails sailing, sleeping, relaxing and eating with long periods of inactivity. The sail configuration doesn't change much, the main is set over the port beam with 1 or 2 reefs depending on the conditions and a preventer to keep it under control in the bouncy seas. The little staysail is set just in front of that on the same side and the foresail is poled out to starboard providing a lot of the drive; again, this is reefed as per the conditions. We seem to maintain good speed and direction during the daytime with less predictable conditions through the night.

Being Sunday, today was a day for rest and recuperation; the fishing rods were set and the men folk were on deck discussing the finer points of life. Today was also shower day so *Spectra* and her crew are smelling delightful. Paul and Peter decided it was time to make themselves more presentable and have haircuts (I hope there's a good barber in Barbados!!) Norma needed to step in to finish Paul's. Half way through Paul's haircut one of the fishing lines started streaming line as a large dorado took the lure, after 10 minutes of excitement and battling with the fish it took a final leap out of the water, shook its head and was gone.

Things then settled into the daily routine again, maintenance, cooking and general chit chat. Peter was obviously content with all that was going on and quietly supervised all the activities (at least that's what I think he's doing with his eyes closed and chin on his chest!!)

At lunchtime, we all gathered in the cockpit to eat, which was a lovely bowl of pasta with pesto prepared by Paul. Not two mouthfuls in, one of the fishing rods bursts into life again. Tony grabbed the rod and, after a briefer battle than before, another dorado escapes the frying pan.

Mother watch entails cooking, sleeping, eating, cleaning, reading and watching movies. In the afternoon this fell to Norma. She took breaks through the day from doing laundry and cooking Sunday Roast, to practise her ukulele in her bedroom, she's not brave enough to go public just yet!

Things continued with the routine. This time it was my turn to do some supervising with Paul, Norma and Tony were having a chat on the deck when, for the third time today, the same fishing rod sprung into life with line streaming and lots of excited chatter.

Tony managed to get this fish alongside, it appeared to be a small wahoo! It was time to deploy the home-made gaff. I'm sure that Mr Heath and Mr Robinson would have been very proud of our engineering skills. Sadly, the gaff operator wasn't up to the task and once again the fish was gone. There then followed a lengthy debate and Gaff Mk 2 has been constructed; we shall report on its progress in later blogs.

Shortly after that we slipped into night time routines: a quick walk around the decks to make sure that nothing was in need of immediate repair, the harnesses were attached to the safety points, the steamer scarer brought on deck and tested and the navigation lights were on. Then Sunday lunch was ready - a superb meal of roast lamb with potatoes and vegetables; no mean feat is the swelling seas.

Ahead of us the sun dips below the horizon, just as it does a small cloud blocks it from view but a fan of light streams from behind and we have a wonderful golden sunset. No sooner has the sun gone down than the moon, which is overhead, is swathing us in its milky light, there is the proverbial velvet blanket of stars above our heads. Orion is the most obvious constellation to make a showing and the Pole Star is out on our starboard beam, but the Plough is reluctant to show itself.

The night then proceeds without any more excitement. Apart from the watch keeper, everyone takes themselves to their beds. At about 3 o'clock the moon has now set and the sky really comes alive with horizon to horizon stars with only the occasional cloud. Even the Plough has finally decided to put in an appearance. Then slowly the sky begins to lighten from the east behind us and the dawn of another day is here. Within a few minutes we get hit by a squall, the wind picks up from its fairly steady mid-teens to 35 knots and, again, lots of frantic activity. Then, just when everything is set, it has gone as quickly as it arrived and the wind has settled into single figures.

For those that don't know, a Bosun's Chair is a very uncomfortable seat that you strap yourself into in order to be hoisted up the mast. From there you have a birds-eye view of the boat.

3rd Dec 2014 13:43:00
Heading West Fourth Blog, Peter has his say
13:30.46N 43:38.727W

Fourth edition of the going west blogs and it is Peter's turn to wax lyrical. We crossed the half way point yesterday and, although a great personal achievement for all on board, it was tempered by the knowledge that it was Jo's funeral on the same day. As always, our thoughts were and are with Martin and those supporting him back at home. Although *Spectra* is normally a dry boat on passage we gathered together in the cockpit and had a beer in memory of Jo as the sun went down. We also launched a Chinese lantern from the stern as the sun dropped below the horizon. As it dipped and then rose on its passage out across the empty water we were five people, isolated by thousands of miles of ocean, thinking of loved ones at home.

As of this morning just under 1,000 miles to go.

Here are the stats so far:

Day 0.5	17.5 hours	84 miles	Average 4.8 knots
Day 1	24 hours	173 miles	Average 7.2 knots
Day 2	24 hours	187 miles	Average 7.8 knots
Day 3	24 hours	168 miles	Average 7.0 knots
Day 4	24 hours	159 miles	Average 6.6 knots
Day 5	24 hours	149 miles	Average 6.2 knots
Day 6	24 hours	147 miles	Average 6.1 knots
Day 7	24 hours	156 miles	Average 6.5 knots

Time taken to half way point: 7 days 1 hour and 30 minutes

And some extra ones:

Generator hours	44
Water maker Hours	20 1,000 litres of fresh water produced at 50 litres ph
Washing machine loads	3
Crew showers	3 x 5 crew = 15 showers

That's it from me; over to Peter.

Peter has his say.

My apologies to all you Blue Water Sailors but I thought that I would describe, perhaps to the non-initiated (particularly my grandchildren), some of the basic living challenges that crossing the lumpy Atlantic Ocean are presenting the crew of *Spectra*.

Many factors affect the living conditions on board *Spectra*, not least the direction and strength of the wind. However, one factor that may not be so well known is the sea state, for example for most of the trip thus far we have experienced 3 metre waves with the wind directly behind us, and this means that we rise and fall 3 metres each time a wave passes. *Spectra* will also speed up as we surf a wave and slow down as we come off a wave. This causes *Spectra* to move violently left, right, up or down without warning, which makes life 'interesting' and even the most mundane tasks such as cooking, sleeping and bathing a significant challenge. In a previous Blog Paul described making a simple cup of coffee, I hope the following will give a more complete description of the simple life on board.

Cooking

(I hate people who take sugar in their tea.)

The kitchen or galley (I call it the torture chamber) on board *Spectra* is well equipped with a freezer, fridge, microwave, double sink and two good sized work surfaces and an oven. If you can imagine a kitchen being bolted to a seaside rollercoaster you will have a rough idea of what it is like to cook on board *Spectra* in these conditions.

Let's start with something simple – tea and coffee. We have three crew who take tea and one who takes coffee; simple so far! However, if you put a mug on a surface *Spectra* will move violently and the mug will disappear at an alarming rate and end up in the main saloon (as I am writing this Steve, the duty cook, has just lost a jug from the galley which just missed me and ended up in the main saloon). Knives and forks can be lethal so one quickly learns not to leave them unattended (I have the scars to prove it). The oven is mounted on gimbals which means that the oven will pivot in rough seas keeping the top of the oven level, but it also means that the front of the oven will be at chest height one moment and then at knee height the next. I have devised a method of trapping the four mugs in the corner of the sink and holding them in one place with one hand while holding on with the other. The oven is opposite the sink so it is relatively simple to grab the kettle from the oven just at the top of the 'up' movement, and wedging myself between the sink and the oven I attempt to pour hot water onto tea bags and coffee. I then replace the kettle at the bottom of the oven's 'down' movement – job done. Not quite. I now have to get the milk from the fridge. I wait for a down movement of *Spectra* and them make a dash for the fridge. I grab the milk and then dash back to the sink in time to catch the mugs (I am not always successful). Job done. Nearly, but not quite – one amongst us actually takes sugar! Can you imagine that? He will remain nameless …. Anyway, Paul has always taken sugar in tea. Unfortunately, the sugar is kept in a cupboard at the far end of the galley. I did, once, try putting my foot in the sink to hold the mugs and then reach for the sugar – this was simply not practical (I am just too old) so I now trust to luck and hope that the mugs do not end up in the main saloon.

Moving on to something more adventurous – sausage casserole made with tinned baked beans and tinned tomatoes. I know – it sounds disgusting – but actually, after a long day's sailing it wasn't too bad. The oven is equipped with clamps which keep the pots in place so, with frying pan in place, I fry the sausages – simple. I take a sausage out of the frying pan and place it on the chopping board ready for cutting up, I then chase the sausage to the main saloon dust it down and put it back in the frying pan. It's ok, no one knows. After successfully cooking the casserole we have the difficult bit – serving. As I have said, nothing stays in place so serving is a challenge. We tend to eat in the main cockpit and fortunately there is a port (or window) between the cockpit and galley so we dish-up one meal at a time and push it through the window to the hungry sailors. Job done. The window also allows the cook of the day to shout obscenities at the helmsman suggesting, for example, that that they keep the *bleep, bleep* boat still!

Sleeping

Sounds simple, doesn't it? But no – imagine sleeping on a fairground rollercoaster; yes, you have the idea now. In order to be kept from being thrown from bed, the bunks are fitted with a piece of cloth, called a lee cloth, that is fixed to the bunk and tied to the cabin roof, once you are in bed. Whilst it stops you from hitting the floor it does nothing to stop you from being thrown about, hence the challenge of sleeping. I wedge myself under the shelf and push one foot down the side of the mattress; this works up to a point, although eventually my shoulder goes numb and I have to move. I tried to make a London tube style loop to put my hand in and hang from, this hurt my hand so, in a moment of inspiration, I dug out the very nice pair of sailing gloves Ken and Jon gave me before the trip. This worked but eventually I had to give this up as my hand went numb. I now simply put up with being bounced about and grab sleep when I can.

Bathing

Spectra is fitted with two heads (bathrooms/toilets) and perhaps the best piece of apparatus on board is the water maker which means we can actually take showers. Many sailors do not have this luxury – smelly bunch. If you can imagine a bathroom being bolted to a ...... Yes, you do have the idea now. Taking a shower is an adventure, and whilst we do have a water maker we do try to conserve water. So, we start by getting wet, turning off the shower, and then shampooing, etc. The problem is *Spectra* is doing her best to catapult you from wall to wall whilst going through this process. All is ok until the 'soapy hand' stage. This means that any little chance of holding on has now been reduced to zero, so bracing yourself as best you can you complete the process by rinsing yourself off. Now the difficult bit – when drying yourself you really need two hands so, bracing yourself again as best you can, bruised and cut you have finished. Simple.

Note: The water maker consists of a series of filters that reduce in density - the last one being a carbon filter – sea water is forced through the filters and after a final ultra violet treatment the water is ready to drink.

Toilet drills

Using the toilet is an even bigger adventure – if you were to bolt a toilet to a ……. etc. Yes, you have definitely got the idea now. Sitting on the loo is a piece of cake – ha – not so when *Spectra* is doing her very best (I think she tries her hardest at this stage) to lift you to the roof. This, in itself, is not so bad; the problem is *Spectra* twists and turns until the toilet seat is no longer in the same position when you land. Result: cuts and bruises galore – job done.

Spectra is in her element in the Atlantic – these conditions are exactly what she was designed for and she is clocking up the miles at an impressive rate, many modern boats will not perform anywhere as well, as was proved when she left eight French yachts in her wake when we left Cape Verde. Steve insisted that it wasn't a race, Norma insisted that it was!

The living conditions, whilst not luxurious, are first class and it is a joy to be part of the adventure. *Spectra* is a good-looking yacht that has attracted many positive comments from fellow sailors and onlookers alike. Paul and Norma are rightly proud of her. In fact, in San Miguel Marina a man on an adjacent French yacht asked if *Spectra* was a charter boat. An affronted Norma replied ''No, she is ours.'' This statement has to be read in an Ulster accent which goes something like this: Nooo shays Ouurghhhrrrs and this translates into French as – ''no its not, you stupid little French man''. (I am well qualified to translate here as my mother came from the same area in Ireland as Norma.) My translation abilities have been invaluable during this trip. For example, when I was driving in Tenerife she was shouting at me to "turn left". I shouted back that it was a no left turn junction. She then said "no! the other left". I understood immediately but missed the right-hand turn anyway.

Love and regards to all and a special hello to my grandchildren who seemed to be concerned that we are not sufficiently equipped to celebrate

Christmas; it's OK, we do have a Christmas tree and plenty of lights!!!!

5th Dec 2014 14:07:38
Heading West Fifth Blog, back to me I'm afraid
13:08.49N 48:04.47W

Fifth edition of the going west blogs and it is back to me as Tony has declined the offer of going into print. What can I say? Nothing much has happened which, on an ocean passage, is probably a good thing. We are into a Groundhog Day routine and the miles keep ticking away. Tony has had several hits on his fishing line, all bar one getting away. This was a new species to us and the best guess so far is that it was a horse eye jack. It was not big enough to feed five, so it has been filleted and put in the freezer, to await a partner or two before becoming a meal for the crew. Everyone is getting a bit adventurous with the cooking and meal times are a real treat. After every meal Steve states with absolute conviction "that was definitely better than the shit we had last night" so we must be getting better. Likewise, the bread making, after a bit of a ropey start, is producing fresh loaves every other day with Steve and I being the nominated bakers. I don't know what it is but there is definitely something almost primeval and immensely satisfying about making bread.

Every night before the sun goes down we have a scheduled 100% deck check. This involves the next person on shift going around the decks and checking every nut, bolt, washer and fitting for tightness, wear, chafe or damage. This process is again repeated at 8:00 in the morning and I have found it works really well having already found several issues before they become problems. Having said that, we still accumulate a string of niggly little faults that need fixing. The main kicking strap popped a couple of rivets yesterday and, of course, my rivet gun broke so it is now supported by a ratchet strap until we get into port. This morning, when we went to shake out a reef in the main, I noticed that the car for the second batten had come apart in the night. We took the car apart and found the bronze nut inside had stripped its thread. No spare nut as it is a bit of a strange one, so the whole unit is now sitting on the saloon table after being epoxy glued in place. It will go back up this afternoon. Fingers crossed nothing has come up yet that is beyond either our skill set or spare parts bucket and we have been able to either fix it properly or at least make a decent running repair.

On a slightly more worrying note, Norma has informed us that we are down to our last 10 chocolate bars. I have placed them in the safe, and I am watching the crew closely for signs of mutiny. On that theme, we have a snack box in the galley which Norma restocks daily with nibbly things for the on-watch crew to pick at. We do that to stop hungry sailors harvesting the food lockers in the middle of the night and completely mucking up the meal plans. It seems to have worked pretty well so far and nobody is in any danger of contracting scurvy, that I can say for sure. A bit of a rambling diatribe, this one, but we are all well and counting the miles down to Barbados...666 miles to go (the number of the beast!!).

As a side note, if anyone has any particular questions about doing this sort of trip please ask via the email below and I will do a blog in a week or two and answer them all together. Who knows? It may be of use or interest to the wider audience. I bet if you have a question, someone else will be interested in the answer, so no such thing as a stupid question and I won't print any names, promise. Also, on that note, if anyone knows of a particularly good place to go or thing to see in Barbados or Grenada please drop me a line on the email below. As always, no attachments please as it will kill the satellite link and/or cost me a fortune.

That's it from me, I am on Mummy watch this morning, the bread is baking after spending an hour or two rising under the covers with Norma while she slept, and it is smelling good! Steve is fishing, Norma and Tony are still sleeping after their night watches and Peter has our lives in his hands as he is on watch.

Here are the stats so far:
Day 0.5   17.5 hours   84 miles   Average 4.8 knots
Day 1   24 hours   173 miles   Average 7.2 knots

Day 2	24 hours	187 miles	Average 7.8 knots
Day 3	24 hours	168 miles	Average 7.0 knots
Day 4	24 hours	159 miles	Average 6.6 knots
Day 5	24 hours	149 miles	Average 6.2 knots
Day 6	24 hours	147 miles	Average 6.1 knots
Day 7	24 hours	156 miles	Average 6.5 knots
Day 8	24 hours	97 miles	Average 4.0 knots
Day 9	24 hours	151 miles	Average 6.3 knots

Time taken to half way point: 7 days 1 hour and 30 minutes

And some extra ones:

Generator hours	60	
Water maker Hours	28	1,400 litres of fresh water produced at 50 litres per hour
Washing machine loads	3	
Crew showers	4 x 5 crew = 20 showers	
Mummy watches each	3	

7th Dec 2014 16:32:53

Heading West Sixth Blog, Special moments, S:@t, Ships, Sails and Soda bread

13:00.412N 52:56.328W

Sixth edition of the going west blogs and we are on the home stretch. We dropped below the 400 miles to go point this morning, during Norma's watch. In the last blog I commented on how it is a bit Groundhog Day at the moment, well I had no sooner finished the blog when the fun started.

Special moments

Dolphins have been noticeable by their absence of late, in fact we haven't seen any since our approach to the Cape Verdes so Tony nearly jumped out of his skin when a dolphin vented right next to the cockpit. Soon there were at least 50 and probably a lot more all around the boat. You could see waves of them coming in from the starboard side leaping clear out of the water and spinning in the air. Pretty soon it was like dolphin soup under our bows as they all vied to be the next one to ride the wave. Tony managed to take some great pictures with his camera and even put it onto the boat hook and dipped it under the water. We have actually got some pictures of a group of dolphins swimming under Spectra's bow from below the water and some of us sailing towards the sunset with dolphins jumping in front of us.

S:@t

The aft heads (toilet) stopped flushing and so the joy of boat ownership was complete. I discovered that the outlet pipe was completely blocked, urghh, yuk. A very memorable time, for all the wrong reasons, was spent dismantling the toilet whilst bent double in the smallest room. Remove the pipe (double jubilee clips on both ends of course), pull it through two bulk heads all in 35 degrees heat and a rolling sea. Then on deck to bash it against the side and force water through it with the deck pump until it was free. Sounds a bit unpleasant, but from your armchair at home manageable at least? I did mention the heat and the rolling sea, by the time the pipe was clear both Tony and myself had been sick over the side more than once whilst the rest of the crew watched from upwind and outside the fallout zone. Put it all back together again, clean up the mess and job done. Three hours that took, and I want to go on record, officially, as hating toilets and all things plumbing related. I will certainly never ever use one again, ever!

Ships

Towards evening we picked up a ship on the AIS, the *W-Eagle* a 754ft tanker, some 20 miles astern and doing 14 knots in our direction. We watched it approach on the plotter and within 45 minutes it was just visible on the horizon. Checking the plotter, it looked like it would pass pretty close and so I radioed up and asked his intentions; no reply. We waited 15 minutes and tried again; no reply. It was now obvious that it was going to come too close for comfort and, as we were the stand on vessel, we continued to call. We tried Channel 16, Ship to Ship, DSC on both VHF radios and finally I got Peter to 5-flash our search light at his bridge; no reply. With 20 minutes left until the closest point of approach I changed our course 30 degrees to port to get out of his way. The *W-Eagle* carried on totally unaware of our presence right through the patch of water we had previously occupied. As he drew level with us Norma noticed his navigation lights switch on. I tried the VHF again and he replied immediately so I can only surmise that someone had just woken up on the bridge to turn the lights on and noticed us calling, or maybe it was half time at the football? When asked why he had not responded or kept clear of us he said they had been monitoring VHF and heard nothing. My reply was short, sharp, and brought his professionalism into question which elicited no reply so I assume his radio had gone into silent mode again. First ship in four days and he tried to kill us, the bugger!

Sails

During my night watch (2:00am on my own) I was happily sailing along with full foresail, stay sail and full main when we were hit by a bit of a squall. The wind went from 15 knots to over 35 knots in a heartbeat, and I frantically wound in half of the foresail. That accomplished, *Spectra* stopped showing off by doing 9 plus knots and settled down to 7-8 knots and peace was restored. Ten minutes later the wind died and the rain came down hard, and I mean 'stair rods'. Not being in sight of the yacht club balcony, I shamelessly put up my umbrella and sat miserably in the corner thinking of the others sleeping below. All was not well with my world and it didn't get better when bang! the main halyard broke and the main sail slid gracefully down the mast and settled into its lazy jacks. There was nothing much to do about it at that point and, with 30 minutes to shift handover, I decided to wait until Tony got up so we could then sort it. We have a rule that no one leaves the cockpit at night alone. Sailing with just the foresails up, *Spectra* rolled like a drunken dog which woke-up Steve and so I now had a fully formed and keen working party. By 3:00am we had run the topping lift in as a spare halyard and got her sailing again, allowing us all to sit in the cockpit drinking cups of tea; honestly just how British are we sometimes?

Soda Bread

I must also mention that Norma made her first-ever batch of soda bread today - one plain and one fruit soda. It was all eaten in one sitting, whilst still warm from the oven which says it all really; it was great.

So that was my non-Groundhog Day. I fervently hope for a really boring day tomorrow with nothing happening from one sunrise to the next. Still, it's Sunday today and Peter is making Sunday lunch; a 'knife and fork day' hooray! At the present rate of progress, we should be in Barbados either late

Tuesday or Wednesday daytime, all looking good so far.

Here are the stats so far:

Day 0.5	17.5 hours	84 miles	Average 4.8 knots
Day 1	24 hours	173 miles	Average 7.2 knots
Day 2	24 hours	187 miles	Average 7.8 knots
Day 3	24 hours	168 miles	Average 7.0 knots
Day 4	24 hours	159 miles	Average 6.6 knots
Day 5	24 hours	149 miles	Average 6.2 knots
Day 6	24 hours	147 miles	Average 6.1 knots
Day 7	24 hours	156 miles	Average 6.5 knots
Day 8	24 hours	97 miles	Average 4.0 knots
Day 9	24 hours	151 miles	Average 6.3 knots
Day 10	24 hours	145 miles	Average 6.0 knots
Day 11	24 hours	156 miles	Average 6.5 knots

Time taken to half way point: 7 days 1 hour and 30 minutes

And some extra ones:

Generator hours	71
Water maker Hours	33 1,650 litres of fresh water produced at 50 litres ph
Washing machine loads	4

Crew showers	5 x 5 crew = 25 showers
Mummy watches each	3

Highest recorded boat speed 10.7 knots (not for long, thankfully)

Highest recorded wind speed 38 knots (same time same comment as above)

9th December 2014 21:03:10
Heading West Seventh Blog, nearly there
12:53.412N 58:20.328W

Seventh edition of the going west blogs and we are definitely on the home run. At the present speed we should be in Barbados by about 4:00 in the morning so this is only going to be a quick update to let everyone know that we are safe and all still speaking to each other. The wind has come up this morning and we are averaging 7 knots today, with a double reef in the main, and a few rolls in the foresail, so no complaints from me or from *Spectra* who is loving the conditions.

That's about it for this one, I will update tomorrow or more likely the day after, once we have cleared Customs, had a good sleep and found out were we can get on line, etc, but first a cool beer.

I will write soon......................

13ᵗʰ Dec 2014 16:11:50
Barbados 1
13:5.45N 59:36.48W

We have been offline for a few days, settling in, and I have discovered that my mails have not been going through. I have now found a semi-reliable wi-fi connection in a local bar, which definitely has fringe benefits as I am currently sitting here on the balcony with a cool beer at my elbow. Here goes for a quick update. We arrived after 13 days and 18.5 hours which gave us an average speed of 6.4 knots for the crossing. Our first anchorage was in Carlisle Bay, where we stayed for a few days but we have now moved into the Careenage, which is the old commercial harbour in the middle of Bridgetown. Our mooring is stern-to a little park which has a Christmas tree from every commonwealth nation in it, each one decorated by a different local school. This all goes to make a great display at night. Norma has decreed that our Christmas lights must go up today so we were all up and busy first thing. This afternoon we are off to watch a cricket match and last night it was a bit of street food and music at the Oistins Bay jump-up. We have also been given temporary membership of the Barbados Yacht Club which looks very colonial and is hugely welcoming.

That's it for now, I will update properly very soon, promise.

17th Dec 2014 13:44:55
Barbados 2, Catch up

Finally, I have made the time to do a bit of writing. We arrived off Carlisle Bay just before dawn on Wednesday the 10th December and bimbled around waiting on the sun before making our final approach. Steve was on watch and had called me up on deck a couple of hours previously as he was seeing some very strange navigation lights which he couldn't fit onto the charts. After studying them for a while we realised that we were actually looking at planes taking off from Barbados airport which after a couple of weeks at sea and a bit of sleep deprivation blew our tiny minds for a while. As the sun came up we tried the Barbados signal station on the VHF and to our surprise they came back straight away and instructed us to come into the commercial port for Customs clearance. We moored alongside a huge concrete wall as directed and as it had no ladders we had a bit of a scramble to get onto the dockside which was a rather undignified way to make our landfall but it was good to get my feet back on *terra firma*. Having read the pilot guides and been warned that the Barbados customs process was convoluted and very strict we were again pleased to find everyone friendly and helpful; the various officials were all keen to encourage us to visit different places and they all welcomed us to Barbados and wished us a pleasant stay. We walked out, thoroughly impressed with the whole experience. Then the bad news, as we came out of the customs shed a huge liner was berthing at right angles to us leaving Norma and Steve, who had stayed aboard, rocking and rolling on deck as they were buffeted about in the massive wash from the ship's propellers and stern thrusters causing a gouge in *Spectra's* port side gel coat, as she pushed against the concrete wall, having crushed a fender. We waited for the ship to berth. Well, we had no choice as we were pinned against the wall by the force of the prop wash, whilst I gave several rude hand signals to the officer of the watch who was hanging over the back of the liner. When my nerves stopped jangling and my heart rate fell back to normal, we pulled down the yellow Q flag, moved out and sailed around to Carlisle Bay in order to anchor up, managing to get the hook to hold on the third attempt. I immediately dived over the side and relaxed, we had done it.

BARBADOS & GRENADA - CHRISTMAS & NEW YEAR

DECEMBER & JANUARY 2014/15

10th December

Later that afternoon we went ashore in the dinghy to investigate and managed to get swamped coming onto the beach; second undignified arrival of the day. Eventually Peter and Steve managed to push the dinghy out again and I went back to pick up Norma and Tony. This time we went up the river and tied the dinghy up in the Careenage near the centre of town. I have said it before, of other places we have visited, but this is really a lovely place and so friendly. We walked along the beach to the Barbados Yacht Club who were happy to make us honorary members for the duration of our stay, and after a few beers on the beach we wandered back into town and out to the Kensington Oval Cricket ground to see if any matches were due to be played over the next week or so. No cricket but there was a jump up/karaoke night going on and the place was packed, not wishing to appear rude, in we went.

During the evening a lot of people came over to say hello two of which stood out; Kelvin who was so drunk he was actually defying gravity and all of the laws of physics just by being upright, and Olvin, who was a much more interesting character. Olvin, as it turned out, had lived in the UK for many years and was a cricket coach for a league team on the island. Anyway, long story short, we're invited to watch a match at the St Andrews Lakes on Saturday, so that's a date.

By Thursday it was apparent that with five aboard and a 3-man dinghy the shuttle back and forth ashore was going to be a pain and so I made enquiries about a mooring in town. Again, the pilot book stated clearly that visiting yachts would not be welcome in the Careenage. After a quick conversation with Godfrey, a charter fishing boat owner, I found myself in the port control office speaking to Tonya who was more than pleased for us to come in. She organised for the swing bridge to be opened at 2 pm the next day and gave us a choice of berths. When I asked how deep the inner basin was she thought about it and then with a smile said "Oh it's pretty deep, I'm sure you'll be right" and that was it, and you know what, it was, so she was right. At 1:30 pm we were on the waiting pontoon and everything went like clockwork; the bridge went up, Tonya was on the quayside with two electricians to hook us up, and the whole town seemed to be watching me manoeuvre in. No pressure there, then. It all went well apart from when we tried to hook up the electrics, and we didn't have the correct plug. No problem said the electrician, and proceeded to take our plug apart, and using an international universal connector (chock block), connected us to the town's supply. He said that it was a 110v feed so he had connected two together which made me twitch a bit, but what can I say? Ten minutes later the electric kettle was boiling and we are all good to go for Christmas. By the way US$25 a day is the fee, and that's per boat, no mention of size and it includes water and electricity, not bad, not bad at all.

Friday night means a trip to the Oistins Bay jump up and off my gallant crew trotted. Unfortunately, as I had been stupid and not drunk enough water, leaving me with a bad case of the shakes, I had an early night to cure my pounding headache while the crew kicked their heels up. By the happy giggles on their return it was a good one.

Saturday and we grabbed a taxi to the cricket ground which was about 17 miles away. Another good choice as we met Adrienne who is a taxi driver, tour guide and all-round amusing chap. He agreed a very good price as long as his girlfriend/wife/mistress (he used all three titles) could come along. We agreed and a brief detour was put into the itinerary past her house, and then past her friend's house because she wasn't in. With the car now full, Adrienne launched into a potted history of Barbados which included a three-question pop quiz for Tony to make sure he was paying attention. *En route* we passed a troop of monkeys in a small village in the hills and learnt an awful lot about life in the island; we were kept entertained all the way.

The cricket match was one of those special days that sometimes come along out of the blue. Everyone made us very welcome at the little club house, even to the extent of insisting that we shared the lunch provided for the players by the local ladies. I must say some of the fast bowlers were truly frightening, you couldn't even see the ball it went that fast. When one batsman got hit in the head Olvin's comment of, "what do you expect that bowler's an ex Windies player, the batsman is showing no respect by not wearing a helmet" rather summed it up. After that poor chap staggered off the pitch to lie under a tree, it was noticed that the follow up batsmen put on their helmets and tightened the chin straps for good measure. The trip back to Bridgetown was by bus and I have a new set of grey hairs to prove it.

Sunday 14th December

That brings us to Sunday and a trip planned by Tony to the Bushy Park race track to see the Race of Champions. But first we had to say goodbye to Peter, who was travelling back to the UK. We have had Peter aboard since mid-October and he has seen us through some tricky times; hand steering all of the way to

Madeira, engine failure on the approach to Madeira itself, lift out and anti-foul in Tenerife, generator failure in Cape Verde and of course the Atlantic crossing itself. He has clocked up 3,844 miles with us and has been great company along the way. Peter will be missed aboard and *Spectra* will always have a berth for him if he fancies helping out on part of the return leg (hint, hint). Adrienne, our taxi driver, picked us up, (minus his girlfriend this time as they'd had a fall out) and gave us another quick history tour on the way to Bushy Park. Again, Tony was given a pop quiz to make sure he had been paying attention which, to my surprise, he passed with flying colours. I thought he had been asleep in the back. It was a boiling hot day and we slowly cooked as we watched David Coulthard win the competition, and also watched some pretty spectacular stunt driving displays. The trip back again was by local bus which is cheap but a white-knuckle ride for sure.

That night the local schools held a carol concert, Caribbean style, in Independence Square behind our mooring which, as mentioned before, has been decked out with Christmas trees from all of the Commonwealth countries. This took place right behind the boat, giving us a ring side seat to our own little concert, whilst sitting on the rear deck of *Spectra*. That brings me up to date, apart that is, from the Mount Gay Rum distillery tour which we did today. I can't remember too much about that and so it must have been good..................until next time.

26th Dec 2014 15:43:17
Barbados 3
5165 Miles from Ramsgate by log.

I think this has been the longest period in-between blogs yet but the days just seem to slip by. First things first, happy Christmas everyone. We are still in the Careenage in Bridgetown, and *Spectra* has benefited from the stay by having lots of maintenance lavished on her. The rails and rubbing strakes have been re-varnished along with the stern woodwork, all the portholes and metalwork above decks has been polished and sealed with varnish leaving her looking very pretty again, but then I am rather biased on that subject. The backup battery charger is still broken, after spending two weeks on the engineer's shelf he said he could not get the parts. When asked which parts he needed he hedged a bit, so I suspect he didn't really know what was wrong with it. I shall try again in Grenada. Steve has pulled the chart plotter's wiring loom apart to try and find why it drops out intermittently, but it still has the problem and so again we will have to live with that for a while. As always, I have backup systems and so it is not a major concern, just a niggle. Meanwhile Tony has been playing with the outboard and it now starts on the second pull and positively purrs along, well purrs as well as any smoky two-stroke ever will. The dinghy will now go up on the plane with one aboard, it still hasn't got the oomph to do it with two up but that is so much better than the useless lump of metal that I had hanging on the back rail before Andy and Tony had a go at it.

As far as sightseeing goes, Norma, Tony, Steve and myself, grabbed a taxi and went to Harrisons Caves which is in the centre of the island. They have a tram which takes you several hundred metres under the ground to explore the limestone caves where runaway slaves used to hide in the bad old days. We also had another night out at the jump up in Oistins Bay which is always worth the trip. Sue and Tommy have been here for a while and we have had several good nights out including a day on the beach and a Bajan buffet at their hotel. We also visited the other yacht club, which is a much more relaxed affair and we were invited to join in their regatta by a Canadian diplomat, but me thinks *Spectra* is not for the race track and so we gracefully declined. As it turned out the race was cancelled, so nothing lost there then. Olvin from the cricket club dropped by for a drink one evening and brought us a spice cake and some marrows from his garden as a gift. I think he enjoyed himself, in fact I know he did, as he fell asleep in the cockpit for a couple of hours before weaving his way off home.

We all gathered for Christmas dinner on *Spectra* yesterday. By decree of Norma, all maintenance and thoughts of fixing things were banished for the festive season. It was a bit of a rainy day but we still managed to have a swim in the morning and eat starters on deck in the sun until a rain cloud stopped play. After dinner, which was a proper turkey and all of the trimmings including mince pies affair, we had drinks on the aft deck and watched Bridgetown's finest promenade past us. Independence Square seems to be the social gathering place to see and be seen in. The children brought their favourite Christmas presents out with them and the square was soon converted into an impromptu race track as remote control cars whizzed back and forth, chased by excited toddlers.

Boxing Day today and Tony will be leaving us in the morning. When Tony stepped aboard in Tenerife his total experience of sailing Spectra had been one trip from Ramsgate's inner to outer marina, now he has clocked up over 3,000 miles and is a hugely competent crew. He has also completed an Atlantic crossing on a small yacht which is something he should be rightly proud of. We talked to Gemma, Duncan and Lily yesterday and with losing Tony tomorrow it is hard not to be homesick, especially at Christmas time. Still Gemma, Duncan, Lily with the new baby on board are flying out to see us in Florida in April so that is something to look forward to, plus Tony hasn't ruled out joining us for at least a part of the return trip.

Barbados has a traditional Boxing Day horse race at the Garrison Savannah Race Track which is only a mile or two's walk from the dock and starts at twelve today. The plan is to meet up with Tommy and Sue there, and after the racing go on to the Barbados Cruising Yacht Club for a drink or two so our day is pretty full on.

While I think of it, congratulations to Stan and the Cruising Committee for organising the harbour Christmas lights in Ramsgate. Malcolm sent us some pictures and Sue showed us some that she had taken, it looked wonderful......... Talk soon ... MERRY CHRISTMAS AND A HAPPY NEW YEAR TO ALL OF OUR READERS.

2nd Jan 2015 13:26:22
Barbados to Grenada 1
12:02.773N 61:44.852W

Sue has just accused me of being far too laid back and even of 'going native' since we arrived in the Caribbean, by being very slack with my blogging, if you can believe it. With that stinging criticism ringing in my ears I have forsaken the wine and sat myself behind the laptop again. What have we been up to? The Boxing Day horse racing was a fun day out for the whole family and took place under clear blue skies and a sizzling hot sun. Norma announced that Duncan, our son-in-law, had given her a tip via the Skype link on Christmas Day and so she would be betting on horse number 3 in every race; she remained committed to that decision despite all evidence to the contrary.

Race 1 started with a cheer from the crowd and ten of the eleven horses thundered along the track. Horse number three, however, stayed in the trap looking pretty miffed that the jockey kept kicking him. Race 2 and horse number three could have been a winner if the rider hadn't fallen off after 20 yards and so it went on. Some of Norma's horses looked like they had recently been retired from the milk round, some looked like they wouldn't have passed the medical in the first place, but Norma stuck to her guns and backed number 3 all day. Finally, on the penultimate race, with my wallet nearly empty, she cracked and actually looked at the odds. After much study, 5 dollars was placed on the second favourite number 6. He could have been a winner if the horse in trap 3 hadn't streaked around the course like a small child on M and Ms, and won by two lengths. Ho hum. Norma's face was a picture of despair whilst we all fell about laughing at her expense. After the races we all went to the Barbados Cruising Club for dinner, at the invitation of the Canadian diplomat, previously mentioned, whose name still escapes me. It was a lovely end to a memorable day, as we sat on the balcony overlooking the beach. This was to be Tony's last meal with us on the island.

04.00 the following morning found Norma and me bleary eyed and sleepy seeing Tony off as he caught his taxi to the airport. It was a sad occasion as it will be next summer before we see him again. Having Tony share this adventure with us has been wonderful; it has been great having him along over the last couple of months, sharing a part of our dream. Later that afternoon Tommy and Sue moved aboard and we all trotted up to the port to clear customs for our departure on the 28th. As always, this wasn't quite as simple as it should have been as the people we needed to see were either asleep or missing, but we kept smiling and persevering finally obtaining all of the stamps and forms required to keep us legal. The rest of the day was taken up with last minute shopping and converting *Spectra* from a floating hotel into a sea-going boat again and, of course, taking down all of those Christmas lights.

11.00 and the bridge lifted spot-on time for us to slip our lines and head out of the Bridgetown Careenage. In true Barbados style, passing locals waved and wished us a good trip as we sailed out. Our last contact with Barbados was by VHF radio when Norma called up the signal station to let them know we were leaving, their response was, "Thank you for visiting our country, happy New Year and we hope to see you again soon" which just about sums up the lovely people of Barbados, I would say.

The weather report was for 15 knots from the North-East, expectation aboard was for a nice smooth downwind sail overnight with no dramas. At 03.00 I was on deck in the driving rain dragging a second reef into the main sail after being woken by Steve, informing me that we had 30-knot plus winds and the swell was over 3 metres. *Spectra* was steaming along at over 9 knots when we pulled the reef in and still doing over 9 knots when we got back into the cockpit, and so half the foresail was put away as well. That brought the speed down to a comfortable 8 knots but, with the confused seas and swell, no one got much sleep. We finally arrived in St Georges, Grenada at 11.30 making our average speed 6.5 knots for the 150ish mile crossing. We are now moored in the Grenada Yacht Club opposite the sparkling new Camper and Nicholson marina which has a clutch of 100ft plus super yachts gleaming in the sun. Norma and I jumped into the dinghy to row across the bay to clear into the customs office located at the marina, and made a bit of an entrance when in full sight of the super yacht flunkies my dinghy's seat collapsed and I ended up flat on my back with my legs in the air while Norma had a giggling fit. I do like to make an entrance. The customs process was a hassle-free affair. Walking back to the dinghy after clearing in, the UK joint services military yacht *Discoverer* came into the marina; the same 67ft yacht that we last met up with in Madeira when we loaned them our keys to the shower block, different crew of course. It is also the same yacht that Steve sailed back across the Atlantic on in 2010, small world. Needless to say, a 67ft yacht looked about as impressive as a mirror dinghy in that marina.

That's it for this one as I am suffering from a terrible, and possibly terminal, hangover after last night's Old Year party but that's a story for next time.........

PS. All of the time I have been writing this, Tommy has been badgering me to only write nice things about him and so I have had a very long think about finding some feature or attribute that I can say nice things about. It has been surprisingly hard but eventually I have found one so here goes – "he knows some really nice people and has a great bunch of friends".

4th Jan 2015 20:43:14
Grenada 2 Andrew & Paula join the party
5318 Miles from Ramsgate by log.

We have now been in Grenada for a week and it has been quite an eventful period what with the Old Year's Party, meeting up with Andrew and Paula and partaking of our usual sightseeing agenda. Unfortunately, Norma has had a little accident. Whilst trying to put a bottle of suntan lotion into my rucksack (fussing) as we walked into St Georges, she managed to kick me in the back of my shoe with her sandaled foot, thereby breaking her little toe. Apart from slowing her dancing down a bit, the main impact has been that I have, with regrets, had to withdraw her entry from the inter-island arse kicking contest where, after years of practice (on me), she was a hot favourite for the gold medal. I, meanwhile, have picked up a stomach bug, the symptoms of which need no further explanation here but let's just say it has also slowed down my dancing a bit! Anyway, enough of the medical reports and onto the adventures.

With Andrew and Paula in the group it was seven for a Caribbean mezze style meal at Patricks near Port Louis on New Year's Eve. The multiple courses delight was accompanied by the ubiquitous thump of reggae music from the next-door neighbours. After the meal, which was excellent, we all walked the half mile back to the Grenada Yacht Club for drinks aboard *Spectra* and a grandstand view of the Port Louis Marina's Old Year's party firework display from across the bay. As the clock struck midnight four or five distress flares were fired off from different yachts around the lagoon, (it is the Caribbean, after all), and then the first firework climbed lazily into the sky above St Georges. With perfect timing, as the firework rose upwards, the heavens opened and an absolute monsoon came downwards. The *Spectra* crew are hardy souls and this failed to dampen our spirits one little bit, we simply dived under the deck sail to carry on the party. Paula and Andrew weaved their happy way down the gang plank at about 1:30am in order to catch a taxi and the party started to wind down, or so I thought. At this juncture Norma, who had been doing one legged Kate Winslett impersonations on the bowsprit, noticed the skipper of the rather nice 80ft yacht *Coconut*, which is moored two up from us, motoring past in his tender and invited him aboard in her usual style which cannot be refused. He duly arrived with several bottles of New Zealand wine from *Coconut's* owner's vineyard and the party resumed. The next time I looked at my watch it was 5:30 am and the sun was rising to highlight the scene of utter devastation that was *Spectra's* decks. Sue had kindly brought a whole pack of party poppers with her, which had fired little coloured stars everywhere. Thanks Sue and I really mean that! Of course, there was the usual litter of bottles, cans and general party detritus to clean up including Steve who was fast asleep on the cabin roof curled up in the foetus position, but not then, definitely not then. It was off to bed for the morning and a large part of the afternoon. The first day of 2015 went by in a sea of pain and discomfort as the whole crew of *Spectra* swore to their own personal gods that they would never, ever, drink again, except for Tommy, that is, who had a beer with lunch.!!!!!!!!!

The second day of 2015 was much more productive and by 10:00 in the morning we were all aboard a busy bus and off on an island tour with Christopher, our very knowledgeable, but not particularly health and safety conscious, guide. The tour included a swim by a waterfall, a spice factory, a chocolate factory, a meal at lunchtime, a trip to the volcano lake with monkeys for company and, of course, a rum distillery. The whole day all for just $150 between the 7 of us, which is not bad at all.

Christopher also described in detail the local homemade fireworks that makes the huge bangs we heard around the island on New Year's Eve.

Step 1:	Get a large fat piece of bamboo and punch a small hole through the internal walls.
Step 2:	Fill with petrol!
Step 3:	Block the hole in the end with clay, allow to dry!!
Step 4:	Place the device onto your bonfire!!!
Step 4:	Stand back and wait for the explosion!!!!
Note:	Do not try this at home, ever - it is very, very, very, VERY STUPID!!!!!

He also explained, with a happy grin, that the bang from a good one could be heard from several miles away and that was why lots of people didn't have eyebrows in January (or heads, I would have thought).

As an aside, after lunch, which was very nice by the way, we were all asked to scrape the leftovers from our plates into a plastic bag for Christopher's dog who is probably deaf and definitely shell shocked.

This is where I must mention BB's Bar and Restaurant. If you ever go to Grenada this is a must. Situated right on the waterfront in the centre of St. Georges it is a jewel in the crown. Credit where credit is due, Steve found the place whilst out for a wander and booked us all in for the night. Paula and Andrew, Tommy and Sue, Norma and myself, plus Steve, of course, were all met at the door by the expansive and hugely welcoming BB himself. Owner, chef and all-round entertainer, BB made us very welcome and served some excellent food. He also provided a box of pens so that we could stand on the table and sign our names on the ceiling which is a custom. After the meal the music came on and we were all encouraged to get up and dance. When BB grabbed Paula's hand, his eyes popped out on stalks and his grin spread from ear to ear as she stood up leaving him barely reaching her shoulders. Without a pause, he signalled his son to put on a slower record and snuggled in for the dance, much to his son's embarrassment. BB is a really infectious character, you just can't be around him for more than 10 minutes without the laughter rolling out. He loves his restaurant and enjoys life, this shines through in his every action. Topping that off with an excellent location and superb menu, I would vote this the best restaurant in Grenada by a country mile.

We had planned to set sail for Hog Island yesterday but the wind was up and would have been on the nose the whole way making for an uncomfortable trip. Therefore instead, we decided on a beach day at Andrew and Paula's very swish hotel which faces onto the lovely Grande Anse beach. It was horribly decadent but I took one for the team and forced myself to endure it, all for the sake of the crew you understand.

Today was Tommy and Sue's last morning with us and they have just jumped into a taxi to head back to sunny Ramsgate via Barbados and all of the delights of a winter in London. Again, it was very sad to see them head off up the hill, and they will be sorely missed until their possible return in May to do a bit of the intra-coastal waterway with us. That leaves us with three aboard and the start of a new chapter in our adventure; Steve, Norma and I will be spending the next few months island-hopping up the Caribbean chain and the intention is to spend much more time at anchor and visit some of the remoter spots. But first I have to get my battery charger back from the electrician and we will be doing a few days day sailing around Grenada with Andrew and Paula...........th that's all folks.

8th Jan 2015 14:32:45
Grenada 4 . . . Hog Island, True Blue Bay and Goodbyes
12:27.40N 61:29.24W
5318 Miles from Ramsgate by log.

Every time I write a blog we seem to be saying goodbye to someone. This time it is farewell to Andrew and Paula who are spending a few more days in their plush hotel before flying off to the bright lights of London, whilst we head Northwards, up through the islands. Before they went we had a couple of days out on *Spectra* sailing on the azure blue seas under cloudless skies. At least that is what the brochure would have said, the reality was slightly different. After one cancellation due to bad weather, and with time running out we set off from St Georges for a quick jaunt around the bottom of the island to Clarks Court Marina, Hog Island, 12 miles and then, after a bit of snorkelling, Andrew and Paula would be able to step ashore and taxi back to their hotel, no problems. Two hours later, with 30 knots of wind on the bow and rain squalls aplenty, I asked Paula how much previous sailing she had done, "including this trip", she said, "that would be just the one". Oops! But game girl that she is, she kept on smiling (or was that a grimace) and even did a turn in the galley helping Norma out, which was pretty good going in my book. *Spectra* looked after us as always and we soon passed Hog Island and turned into the channel for Clarkes Court, a lovely marina as described by Mr Street in his pilot book. Unfortunately, the lovely marina looks like the hillside slipped and wiped it away leaving a building site so it was onto the anchor. The lagoon was pretty muddy and uninviting plus it was still raining and so it was a meal aboard and a dinghy ashore for the taxi. We arrived at the Whisper Cove pontoon as it was getting dark and asked the question reference taxis of the first person to pass. No taxi service and not much chance of getting one was the response but, on a lighter note, the woman was going into town for a meal and offered to give Andrew and Paula a lift; what a bonus! As it turned out, they were dropped off right across the road from their hotel resulting in a dinghy to door service, we should be the holiday hostest with the mostets.

The next morning our intrepid, or is that masochistic, couple returned for phase two, a 6-mile trip around the corner to True Blue Bay. This went much better, same wind strength but from behind which made for a pleasant(ish) sail. The only drama was when the engine stopped in a 20-knot crosswind as we were passing between some coral heads on the way out. I calmly and politely requested that the crew release the staysail and provide me with some steerage (honest) which kept her in the channel. It was then that I noticed someone had leant against the engine stop button. Really, I just laughed and laughed, what little scamps my crew are sometimes, (honestly again).

True Blue Bay was lovely and the water crystal clear so no sooner was the anchor down than I was in the sea swimming around like a dolphin. The pontoon at the head of the bay backed onto the True Blue Bay holiday complex which was very nice and welcoming when we took the dinghy over. After an afternoon of lazing about on their decking, during which Steve took part in a rum tasting and cocktail mixing demonstration, we decided to eat there. As night fell, we had a traditional meal and finally wished Andrew and Paula a fond farewell, we pored Steve into the dinghy and headed back across to *Spectra* while they jumped into a taxi back to their hotel. Again, great crew and good company; they are welcome back anytime.

THE WINWARD ISLANDS GRENADA TO DOMINICA

JANUARY 2015

That brings us onto Wednesday morning (7th) and an early start for the 40-mile trip up to Carriacou. Nothing much to report really apart from that it was a dead beat all the way with the wind gusting from 9 to 28 knots continuously which resulted in it being a motor sail with just the small sails set (Jib and Jigger or forestay sail and mizzen) to keep it all safe and sensible. The only highlights were a small group of dolphins that shared our journey for a brief while and passing over the edge of an active underwater volcano exclusion zone. We are now anchored in Tyrell Bay which is really nice and quite a yachty centre, if the number of boats anchored here is anything to go by. As we came into the bay we were met by Simon, the boat boy, (he is about 10 years older than my grandfather by the way) and his equally aged helper who informed me that he was mentioned in all of the best pilot books and guides, not in ours though. He offered us a mooring buoy for US$20 which we declined and a bottle of red wine for EC$25 which we accepted; this sailing lark is all about getting your priorities right.

It is now Thursday morning (8th) after a truly wonderful meal ashore in the slipway bar, and then spending half the night trying to track down an annoying banging sound that I never did find, I am sitting on the aft deck in shorts watching the sun come up. Tough life I know, but if I didn't do it, you would have to read the Guardian this morning instead of this blog, so I think that you should all be very grateful that I'm willing to take the bullet on this one.

What's next?..... Today explore Carriacou and book out of Grenadian Customs. Tomorrow, onto Union Island to book into St Vincent and then onto the Tobago Cays.

Thanks must go to Mark for the top tips on St Vincent which confirmed what other cruisers have been saying about the likelihood of violent crime and general theft on and around the island. We will be giving the St Vincent main island a miss this time around. Things change and, hopefully, the local authorities realise the revenue they are losing, and will clamp down on the, no doubt, small group of trouble-makers that are giving the place a bad reputation. Next time we pass this way we would like to visit.

Watch this space I will be back soon..................

10th Jan 2015 16:44:52

St Vincent and the Grenadines-Union Island and poison fruit

12:36.205N 61:27.116W

5406 Miles from Ramsgate by log.

I finished the last blog with us going ashore in Carriacou for a look around, then to book out of customs and head onto Union Island the following morning. As seems the norm, a simple couple of days got a bit complicated. We took the dinghy ashore and while Norma booked out of customs Steve and myself filled the spare petrol cans for the outboard. Incidentally, I poured the last 20 litre can of diesel into the main tanks that morning which filled them to the brim. That was the last of our Mindelo stocks, so since leaving the Cape Verdes we have only used about 90 litres of fuel, which isn't bad at all. Anyway, I digress, all going well so far; while Steve took the dinghy back to *Spectra* to drop the fuel off, Norma and I walked along the shoreline of Tyrell Bay, planning to meet up with him further down by a café that we had spotted from *Spectra's* deck earlier. All still going well; after locking up the dinghy we ate a late breakfast and found ourselves relaxed, sitting in the shade of a tree waiting by the side of the road for the local busy bus to take us into town. At this point Steve, ever the curious one, picked up what looked like a little round apple and said, "smell that, it is really sweet". Of course, me being me, I took a sniff, liked the smell, licked it, liked the taste, and so ate it. It had a sweet, not unpleasant taste, and so I encouraged Norma to give it a go. Luckily, she only touched her tongue to it and agreed it tasted not bad at all. Within 10 minutes or so my mouth was tingling, not unlike it would if you had eaten ginger, but this got a whole lot worse a whole lot quicker. Norma also had the same symptoms but thankfully to a much lesser degree. Over the next couple of hours my mouth, throat and lips began to blister. Getting worried, Norma asked in a local shop what they thought the fruit was. The woman looked very concerned and said it was a Manchineel, while repeatedly saying that it was very bad, very poisonous, advising us repeatedly to go to the doctor immediately. Of course, the doctor was shut until 2pm but at least we didn't have to make an appointment, and so we waited for an hour in a bar across the street trying out an old military cure for all ails, drinking beer to sooth my blistered mouth. I had, at this stage, started to form small blisters on the inside of my gums beside my teeth and down my throat which, I can assure you, was bringing a whole new level of joy to the day. As soon as the doctor heard what had happened he prescribed a barrage of pills and ointments and advised us to go to the hospital if we experienced any breathing difficulties, dizziness, nausea, vomiting, or loss of sight. Getting properly worried now I said, "this sounds a bit serious Doctor", which came out as, "wiss founds e bith erious Tractor" to which he simply said, "that fruit is very poisonous, it is very serious!". That was a bit sobering, to say the least. Off to the pharmacy, where we were the subject of much scrutiny. Pills and potions purchased, we were both now experiencing stomach cramps and I was very sweaty and feverish so it was not a pleasant trip back to the boat for anyone on the busy bus. That night the symptoms slowly died down which was a relief for both of us and on checking on the internet we found the comment;

The Manchineel is one of the World's most poisonous trees. The fruits are red or green and are sometimes called beach apples, the Spanish commonly called it, "the apple of death". Even standing under it in the rain can cause blistering of the skin and if burnt the smoke can cause blindness.

Well, we really don't do things by halves, do we? As for Steve, he was fine and resolutely refused to take any responsibility for feeding me the "Apple of Death" no matter how hard I tried to pile on the guilt.

Friday (9th) started bright and breezy for our sail up to Union Island which went more or less incident free, although the last 6 miles or so were a slog, directly to windward which, with my stomach still cramping, was the closest I have ever come to being sea sick. After booking into customs at the airport, which incidentally has a runway narrower than some streets I have lived on, we moved around the corner to Chatham Bay and dropped the hook for the night. After a beach BBQ that evening (my appetite had returned with a vengeance) we turned in, as the wind was picking up for what turned out to be an absolutely rubbish night. Midnight, and I moved myself from the marital bed into the cockpit as the boat was getting a bit bouncy. Two am found me fully awake and reaching for my foul weather gear as 30 knot gusts and heavy rain squalls whistled through the anchorage. At 3 am the wind switched 180 degrees and the large French Catamaran which had been behind us was suddenly in front of us and dragging its anchor. I started the engine and shouted Norma and Steve up and we managed to get clear with only his ensign broken, but we then had to re-anchor in driving rain and some monster squalls. I was seriously debating heading out to sea when the hook finally gripped in 15 metres of depth and things settled down. *Spectra* was soaked inside and out and so were the crew. The conditions called for an anchor watch for the rest of the night as squall after squall ripped across the anchorage.

That leads us onto this morning where we find a bedraggled and tired bunch aboard the good ship *Spectra*. Norma has finally gone to bed after being up for most of the night while Steve and I have just re-anchored yet again to tuck us into the corner of the bay for a bit more shelter tonight, as it is still very blustery. Tobago Cays has been removed from the agenda for today and we are simply going to do nothing, which sometimes is a very good thing indeed.

While I settle down to do nothing, Steve has started to pull the anchor chain out onto the deck to make the depth markings clearer for next time, I don't know whether to applaud his keenness or feed him a Manchineel, I really don't!!

Happy report next time I promise......................

Tobago Cays 11th Jan position update
12:39.6N 61:22.9W

Canouan 12th Jan Position update
12:43N 61:25.5W

14th Jan 2015 14:31:48
St Vincent and the Grenadines- Bequia
13:01.0N 61:15.5W
5446 Miles from Ramsgate by log.

This morning finds the gallant crew of three battling a force 3 zephyr and 1-metre swell as we leave Admiralty Bay on Bequia to pass by St Vincent to starboard, and go on up the chain to St Lucia. A trip of about 60 miles. The plan is to anchor in Marigot Bay tonight but we have a couple of alternatives if we don't make it that far; fingers crossed for a trouble-free day. It has been a few days since the last blog and we have moved around so I am working from a combined memory dump, and a pile of notes from Steve and Norma. If I miss anything I will, no doubt, be chastised later. Here goes.

We finally departed Chatham Bay on the morning of the 11th January. One notable point about the morning was a flock of Pelicans who were busy dive bombing the reef not 25 metres from us; they lined up like Stuka dive bombers in groups of 2, 3 or 4 and then rolled into a dive one by one to smack into the water with their mouths gaping wide; all very impressive and, I am sure, a great way to gargle in the morning. I was rather jealous as my throat was still a bit blistered from the Manchineel fruit. On that note, the Caribbean Compass magazine that we picked up in town had a whole article about the Manchineel; funny how you find all the information after the event.

Our next stop was the Tobago Cays to drop the hook for lunch and what can I say about that? Well, WOW! just about covers it I think. A truly beautiful place. We launched the dinghy and went over to a little island on Horseshoe Reef to do a bit of snorkelling which was a pretty great way to spend a morning if I say so myself; even Steve broke his duck and actually went swimming. Crystal clear, warm water greeted us as we dived under to be met by a multitude of little, brightly coloured fish. I managed to just see the back end of a large turtle as it swam by and I started to follow, swimming as quickly as I could go. At this point Steve spotted a big barracuda in front of us. After a brief pause we decided to bravely swim back to shallower water and leave the turtle and barracuda to get on with their business.

After lunch we headed past Mayreau for the 18-mile run up to Charlestown Bay on Canouan for the night. With the wind still gusting up to 30 knots we finally anchored, tucked up into the north east corner of the bay about 100 metres from the coastguard station, which felt pretty secure all round. Life ashore in Canouan is pretty basic, to be honest. When we pulled alongside the little beach an old man gave us a hand with our lines and, having gained our attention, proceeded to give us his life story. He was, until recently, a conch diver until someone hit him on the head with a conch shell after an argument about prices and now he couldn't dive any more. We shared a drink with him in the only bar on the beach and gave him a few dollars to mind the dinghy as we went for a walk to try and find food and internet access (the never-ending hunt goes on). No success on Canouan, but we did meet a really nice guy who ran the aforementioned Coconut Bar on the beach. When we asked him about internet he said it was planned into his business model but he would need electricity first! He did go on to offer us a complimentary coconut each, so all was not lost. As it began to get dark, we sat at his little bar, drinking first our complimentary coconuts, and then a few of his beers, out of his ice box, by candle light, just to be polite you understand, and he told us all about how he set up the Coconut Bar. A really nice evening as it turned out. Rarely do you find someone so dedicated to, and proud of, a small business which he has grown from a cool box on his shoulder, to a shed, terrace and beach furniture area within a couple of years with absolutely zero capital. His future plans include electricity and a dinghy pontoon. I, for one, wish him well.

Bright and early the next morning we were off again for the 22-mile windward slog to Bequia, which was a horrible trip in very rough seas. *Spectra* even buried her bows under, back to the staysail root, on a couple of occasions which was definitely a first. We arrived in Admiralty Bay wet and tired, having run the engine the whole way which, again, is a first since the trip over from Portugal to Madeira. Bequia is a strange place; the first half of the bay is very neat and tidy, almost French Riviera styled, with a manicured walkway along the seafront and lots of smart dinghy pontoons to tie up to. The second half of the bay, unfortunately, seems to be populated by every down-and-out smack head in the eastern Caribbean. I also think there must be a mental health institution on the island because there were some seriously disturbed people wandering around or, on a few occasions, rolling in the street which doesn't make for a relaxing atmosphere. This was the first time that we felt it necessary to all go to the cash point together, and stay in a tight group when at that end of the bay. As always seems the way, a place we would rather have moved on from results in a stay for various reasons. This time it was the bow thruster firstly refused to start and then, when we did get it going, ran non-stop to starboard, which could get very expensive if it decided to do that in a crowded marina. This called for a maintenance day and, while Steve worked on the control panel, I worked on the main switch which seemed to be stuck on. My bit of the problem required the application of money, unfortunately. EC$100 purchased a new switch as the old one was broken in the 'on' position and I soon had that all working. Steve's end of the fault was trickier, but ultimately cost free. Water had found its way into the switch panel during the previous day's pounding, but after a good drying out and resealing, all is working again. I think the root of the problem is me pushing the buttons too hard sometimes. Mentally it is very hard not to keep pushing the button harder and harder when you have a super yacht right in front of you, the wind is gusting and you need the bows to move quickly. Anyway, I have promised to do better in future. Norma and I also spent a morning scrubbing the water line as *Spectra* has grown a hula skirt of sea grass all around her middle, which is a very modest look, but adds nothing to her sailing performance. We rigged a rope around the boat to hang onto and I went along first with the scraper getting the big bits while Norma followed with a plastic scouring pad to make it all smooth again. All very efficient until Norma let out a scream. I looked up as she screamed again that something was grabbing her foot. I dived under to see the tail end of the rope brushing her leg which, for some reason, I found much more amusing than she did. A cup of coffee and a cigarette later, all was well with the world. That afternoon to celebrate we went snorkelling at the posh end of the bay and added an octopus, several interesting shells and a puffer fish to our list of underwater sightings. Unfortunately, there was also a couple of turtle shells lying on the bottom which is a sad sight. Apparently, they still hunt passing whales from Bequia on occasion so the odd turtle is probably seen as fair game.

Well, that brings us up to date. Steve and Norma are still standing out in the rain while I type away and all is well with the world. The only future fly in our ointment, at the moment, is that we have just found out that we will need full visas to get into America on a private yacht. I had been assured by someone in the know, back in the UK, that our ESTA registration would cover us, but apparently not. At the moment the nearest US embassy is in Barbados, which is galling as we spent several weeks there over Christmas moored virtually outside the place. Had we but known, we could have got them organised then. On the bright side, we have a few months to get it sorted before we have to change plans, so if anyone has a suggestion of where we can get full visas issued between St Lucia and Miami or, even better, the American Virgin Islands, please drop me a line.

Until next time..................

Marigot Bay, St Lucia 15th Jan 2015 14:40:40
13:57.96N 61:01.47W

5510 Miles from Ramsgate by log.

Guess what? It is still raining! I was just about to go ashore to complete the customs formalities in Marigot Bay, St Lucia when the skies opened up and torrential rain came down which, even though it is warm rain, has definitely put the stoppers on that manoeuvre. We arrived at 5 O'clock last night with the boat and crew covered in salt crystals from stem to stern and head to toe respectively after another bit of a bashing by the weather on the way over. The wind was just free enough to sail but, in order to make real progress, we also ran the engine at slow revs to help push us through the confused seas, and oh boy was it a confused seaway. With the wind steady at 25 knots the seas heaped up at the top end of St Vincent and came at us from all directions at once. Poor old *Spectra* had the decks awash on several occasions and, if you know the boat, suffice to say water was pouring out over the top of the bulwarks at times, as the scupper could not deal with the volume. Not nice at all. As if that wasn't unpleasant enough, a rather large wave washed a giant flying cockroach out from under the life raft on deck which immediately instigated a manic hunt as there is no way I'm sharing cabin space with any of those little (big) buggers. Steve attacked it from the safe end of a long broom, while I chased around with two dust pans trying to herd it into a corner. Norma, meanwhile, accused us both of squealing like little girls whilst standing a very safe distance away.

Finally, the battle was won and Mr Cockroach was consigned to the deep, hopefully he didn't fly in with any pals, as they will be grandparents by the morning. Strangely enough, when we looked up from all of this activity the seas had calmed considerably as we were now coming under the lee of St Lucia.

The Pitons rose ever higher as we sailed past, busily snapping pictures, and headed up to Marigot Bay for the night. After studying Mr Street's instructions on finding the entry to Marigot Bay, I gave up and followed the plotter, which as always took me straight in. I am sure there is a conspicuous red roofed house on the hill Mr Street, but it is hidden among all of the other not so conspicuous red roofed houses that have been built since you wrote your guide. Marigot Bay is really, really, nice; a proper picture-postcard type of Caribbean port. We decided to have a good night's sleep and accepted the boat boy's offer of a mooring buoy at $80 EC a night, which was a bit steep, I thought. As it turned out, the fee covers taxi rides ashore and to the restaurants, showers, garbage removal, etc, so it didn't turn out too bad after all.

When Norma and Steve had finished tying the lines onto the buoy I switched the engine off and Norma stood up announcing to the world in a really loud and clear voice that definitely carried to all of the adjacent yachts, "I am always happier when I get on a buoy at night". My ghast was absolutely flabbered I can tell you, and the boat boy went away with a huge grin on his face.

Must go, rain has stopped. I will update next time from Rodney Bay when we get there, tomorrow probably.

18th Jan 2015 14:57:21
St Lucia – Rodney Bay
14:04.431N 60:56.93W
5520 Miles from Ramsgate by log.

We have now had one complete day without rain which is a first in several weeks. The trip up to Rodney Bay was an uneventful but busy 10 miles, of which we managed about 6 under sail, before the constant wind shifts (5 to 25 knots and winds shifting through 100 degrees constantly) became too much of a pain and we switched the donkey on.

Rodney Bay itself is a very well-run marina which we found to be still well stocked with ARC boats all flying their ARC flags and general bunting. It has expanded over the years leaving no real opportunity for anchoring in the lagoon so it was onto a pontoon for us. Actually, getting onto the pontoon was unnecessarily complicated by a local boat boy in, what can only be described as, a floating bush covered in the flags of all nations, who repeatedly tried to get between us and the pontoon in order to sell us fruit as we made our final approach. Finally, I told him to bugger off and come back later, to which he smiled and said, "no problem boss, keep it real". I suspect he had been smoking some of his personal jungle.

We have rather enjoyed being on a pontoon for a few days, the first time tied up since Grenada, and have made the most of it by getting a few jobs done on the boat. The water maker is working again after clearing a faulty valve on the output. It had been indicating 50 litres an hour of good water produced, but nothing was actually coming out of the end of the pipe into our tanks! I suspect that the slight blockage in the valve had caused back pressure which made the machine dump the fresh water over the side with the brine. Oh well, all working now. I have made up a new bridle from some spare 18mm anchorplait that we can use with our sea anchor or drogue, this now only needs a good test in storm conditions (joke). If that stays in the locker for the next ten years I will be a happy bunny. My bow roller now rolls again which is a novelty, and we have a new kill switch for the outboard. I also replaced the bungee cord that holds the main preventer under the boom when not in use and all of the bungee cord on the deck sails which were looking rather tatty. Whilst this was going on our empty gas bottles were being filled with propane, regardless of what it says on the bottle, this is the Caribbean after all. This gives us four large and one small gas bottles all topped up. The sailmaker could not fix our spinnaker storage bag in time and I will sew that myself as we go along, which will save some pennies. Our engine battery charger is sitting on another technician's bench (number 3) so we will see what happens there. I remain full of confidence. I did take it to the on-site electrical repair shop but the conversation with the sleepy girl who was busy doing her nails, at the reception desk went a bit like this:

"Hi, I have a problem with this battery charger. A technician in Grenada has identified the broken parts but he couldn't get them delivered in time before we departed. Could you have a look at it?"

"Ooh, we probably couldn't get the parts either" ... back to the nails.

"Could you get someone to look at it and tell me?"

"Well probably, but when do you want it?" ..... looking up briefly from the nails.

"Next Monday?" (this was on Thursday)

"Well I don't know, maybe Tuesday would be good"...fully focused on the nails now

"No, I leave on Monday. Do you want to know what parts you would need so that you could check?"

"Probably, but I don't think we could get them" .... Looking at the nails from arm's length now.

"I tell you what, I don't think I will bother, I'll try somewhere else" says I.

"Ok, you have a nice day then" ... nails looking good, another satisfied customer leaves the store.

...................Bloody hell! It is hard work to just give money away sometimes!

After that little exchange Norma had to give me an emergency shot of beer to get the blood pressure down and I then found a computer repair shop right under the customs building. The man in there was not only keen but he was actually interested in doing the job and so my battery charger is in pieces spread across his bench, chair and parts of the workshop floor the last time I checked. He assures me it will be done by Monday morning and I am brimming with faith.

While I was pottering about doing boaty bits Norma reorganised the nest. Most of the boat's contents were pulled out, rearranged, cleaned and put back away again, leaving *Spectra* a very refreshed and clean girl indeed. Good news, no evidence of cockroaches, or other creepy crawlies, was found anywhere.

With all of the immediate tasks completed, yesterday was a down day. Steve took a walk up to the fort on the hill at the entrance to the bay and sampled some of the local produce (rum) in the rebuilt Napoleonic officers' mess. He declared the rum an excellent brew and so had another. Meanwhile, I went shopping with Norma, which was an absolutely fantastic fun-filled day for the whole family. Even Norma agreed that $70 US for a pair of shorts duty free was a bit steep and so we brought a new set of hair clippers for me. Last night I was pinned to the floor and sheared like a sheep by Norma leaving me looking a lot less of a hippy, even when I wear my banana hat. I am rather proud of my banana hat which I haggled for at length with a boat boy in Marigot Bay; $5 EC and a can of beer. Absolute bargain, I say. Everyone else we meet says he saw me coming.

Our American visa, or lack of American visa to be precise, issue has also progressed. Steve returned from a trip to the marina toilets and announced that he had met a very interesting man in the toilet and got a result!!!! As you could imagine, all work stopped and we were all ears to hear further details of this life changing moment. Unfortunately, he was only talking about visa applications but Norma and I had suffered a premature innuendo overload, if you will excuse the innuendo. He had met a man who had been told that you could take the commercial ferry across from the British Virgin Islands (BVI's) to the American Virgin Islands (AVI's) and do the visa in a day. You then go back, pick up your boat and sail into American territory. On further investigation this proved to not be completely correct in our case, as he was booking his boat in as cargo to get shipped back to the UK on a freighter, whereas we wanted to sail around a bit. Nearly there but no banana this time. We have started to fill in the D-160 forms for the American Embassy and will then book an interview in Nassau, The Bahamas, sometime in mid-March. This should allow plenty of time for us to get to Florida and meet up with Gemma, Duncan, Lilly and baby MacDonald by the beginning of April. Unfortunately, we will have to miss the American Virgin Islands and Puerto Rico as they come first and with no US Visa we can't get in. The problem now is that we were going to drop Steve off in Puerto Rico to catch his flight home. He is now looking at ways to get from the BVI's to Puerto Rico by commercial flight/ferry, but that is a problem for another day. Our itinerary will now be from the BVI's to the Dominican Republic, possibly Haiti or the Turks and Caicos, Cuba and then across to the Bahamas which is all good.

Last night we had a bit of excitement when a police boat started stopping boats in the harbour for checks, blue lights flashing, etc. He seemed to be concentrating on the local open boats which buzz about after dark with no lights on so perhaps there had been a tip off. Speculation ran rife aboard *Spectra* and we were in full expectation of a "Miami Vice" style drugs bust and shoot out. Instead the police went home and it all went quiet; except of course for the local open boats who all started to buzz around the harbour without any lights on again. That's it for now, beach day today, (Sunday 18th), and then set sail for Martinique after clearing customs and picking up my fully repaired battery charger on Monday morning. What could possibly go wrong with that plan, I ask you?

22nd Jan 2015 18:00:14
Martinique – Forte de France
14:33.531N 61:06.83W

5570 Miles from Ramsgate by log.

Well what can I say, I have my battery charger back on board and it is still not working. Again, the problem is spare parts, or lack of them. However, all is not lost, what I do have is a list of components that are needed so I think a visit to ebay is in order, get all the bits and solder them on myself. The good news is that I have still not been charged any money for the accumulated technician time, so free tech advice I suppose. The customs clearance at Rodney Bay was all very smooth and efficient, our government costs for the stay were $100 EC for customs/light dues which is ok, as most of the navigation lights on St Lucia did seem to be working, even if they didn't necessarily line up with what my chart said. The commotion with the Police boat on Saturday night turned out to be a break in on a yacht which was moored on a nearby pontoon. Although these things happen everywhere in the world, it is still not a very good advert for St Lucia, particularly considering the yachtsman's murder last year during a failed robbery attempt while at anchor. Back to the customs clearance; it all went well and we were even offered, and declined, a free AIDS test as part of the process, which is a first. To explain, St Lucia is running a health campaign which can never be a bad thing. While we were waiting for the immigration chap to turn up for work, we got talking to a local guy, who turned out to be the St Lucia National Swimming Coach. He was at the marina to teach some swimming lessons in the on-site pool. He was a very interesting chap and, although originally from Grenada, is now a very patriotic St Lucian. He said that only about one in ten locals can swim and amongst the fishermen it is probably even lower, which is a pretty poor statistic for a small island. His mission is to turn that around and he was very passionate about it. As an aside, he also proudly pointed out that St Lucia is one of only three countries in the world where you are more likely to work for a woman than for a man, answers on a post card, reference the other two, and chaps just saying, "my house" and putting your home address down is not an acceptable answer.

    The trip up to Martinique was uneventful and ended up as a motor sail in 5 knots of wind, just enough to keep you cool. We spent one night in the 'Cul-de-Sac Marin' anchored closely outside the 600-berth marina. We rowed ashore to clear into customs and have a Ricard or two; we were now back in France after all. The customs process involved nothing more complicated than completing a form on a computer pushing print and paying 5 Euros (yes, we are back in Europe) and that covers us for arrival and departure, so simple. The next morning, we moved the 20 or so miles around the corner to the Fort De France Bay and anchored right up under the dominating walls of Fort St Louise in 3 metres of water, and only about 30 metres from the promenade and beach, which is a lovely spot. When we looked at our neighbours I thought for a moment that Paul from Ramsgate, who lives in a 20 something foot yacht that often has more piled up outside than could ever fit inside, had beaten us across the Atlantic. On closer inspection this turned out to be an intrepid American in a very small boat.

This really is a bit of France, the whole feel of the place is more French Mediterranean than Caribbean, they even speak all funny. No matter how loudly I shout they still adamantly refuse to understand a word I say, blooming typical. An added bonus for us was that the Lanzarote to Fort De France Classic Yacht Race was due to finish the same day and the winner's pontoon was only 100 metres from where we were anchored. This gave us a grandstand view of the first yacht, *Altair*, crossing the line under an absolute mountain of cream coloured top sails and multiple jibs, closely followed by a press helicopter and fire boat with water cannons shooting a fountain into the air. Her varnish and brass work had such a depth of shine that it looked like you could dive right into them. The crew were also resplendent in matching T-shirts and shorts lining the side decks for the arrival celebrations, and this was at the completion of an Atlantic crossing/race!! It sooo reminded me of *Spectra's* arrival in Barbados.

They must have done extremely well as it was two days later that we caught sight of the next boat coming in, as we sailed out at 5 in the morning for the trip up to Portsmouth on Dominica. Over the previous two days Steve and I had taken a trip up to Fort St Louise while Norma went shopping. We all had a good look around the town and had a very French, and very good, meal ashore. The fort is still an operational French Naval base and so the tour was very restricted, to be honest. What it did provide was a walk along the battlements and glacis plate giving us a great view across the harbour, with *Spectra* bobbing around on her anchor many feet below. One notable point of the tour was the iguanas which infest the place, apparently there used to be a zoo in the fort and these are the offspring of the escapees that have gone native.

And that brings me up to date. It is now 8:00am and we are abeam of the northern point of Martinique and Dominica is just visible nestling amongst the clouds on the horizon. A small pod of dolphins has just dashed past in the opposite direction, these being the first we have seen in I don't know how long. They must have been hungry as they didn't stop to play, or maybe they only speak French and so couldn't understand what Norma was saying? The plan is to travel most of the way up the coast of Dominica to Portsmouth Bay, and then tomorrow take the Indian River tour up into the mangrove swamps and rain forest of the interior, before moving on again. The guide book is not very flattering about the honesty of the locals and advises paying a boat watcher if you leave the boat unattended for any time. But, as always, we will take it as we find it; the guide book has been consistently wrong about most things so far. That's all for now; sausage and bacon baguettes are being prepared and my stomach is rumbling, I will send this as soon as I can get connected.

26th Jan 2015 13:39:33
Dominica, Swamps. Mosquitoes, and Pirates of the Caribbean
15:34.848N 61:27.807W
5640 Miles from Ramsgate by log.

I have just written that we really enjoyed sausage and bacon baguettes for breakfast, and I have been soundly chastised by Norma for lack of literal accuracy. I have therefore now corrected this to read, the sausage and egg baguettes were really enjoyable. I will go on to say, at the risk of further chastisement, that they were a culinary masterpiece and just what the doctor ordered. I'm glad I got that sorted out as it could have been a disaster to my readers understanding of the trip. Here we go with today's blog.

The sail, and it was a sail for a change, up to Portsmouth in Dominica was a long 70-mile day sail which took us a very respectable eleven and a half hours from anchor up to anchor down. Approaching the final headland before Prince Rupert Bay and Portsmouth town we were met by Alexis in a high-speed punt who introduced himself very politely and explained the PAYS (Portsmouth Association of Yacht Security) system. This is a cooperative of boat boys, tour guides, local restaurant owners, chandlers and taxi companies who have got together to sort out the problems that Dominica was experiencing with rogue traders, boat theft and the like. They share out the work amongst other PAYS members, provide security patrols at night, do the official tours in the areas and, in general, as they are answerable to the cooperative for their actions, seem to have sorted out most of the theft and general abuse problems that have been reported in the sailing press, certainly in my pilot book anyway. They also host a big beach BBQ on Sunday night for all of the yachts in the bay at a very modest price of $5 US which covers the administration costs of PAYS. That was our introduction to PAYS and Alexis, which as it turned out after some initial trepidation on our part, was all good. Once we had dropped our anchor and got it well dug in Alexis returned and offered us several local tours and a general rundown on what was available in the area. We booked ourselves onto an Indian River tour for the following day with Alexis at $20 US each, plus $5 for the national parks permit, and then spent an hour or two putting the boat to bed and having a bit of a siesta before going ashore to test out the fleshpots of Portsmouth. On a side note, as I walked towards the back of the boat to untie the dinghy in my bare feet I kicked one of the large bronze cleats at the stern, my foot slipped under it and the sharp end met my instep with a crunch. It started to swell immediately and I spent the rest of the night hobbling around as my left foot got bigger and bigger. Not to be deterred we went ashore anyway and soon found the Blue Bay restaurant that had limited Wi-Fi and cold beer. We settled in, sent those all important messages and caught up on the gossip from home.

Here is a bit of local history for you. Portsmouth used to be the capital of Dominica but it was abandoned pretty early on in favour of Roseau in the south of the island, the reason being Portsmouth is essentially a swamp. The problem with swamps is that they are full of mosquitoes and at that time they carried yellow fever which had the nasty habit of killing off anyone who tried to build a house there. Luckily for us the yellow fever has been eradicated and the town has been able to thrive. Unluckily for us, and in particular for me, the mosquitoes are still here. Why me you say? Well, Steve has not been bitten once, Norma has five bites on her legs, while little old me has over 100 on my legs, arms, back and neck. Norma counted them. Why, I don't know, but they just love a bit of vintage Russell 2015 and tuck right in every time I step ashore. In fact, I look like I am at an over 50's disco as I twist and turn scratching all of my little itchy bits all day and all night. With that bit of background knowledge, you can understand why we beat a hasty retreat back to the relative sanctuary of *Spectra* and her supply of citronella and why I was looking forward to the Indian River tour (which definitely is a swamp) with some serious reservations.

Day two broke with gloomy rain clouds overhead and Alexis arrived smack on time 0800 to pick us up for the tour. We picked up another English couple from the boat next door and then three Norwegians from their boat at the other end of the anchorage before heading up the river. At $20 a head that's a pretty decent payday for Alexis. The Indian River has been designated a nature reserve meaning that once we had passed below the concrete bridge at its entrance the outboard had to be turned off and Alexis rowed us up the shallow mangrove lined waterway.

What a great morning. Alexis was entertaining and very knowledgeable about all of the plant and animal life that we encountered. Soon the canopy of trees closed over our heads and Alexis told us tales of his youth playing in the woods, hunting for the land crabs and eating the forest fruits with his friends. He told us of the Carib Indians that used to live in the area and how they now live on a 30,000 acre reservation on the island. He showed us the remains of the light railway that the British built through the swamp which was finally destroyed by Hurricane David in the 1990's. He then took us up a side river a short way and we came upon the film set from The Pirates of the Caribbean, with the shack that Calypso the witch lived in, still in place. He also commented on just about every living thing that we saw, from land crabs through iguanas and onto white cranes, finishing each description with, "they taste pretty good, you know, just like chicken". Coconuts were his passion and he swore blind that everything to do with coconuts was good for you, except for standing under a tree and having one fall on your head, that is. As proof of this he quoted the oldest woman in the world who lived in Portsmouth until her death at the age of 128 who drank coconut milk every day and claimed to have never been ill. So, now you know; stop reading this and get down to the supermarket for some coconuts before they sell out.

At the furthest point upriver that our tour reached we stopped at a bar, conveniently placed there by a PAYS member, for a walk around. Alexis took us about a mile through the woods which was a bit of a struggle for me as my foot now resembled a melon after my bare foot kicking match with the cleat on *Spectra*. It soon became apparent that most of this seemingly virgin forest was actually cultivated but it is done in such a low impact way that you have to look hard to see it. There were pineapples, passion fruit, bananas, coconuts, cucumbers, lettuce, cashew trees, cinnamon trees, ginger, grapefruit, mint, rosemary, thyme, a little plant like a Venus fly trap that closed when you brushed against it and, rather bizarrely, a cow, all in the middle of nowhere. The trip through the woods finished with some local rum cocktails made by a friend of Alexis in another shack and the opportunity to buy some fruit from the farmer, another friend of Alexis. We purchased 10 grapefruit for $1 which were so tasty you could eat them like oranges and they tasted really sweet; absolutely delicious.

On our slow meander back down the river it became clear why Alexis encouraged us to go early, not only was the river getting busy with other trip boats (all rowed) but the mozzies were beginning to bite as the day warmed up. As promised, Alexis took us down to the South end of the bay to clear into customs on our way back to *Spectra*, I suppose officially it should have been the other way around, but heck who's counting. Customs was a very easy process and for $14 EC you book in and out at the same time and can stay for up to 14 days. The only thing that marred the experience was the stroppy little mare behind the counter who made full use of her moment of power to be borderline rude throughout the process. Anyway, I kept smiling and very politely pointed out at the end, once my passport was safely back in my pocket, that she had only given me a receipt for $12 when I had paid her $14. She said the $2 was for the paperwork and then, under the close scrutiny of her boss, changed the figure on my receipt to $14. I'm not proud of it, but I have to admit I really enjoyed deflating the little madam, just that little bit.

On getting back to *Spectra* we unpacked our goodies from the walk through the forest. We had grapefruit, lettuce, coconuts, passion fruit and one frog. Norma found the frog when she washed the lettuce and, after an initial squeal, rushed up on deck to show us our latest crew member. At that point, no doubt having seen Steve and me, the frog abandoned ship and jumped into the sea. He was last seen floating out to sea belly up, I'm afraid. After that commotion, I commented that my feet were sore from the walking and Norma pointed out that my toes were filthy from the forest mud so I rinsed them in the sea. Unfortunately, it was not all dirt and three of my toes and the top of my foot had gone black with bruises from kicking the cleat. Later that afternoon Frank and Mandy, from *Infinity B,* another yacht in the bay, the English couple who had been on the tour with us in the morning, came over to talk about our HF SSB radio. They are members of the Ocean Cruising Club which is very active in these here parts and they have a daily catch up across the Caribbean by SSB radio. Anyway, to cut a long story short, Frank gave us all of the frequencies and times that we need to listen in on, meaning we have another good outlet for information now. That night we went ashore again for a drink with Frank and Mandy and to meet up with Simon and Hilda another OCC couple who have been sailing around the Caribbean for over 9 years now. We gained an awful lot of good information from the two couples, particularly in reference to sailing in America, but unfortunately no new information about Visa applications. Later that night the three of us had a farewell to Dominica meal, the plan being to have another look around the next day and then head up to the Ile de Saintes about lunchtime. We ate at an open fronted and sided restaurant on the beach called the Purple Turtle where the bats flew in one side and out of the other, dodging around the tables and our heads as they came through at breakneck speed hunting for insects. The food was good but the mozzies were ferocious again and so the dots on my legs have all now been joined together. Noticing my discomfort, the lady owner stood me on a chair in the middle of the restaurant and sprayed me with a local concoction that actually worked and kept the little blighters at bay. I don't know what it was, DDT for all I care, but it gave me a window of relief, enabling me to enjoy a very pleasant meal, if not a good night's sleep.

After a truly awful night of scratch, scratch, scratch I awoke in a foul mood and absolutely no desire to set foot on shore again. Norma and Steve concurred and so we pulled up the anchor and headed North again for the 20-mile jaunt to the Ile de Saintes.

A final note on Dominica, we found absolutely no problems there at all. The locals were all friendly, bar the customs girl who, to be fair, was a typical teenager, and we really enjoyed our short stay. It is a beautiful country, much greener than some of the other islands, and I will certainly return again but for longer next time. What I will do, though, is pack enough noxious-smelling substances from Boots to declare full scale chemical warfare on any flying insect that even thinks about coming close.

Next blog will be from the Ile de Saintes...........................

THE LEEWARD ISLANDS, ISLE DE SAINTES TO US VIRGIN ISLANDS

JANUARY TO FEBRUARY 2015

26th Jan 2015 15:21:26
Ile de Saints
15:52.11N 61:34.56W

We arrived safe and sound, all is well but internet very flaky. I will give a full update soon on our adventures in the Ile de Saintes. Lovely place by the way.

26th Jan 2015 23:32:02
Iles de Saintes 2 …………..Beaches and ice cream
15:52.11N 61:34.56W
5662 Miles from Ramsgate by log.

As promised, an early update on our latest travels which should bring everything nicely up to date. We arrived in the Iles de Saintes at lunchtime on the 24th and decided to spend the first night anchored off the western island in the group, Terre-de-Bas, as this is often missed by passing yachts. Unfortunately, it only has the one anchorage that could be considered safe for an overnight stop, particularly as the wind was gusting well over 20 knots from the east and, as luck would have it, there was no room at the inn. The way it seems to work is that the first wave of boats to arrive grab the prime spots close to the beach or pontoon, but at a safe distance, no problems there. The next wave to arrive anchor further out, still all very gentlemanly. The next wave, finding no obvious good spots, muscle their way in between the first boats and the beach, the next wave squeeze themselves in between the first and second boats, and so it goes on until you are left with two or three boats (usually French as they don't give up as easily as us Brits) motoring around the bay at ever higher speeds trying to find a non-existent spot and shouting a lot of nonsense like, "where is your anchor?", or "how long is your chain?" To which the answer, "it is in front of my boat, where else would it be?" or "my chain is just long enough to go from my boat to my anchor" does not seem to please. At this point we decided to go elsewhere, instead of adding to the spaghetti junction of anchor chains littering the seabed. We went the mile and a bit across to the

Eastern Island, Terre-de-Haut, and tried to pick up a buoy but alas for us again no room at the inn. Eventually, we dropped anchor just outside the buoyed area in 15 meters and the hook dug in first time, 1500 revs in reverse for 5 minutes and we did not move so I was happy for the night.

We stayed aboard for the first night and, whilst we were eating breakfast on Sunday morning, the first yachts began to leave the buoys. By 09:00 we had moved and were snugly attached to a buoy about 50 metres from the landing pontoon and town centre. "Good things come to he who waits" say I, amongst other very smug comments at inopportune moments, but that's just the way I am I suppose.

Ile de Saints is a real picture postcard sort of place. The small town has lots of little tourist shops and restaurants aplenty along the beach, there is a fort on the hill (called Napoleon of course) and you can walk from one end of the place to the other in half a day. That first day we had a look around the town, which was half closed because it was Sunday, and walked across the island to a lovely beach before eating a really nice meal for lunch and then heading back aboard.

That night my generator decided it didn't want to run for more than twenty minutes at a time before stopping, so out with the tools and into action. What I found was that it was full of loose connections. It does vibrate a bit and to be fair it has taken a hammering this year. I tightened up everything, only causing big sparks once, which is pretty good for me, and I'm still not sure which loose connection fixed the problem but it is running as sweet as a nut now. Point to note: Everything, and I mean everything, on a yacht is in a permanent state of decay. From the moment you tighten a nut or fix a loose thread it is trying its best to work loose, fray or just break, so keeping on top of it is a full-time job if you are travelling any distances. Whinge over, onto what the "*Spectranauts*" did next.

Monday morning 0730, bright and early, I was listening to the SSB radio net catching up on what was going on in the cruising world when our croissants and baguettes were delivered to the boat by the harbour master; good service here in little France. By 10 O'clock we were shore side and ready to go. Steve was heading up to Fort Napoleon for a look around which I rather fancied, but a big hill and my sore foot would not have made a happy partnership. Instead, I spent the morning booking into customs with Norma. The Saintes is another French outpost in the Caribbean meaning the customs process, like Martinique, was very simple: fill in an online form, pay an admin fee €2 and you are good to go. What slowed it down was that there was only one computer and we were 3rd in line. To top it off the American guy who had control of the keyboard could only type with one finger, could only remember one letter at a time and, to put the icing on the cake, had a crew of eight all of whose passport details had to be typed in laboriously one digit at a time. Clack....clack....clack went the keyboard as we all looked on. Forty-five minutes later we were at the front of the queue and the printer broke down! We had to wait while the nice French lady installed a new one, arrghhh! Actually, it wasn't that bad and we met some interesting people in the line, an American from a massive power boat and a French man from a 30ft single handed sailing boat, both of whom were very friendly and happy to chat away as we listened to the metronome slowly clacking away in the corner. Clearance completed and €2 fee paid we were all legal and above board until the 30th, and so it was off to the café for coffee and internet. After that we headed back across the island to the beach that we had spied from yesterday, but this time we were prepared, with swimming costumes and snorkelling gear. We met up with Steve on the beach who informed us that it was the best fort so far with a museum that actually gave you the whole story of the place. He was lent the only English guidebook on the understanding that he had to return it before he left, which of course being an English gentleman he did. I, also being an English gent, hid my disappointment and jealousy behind my stiff upper lip, but inside I was crying like a baby. I hate my foot and I hate that vindictive cleat on the aft deck.

That's it really, only a short stay and mainly beaching but hey it's not all work you know. Tomorrow we head across to Guadeloupe having spent a really relaxing and above all mosquito-free couple of days. By the way, my mozzie bites have started to fade and my left foot is now only one shoe size up so all is well with the world....

30th Jan 2015 14:53:33
Guadeloupe-Antigua............Turtle rescues and Cul de Sacs
17:00.307N 61:45:632W
29th January 2015
5686 Miles from Ramsgate by log.

Our journey over to Pointe-a-Pitre in Guadeloupe was all going very much to plan. We left the Saintes at 0900, after taking delivery of our Croissants from the harbour master, and headed across to Guadeloupe which was clearly visibly about 6 miles away. Our route up to the marina in Pointe-a-Pitre was, in fact, closer to 22 miles as it is at the head of the Petite Cul de Sac Marin and would give us easy access to the river Salee which bisects the two islands that make up Guadeloupe. The cunning plan was to spend a night at the marina and then move out to anchor near the first of the two lifting bridges on the river for the next night. This would give us a flying start for when the bridge would open at 0430 am to allow us to pass through and head on up to Antigua in one easy day sail. That was the plan anyway, but more of that later.

We just managed to make the headland at the south end of Basse Terre after having to take avoiding action to miss a really big turtle on the way and shot into the Petite Cul de Sac Marin doing a respectable 7 knots when we sighted the first of many fishing buoys. The whole area is absolutely littered with them and the markers are usually no more than a coke bottle or a small piece of polystyrene which makes spotting them a bit of a trial in the choppy seas. As we crossed the bay we reduced sail to better spot the markers when Norma, who is our champion buoy spotter (no pun intended) shouted out that there was another turtle dead ahead. This one didn't seem quite right and we slowed down for a better look as we passed close by only to find that it was well and truly tangled in a fishing net that was slowly strangling it. We dropped all sails and went into man overboard mode in an attempt to save the turtle. Steve steered, I grabbed the boat hook and Norma prepared a line while keeping the turtle in sight as we manoeuvred around. The problem was that Mr Turtle did not appreciate our efforts and every time we got close he dived down only to resurface gasping for air a few minutes later. I finally managed, on about the tenth attempt, to hook the net and get him alongside but he dived deep ripping the boat hook out of my hands and nearly taking me and Norma with him. At this point a large yacht race came by complete with attendant umpires on ribs. One of the boats broke away from the race to see if we needed any help, it was a kind offer but there really was nothing they could do and so they sailed on wishing us good luck (in French of course).

After recovering the boathook, we had another go and on the second attempt Mr turtle dived under our bows and I heard him thumping along under the hull. Rather speculatively, I leant out as far as I could go and reached down under the hull with the boat hook and, more by luck than judgement, I managed to snag the net that was trapping him. This time I was not letting him go and so with a heave I managed to jam the boathook and net behind one of our mid ship rail cleats. That had him safely attached to the boat at least but he was still under water and slowly drowning. The next step was Norma quickly passing me the fishing gaff hook, which is on a pole, so that I could snag the net lower down. Putting all of our effort into it, (a struggling one-metre long turtle is a heavy and powerful thing), Norma and I hauled on the boathook until finally the turtle surfaced with a big gasp for air. We managed to hold him just long enough for Steve to lean over and attach a rope to the net close to his body which was also fixed to a cleat; now we were in business. Norma dashed below for our sharpest knife and then, while I hauled up on the net to try to get as much of the turtle out of the water as possible, Steve lent over the side, with Norma sitting on his legs to stop him joining the turtle, and began to saw away at the net. It took quite a while and it was distressful hearing the turtle gasping for air but, after repositioning the ropes and hooks a couple of times, the turtle finally slipped free and without a backwards glance swam away at speed. Although pretty tired we decided the best thing would be to bring the net aboard so that it didn't snag any more wildlife and we all began pulling it up, and boy was it heavy. After a while the reason for the weight became clear, there was another, equally large, turtle trapped in the net further down! This one had been under the water the whole time and so we thought it must be dead but, to our great relief, when we got it to the surface its eyes opened and it took in an enormous gasp of air. Again, I hauled, Steve cut, and Norma sat on his legs while pulling lumps of netting out of the way. This one was well and truly entangled, it took a while, but we got him cut free eventually and watched him swim away which, to be honest, was quite emotional. Only after the event did Steve notice that he had cut his hand on the turtle shell but small price to pay I think.

As if that was not enough excitement for one day, as we entered the channel to go up to the marina the biggest dolphin we have seen yet surfaced right next to us, it must have been about 10 feet long, an absolute monster, and we mistook it for a shark at first. Norma stated, very confidently, that he was the king of the dolphins and had come over to say thank you to us for saving the turtles. Nice thought, but Steve and I still extracted the Michael all the way into the marina. As we entered the marina, which is a huge, thousand-berth affair, the large, international racing fleet were moored on the first few rows of pontoons inside. This fleet included a brace of truly massive trimarans, one of which, we later found out, had crossed from St Malo to Guadeloupe in 8 days!!!!. One of the guys shouted across to ask if we had saved the turtle to which Norma replied (while holding up the remains of the net) that there were two turtles and we had saved them both. The whole racing fleet gave us a huge round of applause, clapping and cheering as we went by. What an entrance!

The next day we all trekked into Ponte-a-Pitre town, the capital of Guadeloupe, for a look around and for Norma and me to get some photographs taken. Our UK passport pictures do not meet the requirements for a US visa application and so we had to get new ones (the saga goes on). The lady in the shop said that our t-shirts were too light and so we went and brought two black ones (the saga goes on and on). Once that little task was completed and my wallet was €30 lighter we had a wander around the old town. I wouldn't say that it was a nice-looking place but there were parts that showed its faded grandeur from days gone by. Unfortunately, the road we took was lined by ladies of the night working in the day, but I am sure you get my point, which rather clouds one's opinion of a place.

That nearly brings me up to date, apart from to say that when we moored up we discovered that the lifting bridges on the river Salee were broken and there didn't seem to be any plan to fix them in the next year or so. We would have to go back the way we came and go around Guadeloupe making it a 76-mile trip up to Antigua. Oh well, it is an adventure after all.

On the afternoon of the 28th we slipped from the marina with the plan of heading up the coast a bit and dropping anchor for the night before heading onto Antigua the next morning. Again, the gremlins struck and my engine alarmed showing water in the diesel. No problems, open the valve at the bottom of the filter and let the water out, all fixed. No such luck, the valve was seized shut meaning I had to remove the whole filter. The only way to get the valve off was by cutting up the filter which only proved that the valve was completely buggered and I now have a new filter fitted. I always carry a spare or two, but no water release valve. This is not a show stopper but annoying none the less.

As I write this, I am actually sitting at anchor just inside English Harbour eating the last of the grapefruits that we gathered on our Indian River tour in Dominica. The trip over yesterday took 15 hours, including a couple of hours trying to find a place to anchor. We didn't finally manage to get the anchor set until just before 23:00hrs and even then, the holding was so poor and the anchorage so tight, I dropped all three anchors to make sure of the job. It is like trying to get an anchor to hold in thick soup. One strange coincidence this morning; we woke to find the yacht anchored behind us is *Dark Horse*. This 60ft schooner is the ex-Lloyds Bank Sailing Club yacht that Norma and I sailed from Cadiz to Tenerife via Madeira way back in 2002, small world. That's it for this one; Steve has just got up at 09:30, the sleepy bugger. I am going ashore to complete customs, find a fuel filter and sensor and look at all of the millionaires' pretty playthings moored alongside Nelsons Dockyard.....talk soon.

4th Feb 2015 03:39:19

Antigua.......Big boats, Mademoiselles in distress and Jump ups.
17:03.95N 61:53:01W
3rd February 2015
5778 Miles from Ramsgate by log.

Today finds us still in Antigua, snugly moored in Jolly Harbour marina some 14 miles around the corner from English Harbour. We arrived here yesterday, after a very squally run up the coast. The forecast was for force 4-5 winds with occasional rain showers, so no surprise when we sailed out of English Harbour to find a 153ft Dutch super yacht laying right over on its side having been caught out with all sails up in 37-knot prolonged gusts. Pre-warned by his misfortune, we kept the sails small and had a relatively dry and comfortable run. Steve and Norma did anyway, as they found important jobs to do below at first sight of any black clouds, not that I am one to complain you understand. Anyway, bright sunshine now and Norma and I have just returned from the beach. So that's how we got here, but what have we been up to over the last four days?

As mentioned before, we initially anchored in Freemans Bay in English Harbour which, although the holding was pretty poor, did give us a grandstand view of a super yacht regatta that was being held just outside of the harbour entrance. Every morning a procession of yachts passed us by, going out to do battle, and what yachts they were. One, which was bright green in colour, was noticeably smaller than the rest and seemed out of place amongst the big boys. We looked it up on the internet only to find that it was, in fact, 105ft long, so not such a tiddler after all. The largest was 195ft and had, what looked like, the entire staff of London Underground, but much better dressed, standing on the side deck every morning. As I am waxing lyrical about the posh boats, I must mention *Leander,* the 50th largest motor yacht in the world, which was moored behind us, just across the bay, and is magnificently maintained. I could go as far as to say we were harbour buddies. Anyway, being nosey, we also checked this out on the internet. Owned by Sir Douglas Gosling, (a Royal Temple Yacht Club member, I am told) and apparently hired by the Prince of Wales and Camilla for their last official Caribbean cruise, in order to reduce their carbon foot print by avoiding air travel. 22 crew for 11 guests and it could be all yours for a mere $490,000 per week, plus expenses and tips of course. I was going to enquire about a booking but I just couldn't be that disloyal to *Spectra*, now could I?

Nelson's Dockyard, for those that haven't seen it, is a real treat for a history buff like myself and we topped the week off with a meal out in Nelson's Officers Mess which, like so many of the buildings, has been tastefully restored to its former glory or maybe better. It wouldn't have been right not to include a visit to the Shirley Heights jump up on Sunday night. On went the dancing shoes, we jumped in a cab and off we went up to the old gun battery that overlooks English Harbour and Falmouth Bay. A great night was had by all and I even spotted Steve's feet moving to the music at one stage. The night started with watching the sun go down, (no green flash I'm afraid), went on to a BBQ which was really good (and I generally hate BBQs), the best steel band I have ever seen or heard and ended with a reggae band. So, to say it was good would be the understatement of the week. After that lot we cadged a lift back down to English Harbour to find the Super Bowl still in full swing. Me being me, I identified a group of Americans at the hotel bar transfixed by the screen and asked them if they would mind if I turned the television over as I thought there was some cricket on the other side. One of the 'Americans' turned out to be British who, quite seriously, asked me who was playing in the cricket. God, you have to spoon feed humour to some people. Anyway, we had a chat and it turned out that they were all crew on one of the super yachts. We chatted about Atlantic crossings and island hopping, boats and bits as you do. They asked how big *Spectra* was to which I replied "53". "Oh, about the same size as ours" they said. Trouble was, they measure in metres and I measure in feet!!

That night the wind picked up and swirled around the anchorage which, with twenty or so yachts crammed in, resulted in, among other dramas, the French catamaran that had anchored far too close in front of us ending up about 5 metres from our bows by the morning. I watched for a while and then decided that I would have to encourage them to do something, so I went up the front and asked if they were happy about how close they were to us. At this stage all three of my anchors were underneath them somewhere so I was a bit short on manoeuvring options, plus they were now about three metres from our bow. A rather excitable French lady replied that all the men were ashore jogging and they did not know what to do. This would never have happened on *Spectra* for two reasons: one, Norma knows how to work the boat and is very good at it and two, I have a policy of never doing anything physical in public. That left us in a bit of a stalemate, as they slowly inched closer, after five or ten minutes I heard their anchor chain clanking in so thought all was well. The problem was that between the four of them they had found out how to pull the anchor up but not how to start the engine and so the inevitable happened, their anchor popped off the bottom and they drifted back onto us at a rate of knots. Luckily, we managed to push them around our bows and secure them alongside before they committed further carnage to the yachts behind us. At this point a rather bemused French jogger appeared on the jetty about 100 metres away to be met by a tirade of abuse and arm waving from his wife, much to the amusement of the entire anchorage. We found out later that he was the skipper and had the engine key but the other guy, who was still jogging, had the kill switch to the dinghy. This was now getting a bit like an Ealing Comedy or Carry On film and we settled down to watch. With a large dose of Gallic flair he dived in and started to swim towards us. The trouble was he was of advanced years and had just been jogging so after 30 metres he rolled over onto his back and started blowing like a pregnant walrus. Enter stage left the second Frenchman, returning from a pleasant jog, to find his floating home attached to an English yacht (the shame, the shame) and his skipper floating around the harbour doing a very presentable walrus impression. All four women now gathered on the foredeck to shout, advice, encouragement, admonishment, and probably the addresses of several divorce lawyers but, as I can't speak French, it may have been just general abuse. Frenchman number two now leapt into action; he untied the dinghy, started it up (he had the kill switch in his pocket, remember) and roared across the harbour towards Frenchman number one who was still gallantly trying to swim across to rescue his ladies. On approach he slowed and Frenchman number one with obvious relief grabbed the dinghy grab handle. Frenchman number two now opened the throttle nearly drowning Frenchman number one who was left behind in a welter of salty foam as the dinghy roared away. Number two noticed his error, returned and circled his now desperate skipper several times at high speed nearly drowning him with the wake he created on each circuit before heeding the desperate pleas of the skipper to leave him alone to die quietly and speed toward us.

At this point it must be noted that Norma had made us all a nice cup of tea and the three of us were being very British and hardly smirking at all.

Frenchman number two arrived alongside the catamaran in a welter of spray and leapt aboard to the relief of all. I think I have mentioned that I don't speak French but, by observing the body language, it became apparent that although Frenchman number two had the dinghy keys and had indeed arrived to save the day. Frenchman number one, who was still spluttering towards us across the harbour, had the yacht keys in his pocket. Oh dear, the ladies were not impressed....

It must be noted at this juncture that the gallant crew of *Spectra* were risking serious injury by burying our quivering stiff upper lips in our scalding hot tea.

Frenchman number two duly made himself busy by first saying a pleasant "bonjour" to us and then checking his anchor, which was hanging about two foot below his bow doing absolutely nothing for anyone. He then, with his head firmly down and eyes averted from the ladies and the watching English, busily checked all of the lines that were attaching the two boats together.

Our tea finished, we tried to make pleasant conversation and I even asked whether they had any spare croissants. They didn't.

Enter stage right one very wet, very tired, and very embarrassed Frenchman number one who, although clearly on his last legs, was leapt upon by a gaggle of furious women. He gave us an apology, a sheepish smile and then with his last ounce (or should I say gram) of Gallic flair produced the keys and saved the day........Hooray!

As an aside, they did give us a bottle of rum as a thankyou and quickly moved into our spot when we left, so all's well that ends well.

Jolly harbour is well run and accommodating. On arrival we were hailed from the quayside by a chap that had been aboard Spectra when she was under previous ownership and doing the Blue Water Rally, small world. Basically built in a swamp, they have an anti mossie truck that drives around every evening blowing smoke into the hedges which seems to keep the insect population down. Customs clearance was easy with everything next to each other within the harbour limits so we were quickly cleared and ready to go.

Tomorrow we head for Montserrat and then onto St Kitts from where I will blog again. Until next time.................

5th Feb 2015 16:21:54
Montserrat....Whales, a horrible night's sleep at anchor and lost Irish Kingdoms
16:48.046N 62:12.485W
5834 Miles from Ramsgate by log.

Yesterday we dropped down from Jolly Harbour, went around the bottom of Montserrat and spent the night in the only surviving harbour, Little Bay, a distance of around 42 miles. One point of interest as we crossed over was a pod of 4-6 whales that came within 25 metres of us. I'm not sure which make or model they were but they measured about 15 feet, were all black and had very blunt noses. They certainly caused a flurry of activity on board as cameras were grabbed from below but all to no avail; all we managed were pictures of empty ocean.

On approaching the South West coast of Montserrat the devastation from the volcano is still very much in evidence and even from 1.5 miles offshore you can see the ash flows running down the volcano's side. When we turned the corner at the bottom of the island the old capital of Plymouth came into sight which had two great swathes of devastation running right through it, leaving a small island of houses and greenery in the middle. The volcano is still giving off steam and smoke which meant that when we finally got down wind of it, the air became laden with a strong sulphur smell which was not pleasant at all. As most of the southern part of the island is still under an exclusion zone, as the volcano is still very active, the only harbour and port of entry remaining is Little Harbour up on the North East coast. It is really just a small dock and a Customs shed with a few buildings around it. The only real point of interest was *HMS Severn* anchored in the bay which is on Caribbean (anti-drug smuggling) patrol. In traditional form we dipped our ensign to salute them as we passed and awaited their response which turned out to be a damn good ignoring but at least we tried.

No sooner had we dropped our anchor than an inter-island trading ship came into the harbour which needed room to manoeuvre and the room it needed was right where we had parked. It was up anchor and move over. By the time we had re-anchored it was getting dark and as customs was closed, we decided to eat aboard and get a good night's sleep. No chance of that, even in the fairly light winds a swell worked its way into the anchorage and we rolled like a drunken dog all night. I dropped our flopper stopper over the side in an attempt to cut down the roll, which was its trial run. The small parachute affair did slow the roll down but it was still extremely uncomfortable. A small Dutch yacht to the side of us was dipping his rails under in the bigger rollers, it must have been like trying to sleep inside a tumble dryer in that boat. As the sun came up I gave up on sleep and started getting *Spectra* ready for sea there was no way I was spending another night there. By 0715 we were away, just behind the Dutch boat, who had also given up the struggle. We passed *HMS Severn* again at 0730. I was debating dipping the ensign again as I am a bit of a traditionalist but, considering the fact that they hadn't even put their ensign up yet, it seemed a bit pointless and so I didn't bother.

Today we are heading for St Kitts where we will spend two nights in the marina, as my generator is playing up and I don't want to fix it while we are rolling around. I have also got to go up the main mast again and rerun the main halyard as that has broken. The jobs just never stop when you are using the boat a lot! As an aside we have just passed the islet of Redonda which is 9 miles from Montserrat but owned by Antigua. While reading up on its history, I discovered that an Irishman living on Montserrat had realised that it was unclaimed land back in 1865 and so, seeing an opportunity or maybe just being eccentric, claimed it for himself and a few years later crowned his son the King of Redonda. Not much came of the claim as it was generally ignored by the rest of the world but on the son's death a society was formed which to this day elects a new King of Redonda when needed. Apart from a few phosphate miners back in the 1800's and early 1900's the island has never been inhabited and remains abandoned to this day.

That's it for now, go on try and resist looking up Redonda on the internet I challenge you....

7th Feb 2015 17:56:19
Sint Maarten position update
18:01.095N 63:02.856W

Safe and sound in Sint Maarten blog update soon........ promise

14th Feb 2015 12:51:00
St Kitts, Eustacia, Sint Maarten, St Martin and Anguilla
18:12.204N 65:06.04W
5954 Miles from Ramsgate by log.

I have really got behind with this blogging malarkey and so this, and the next one, will have to be a bit of a catch up. We arrived in St Kitts on the 5th February and, by sheer luck, managed to bag the last place in the marina. It was a bit of a tight squeeze but with the help of a friendly American chap who took our lines, all went well. There was a moment of comic confusion when, after the American chap had called me Captain for the umpteenth time, I started to call him Captain in return and it went on, "Thanks Captain, You OK Captain? I'm OK Captain, are you OK Captain?" etc, etc, etc, all to the amusement of the dock master who had obviously seen it all before. As for the two Captains we shared a beer later and got on famously well. Anyway, St Kitts; after studying the guide book we rather fancied a ride on the only working railway in the Eastern Caribbean but at $60 per head for a short ride up the coast we decided to give it a miss. The capitol, Basseterre, has been taken over by the cruise liners, and the whole dock area of port Zante resembles an outlet centre. Seven days a week the cruise liners come in, all the shops and restaurants open and when the passengers head back to the ships, all of the shops and restaurants shut up again. To be honest, the place had no soul but, on the bright side, being in the marina did give me the opportunity to climb the mast yet again and re-run the main halyard which had come undone and typically fallen back down inside of the mast. Usually I splice all the halyards or use a bowline but this time I had tried a new knot which was recommended by a rather glossy yachty book. I'm not even going to dignify the knot with a name, it was rubbish, and came undone causing this trip up the mast for me. Why I changed I don't know but it will be splices or bowlines from now on for *Spectra*. Going to the top of the mast was no problem and even provided a point of interest for the hordes of tourists pouring ashore from the cruise liners. Nor was dropping the light mouse line down inside of the mast, but trying to fish the little bugger out of the bottom took the best part of three hours and ended up with me applying a good dose of industrial language to the problem. Finally, I admitted defeat and removed a riveted cover plate from the side of the mast in order to get better access.

Anyway, job done. *Spectra* now has her full complement of halyards and is all ready to go. The second night in St Kitts started off with an Indian meal ashore, which was a nice change and, ironically, reminded me of home. This was our first curry since we had a rather dodgy one in a joint Italian and Indian restaurant (now there's a combination to delight the taste buds) with Peter and Norma back in Lisbon, Portugal, all those months ago. After the meal we took *Spectra* out of the marina and spent the night just outside the entrance channel at anchor in the bay. After sighting a shark type fish swimming around the boat in the night, which was all very spooky, we had a very peaceful night and headed for Eustatia early the next morning.

Eustatia is a tiny little place, with an interesting history. It was used by the Dutch as essentially a customs dodge during, and shortly after, the American Civil War, allowing trans-shipments of goods from and to the newly independent America.

This created a legal loophole which bypassed the nasty old British blockade of trade with America and made the inhabitants of Eustatia extremely wealthy in the process. That was until the British had had enough of that and sent Admiral Rodney in to sort it out. He did in the true English style of the times by invading the place and stealing everything he could lay his hands on, making himself and his captains extremely wealthy in the process. Well that's the history, the reality today is that it only has one very small exposed anchorage which, as we approached, found it to be packed with local boats all bobbing about crazily in a dangerous swell, making it impossible to land. After a slow sail down the leeward side of the island we turned around the northern tip and headed for Sint Maarten which we could see in the distance.

Sint Maarten is the Dutch side of this island. We went straight into Phillipsburg, the main town, and dropped anchor quite close to the entrance of Bobby's marina, on the afternoon of the 7th. After putting the boat to bed in record time, we dashed ashore as the sun went down for a walk along the promenade and a beer in a beach bar which was all very nice and civilised. The next morning Steve went for a wander over to the salt lakes behind Phillipsburg while Norma and I went up the road out of town into the main docks to clear into customs. Not a nice way to start the day; why, oh why, do so many customs officials feel it is part of the job to be so miserable? It really is a downer doing business with them! After parting with a ridiculous amount of money, putting up with one-word answers, sullen looks and having a hatch slammed shut after every muttered syllable, we were in. They had annoyed me so much that I decided not to stay on that side of the island and booked out at the same time, which is a shame. These people are representing their country and if that country's main income is tourism you would think they would make a bit of a connection there wouldn't you, and abusing the golden goose? Moan over, the rest of the day was spent doing the tourist bit around Phillipsburg, but to be honest it was very much like St Kitts i.e. one big outlet centre for the cruise ships and so the following morning we up anchored and moved over to the French side of the island St Martin which involved a pleasant 10-mile sail around the coast. Again, we dropped anchor and went ashore, what a difference. Vibrant, friendly and a customs process which involves 5 Euros and ten minutes on a computer. At least it would have done, but the office was closed, so we went out for a meal instead. We know where to go next time for sure, especially as you can cross the land border into the Dutch side with zero checks; you live and learn. The French side of the island is actually bigger than the Dutch side, and they are separated by a large Salt Lake, "the lagoon", in the middle. You can enter the lagoon via a swing bridge from either side of the island and there are a multitude of marinas dotted around its shoreline. It would make an excellent place to spend a week or two refitting the boat, as every kind of boat fixing service you can imagine is dotted around the lagoon. Unfortunately for us, we had set ourselves a schedule to meet up with Mike and Kate aboard *Right Turn* in the BVI's and so again we had to head on after far too short a stay. Incidentally, the division of the island, so local folklore has it, was achieved very amicably. A Frenchman carrying a bottle of wine started walking from the North shore while a Dutchman carrying a bottle of gin started walking from the south shore, where they met was to be the border. As gin is far stronger than wine and it was a hot day the Dutchman sat down for a rest after a short time of walking. The Frenchman fortified by his wine, covered much more ground meeting up with him a long way into the southern section of the island, and that is where the border remains to this day. That's the urban legend anyway. We did have a good meal and met a lot of interesting people from the cruising world. This is a major refit centre and well worth the stop off, but keep an eye on your dinghy as just about everyone warned us about dinghy theft.

Anguilla is literally a stone's throw away to the north of St Martin and the journey over was enlivened when a mayday with a medical emergency on board came in from a yacht heading into St Martin. We listened to the radio chatter avidly as the local coastguard handled the situation very calmly and competently, arranging a boat to ferry the casualty ashore where an ambulance was ready and waiting. We thought we had our own emergency later in the day when we sighted a jet ski afloat in the middle of the sea, minus a driver. Thinking that we had a bit of a situation on our hands, and potentially a missing person from the jet ski floating out there somewhere, we changed course and closed the gap. When we got close, we realised that it was a complete wreck. No seat, engine or instruments and it had probably been washed off a beach somewhere, so no excitement after all.

Anguilla has the reputation of being a rich man's playground with prices to match, so it was with some trepidation that we went ashore to visit the customs office which is nestled in a picture postcard bay with crystal clear water and miles of white sandy beaches.

The total cost was $8 US for booking in and out. Wow what a bargain. Road Bay is the port of entry to Anguilla and just about the only place that is outside of the national park. If we wanted to leave the bay to visit any of the other anchorages we would have to buy a permit at $56 US per day for *Spectra* which, at just under 20 tonnes, is in the small boat category. The permit only lasts during daylight hours as you are not allowed to stay overnight. As a side note, the next category is 20-50 tonnes and would cost you $104 US per day, ouch! Just imagine what all of those super yachts are paying! To counter my moan from earlier, the customs and immigration in Anguilla were very friendly, welcoming and enjoyed joking with the visitors. Sint Maarten take note: that's the way to do it, we will be back in Anguilla for sure.

We had a great night out at the Elvis beach bar and grill which consists of an old wooden boat dragged up the beach, split in two, spread apart and turned into a bar, half buried in the sand. The night's entertainment included lots of beach games, bean bag throwing, catching a hook on a ring, etc and we met a great bunch of people. A crew of Texans were passing through, who filled us in on details and dire warnings about the intra-coastal waterway which we hope to attempt later in the trip, (visas pending). We also met a Welsh guy sitting at the bar/boat who owned a B&B in Pembrokeshire and worked short term contracts as a cook at a luxury villa on the island during the winter months. The villa has ten staff on site and could be all yours for only $200 grand per week. If anyone's interested, I have the contact details. If you're really interested and can afford it, I really want to be your friend.

We, (well Steve really), met a lady from Canada who was on a long-term holiday and had a hobby picking up dead coral from the beach. The nicely eccentric lady opened the conversation with," Hi, I'm a bit sad as my friend has just shot himself in the head back in the States". After that pretty impressive opening line she went on to explain how she looked for interesting pieces of coral and then pencilled in a few marks turning them into shapes, dogs, cats, chickens and so on which she sold via a local craft shop for a dollar each. It sounds a bit odd, and was to be honest, but nowhere nearly as odd as her opening statement perhaps. The little coral animals were actually rather clever; Steve now has a seal and Norma has a puppy dog which they paid for by buying her a beer. Later as the sun went down in spectacular fashion (no green flash though, although Norma claimed to have seen one) a crowd began to gather on the beach. Pretty soon a van pulled up and a couple of guys got out with a set of scales. I thought it was dodgy dealings but they were fishermen selling their catch direct to the market so to speak. The Welsh cook dived straight into the throng and came out with two big lobsters for $10 which he assured us were destined to be his breakfast and were going nowhere near the guests.

After a great night out we went to bed in a very happy state of mind and all was well with the world aboard *Spectra* that night.

Our generator has been playing up for a while now, it runs for about 30 minutes and then stops, showing a red fault light. Typically, the fault light indicates either low oil pressure or overheating and so you have two possible faults to go for. I replaced the water filter and the fault stayed, I replaced the impeller and the fault stayed, I replaced the oil and the fault stayed, all of this over several days. It was with this in mind that the next day, after a late start, I decided to scrub the bottom of the boat, as we have a grass skirt hanging from our waterline. I also decided to scrub the water inlet for the generator to see if that would improve the cooling. Unfortunately, I only managed to clean the water inlet grid with a wire brush while floating upside down under the boat on one side, before the battering I was getting from the swell coming in got too much for me and my hangover and I gave it up as a bad job. Even at under 20 tonnes (a small boat in Anguilla) it still hurts when a boat hits you on the back of the head every 5 minutes! I will finish the inlet cleaning on a calmer day.

That's it for this one, the next exciting edition includes our night sail over to the BVIs, meeting up with Mike and Kate aboard *Right Turn* and a fun-filled day out for all of the family to visit the American immigration officials in St Thomas, all great fun...... I will blog very soon I promise.

18th Feb 2015 12:48:31
Anguilla to Virgin Gorda and onto Tortola
18:25.442N 64:36.696W
6040 Miles from Ramsgate by log.

Again, apologies for not writing earlier but I have been rather tied up with generator and IT problems. First the good news; we are in the Virgin Islands and they are amazing. Secondly the even better news, we have received a scan picture of my next granddaughter, due on the 4th of July and I must say she is definitely showing early signs of brilliance and beauty in equal measures. I have suggested Pauline or Paula as a name, what do you think?

We checked out of Anguilla and set sail for Virgin Gorda at 14:30 on the 11th of February planning an overnight sail of 80 odd miles. All went well at first and we managed to dodge a myriad of fishing buoys before reaching deep water as night fell. We drew lots for the night shifts and it ended up with Steve doing

22:00-00:00, me on 00:00-02:00 and Norma on 02:00-04:00 and so on but it didn't quite work out that way. On Norma's early shift 20:00-22:00 a lot of lightning developed over on our starboard side, which is never nice but it didn't come our way. As night fell the wind steadied from the South West at force 4 which was perfect for our needs and so all was well with the world, that was until the end of Steve's watch. As I took over at midnight Steve commented that the wind was dying and heading more into the North which was pushing us quite a way off course. I settled into my watch but it was busy, as the wind kept on shifting right through to North East until at 01:00 I finally tacked the boat around and we managed to resume our original course again. The wind was now down to Force 2-3 with the sails beginning to slap and bang as they wouldn't stay filled in the swell. Steve, hearing the commotion from his bunk, (the winches are right above his cabin roof), called up to see if I needed a hand with the tack but I replied all was ok. Ten minutes later the wind was up to 30 knots and we were definitely leaning on our elbow. I called that any help still on offer would be greatly appreciated and Steve, good man that he is, came up to help reef the sails down just before the heavens really opened up. I have rarely seen rain so heavy, it was literally bouncing of the decks. Steve dived below to dry off after half an hour and I stayed up huddled under my umbrella, (I know it's not very yachty sailing with an umbrella but at least it is very British).

Umbrella or not, I was soaked to the skin in no time at all and so I thought it was pointless waking Norma up at 02:00 as she would just get soaked as well. I carried on until 04:00 by which time the rain had finally stopped. Norma's comment when I woke her at 04:00 looking like a drowned rat and explained why she had had an extra two hours in bed was, "Oh! I've got the 4 to 6 shift now, I hate the 4 to 6 shift". Tch, Tch, I just laughed and laughed I can tell you.

As the sun came up we sighted the BVI's through the gloom and here is a direct extract from the log:

Time 09:00, All up for tea and toast.

Sounds like an extract from an Enid Blyton Famous Five novel, doesn't it? Five Go Sailing perhaps, or maybe the Secret Seven Bugger Off to the Caribbean. Anyway, I digress.

We passed through a gap in the islands west of Virgin Gorda and turned right heading for Spanish Town and our pre-arranged rendezvous with Mike and Kate. As we approached the bay our radio crackled into life, it was Mike and Kate who were already inside and waiting for us. They advised that it was very lumpy and uncomfortable in there, and so suggested we moved over to Tortola. Never one to ignore a bit of local advice we readily agreed and after a short wait for *Right Turn* to come out of the bay, we followed them over to Road Bay in Tortola.

By 11:20 we were anchored right up at the head of Road Bay just outside the marina entrance and very shortly afterwards we launched our dinghy and went over to visit Mike and Kate aboard *Right Turn* for a beer and catch up. Later that day we all trooped ashore for the customs entry procedure which was the usual fun and games but nothing particularly problematical. After filling out a multitude of forms, in quadruplicate of course, and paying $17.80 US, we were in and celebrated with a meal at the marina. Mike and Kate were at the marina bar taking advantage of the WI-FI connection and invited us aboard for a meal, we gave it a rain check, no pun intended, but it was raining again though, and we were all pretty tired from the night before plus our beds were beckoning. On top of that, as it was Friday the next day, we had decided to catch the ferry to St Thomas in the USVIs before the weekend in order to get our passports stamped, so that we could take *Spectra* into the USVIs and onto Puerto Rico which is a whole new story, and involved getting out of bed at 05:30. All of which will be covered in full in the next edition. For now, I am going to take the generator apart again to see if I can find out why it keeps stopping (I am beginning to think it is personal).

PS: we are still looking for some crew to come back across the Atlantic at the beginning of June. Three legs of about 2 weeks each; Norfolk to the Bahamas, Bahamas to the Azores, Azores to Cork…. anyone interested in all or part? Drop us a line.

21st Feb 2015 17:36:18

BVI's and USVI's
18:20.32N 64:55.83W
6100 Miles from Ramsgate by log.

Today we are leaving St Thomas in the US Virgin Islands after a week of cruising in the company of Mike and Kate aboard *Right Turn*. I must say this is an absolutely brilliant cruising area. It is a bit like the Solent in that everything is only a few miles apart and the choices of marina or anchorage are just about endless. Also, just like the Solent, it has rained on most days but it would be churlish to complain when a rain shower involves nothing more than getting your T Shirt wet (ooh er missus) and maybe ducking under the bimini for half an hour. In fact, you could quite easily spend an entire season here and not be bored at all. So, what have we been up to?

On the first full day we caught the ferry from Tortola across to St Thomas in the USVI's to get our passports stamped.

This is an anomaly of the system, in that if you haven't got a full US visa on your passport and only have an ESTA you, as an individual, are allowed into the US, but you cannot enter on a private boat. What you have to do in order to get around this bit of bureaucracy is park the boat in the BVI's, get a commercial ferry across to St Thomas, book into the US under your ESTA, which gives you 90 days entry, and then get the ferry back, to pick up your boat, on which you can then enter into the US. Crazy but true. This will cover us for the USVI's and Puerto Rico but, unfortunately, we will still have to go to the US Embassy in the Bahamas to get our full visas, as we want to stay in the US longer than the present 90 day allowance. Are you confused yet? Because we certainly are. Anyway, to sum up, the nice American man with the uniform, sunglasses and big gun said this is what we have to do, so who am I to argue? That paints a nasty picture he was actually very helpful, but he did have a big gun. Having spent an absolute fortune on ferry tickets, departure tax and arrival tax (this was all levied by the BVI's, the US is free) we had to wait in a queue for nearly two hours to get our passports checked again going back into Tortola. Gosh, we just laughed and laughed, I can tell you.

The plan had been to take *Spectra* over to Peter Island and meet up with Mike and Kate on Friday evening, but by the time we got back aboard it was dark and raining and so we gave it a miss and went straight to bed. Early next morning we were up and off to Peter Island, all of 5 miles away, where we dropped anchor next door to *Right Turn* in a lovely little anchorage that was teeming with wildlife. My generator only ran for 30 minutes before shutting down and so I spent the day with it in pieces on the saloon floor. That night after a beer and internet catch up at the only bar, and indeed the only building on shore, we trooped over to *Right Turn* for a meal aboard which was a great feast and great night out/in. I must mention at this point that Steve deserted us and went ashore with Mike and Kate on their much larger and more luxurious dinghy and so earned himself the title of 'Boat Tart'.

The next day we sailed past Virgin Gorda and hung around Necker Island for a while to see if Richard Branson was in, as this is his very own private island. He must have been back in the UK on business as we didn't get an invite to go ashore and so we turned right and went through the reef, finally dropping our anchor outside of the Bitter End Yacht Club. After the obligatory few beers ashore (Steve elected to go ashore in *Right Turn's* dinghy again which is fine by me as Kate is now referring to him as their 'Dinghy Bitch'), we all went back to *Spectra* as it was our turn to cook. Again, a great meal was had by all (no bias but I did cook it) and, luckily enough, we all had somewhere to sit as I had put the generator back together earlier. It had failed again after 45 minutes this time and so I had stripped it apart again.

Mike and Kate headed over to Trellis Bay on Tortola the next morning leaving us at anchor because, you guessed it, I had the generator in pieces still trying to find out why it was overheating. When I finally put everything back together we headed down to Spanish Town on Virgin Gorda so that we could clear out of customs and then, rather sneakily, headed over to Trellis Bay to meet up with Mike and Kate again (please don't tell the BVI customs that we were naughty). Another evening of generator repairs, or lack of them, was followed by a walk along the beach which is directly under the little airport on Tortola's flight path. Fortunately, the planes were mostly small, private, propeller jobbies and the noise wasn't intrusive at all. PS: The 'Dinghy Bitch' is still playing with his new friends.

That was it for the BVI's, the next morning we headed for St Johns in the USVI's and our destiny with the immigration people. As it turned out, we went south around the islands while *Right Turn* went North and we both met up outside of St Johns main harbour, Cruz Bay. This was absolutely packed and was also suffering from a rough swell working its way into the bay. The decision was made to head on over to Charlotte Amelie in St Thomas. We spent two days and three nights at anchor right next door to the Coast Guard station, managed to clear customs and to head on up to Puerto Rico, which I must say was a completely pain free experience.

During this stay I finally lost all patience with the generator, and for the first time on the trip I really had just had enough of the whole thing. Too much hassle and too much stress about how to get the simplest of things done. In short I had a right good sulk, threw my teddies out of the cot (or dolphin out of the dinghy I suppose) and said I wanted to go home, start working again and be done with the whole ?"£**& thing. Kate gave us some really good advice which essentially boiled down to "if something (the generator) is dominating your life and ruining the trip just get rid and start again". It is just not worth stressing about it. Norma also knows me of old and poured good sense into my ear until I stopped being a baby and started working on the generator and other solutions again. Then miracle of miracles, an email from one of the suppliers came through with a comprehensive test schedule to isolate the fault. Most of the things I had already done but the next step was to remove the sensors one at a time to see which one was stopping the engine. I now have the sump oil pressure sensor removed and the generator is running. This is not ideal, but it is a solution until we can find a replacement sensor, the engine is not losing any oil, I have given it an oil change and there is no leakage, so the assumption is that the sensor itself is at fault. Fingers crossed it is fixed. It has now run for five one-hour stints without problems and my bottom lip is beginning to retract.

That's it for now, we are en route for an overnight stop in the Spanish Virgin Islands before reaching Puerto Rico on Saturday afternoon, and our next encounter with US Customs and Immigration. Wish us luck, they are scary people.

USVI'S TO THE BAHAMAS

FEBRUARY – *MARCH 2015*

26th Feb 2015 19:46:53

18:19.22N 65:12.75W
21st February 2015
6170 Miles from Ramsgate by log.

Here I am playing catch up again, I really must stop enjoying myself and spend more time down below typing. Firstly, I have been told off for not mentioning our trip to Bluebeard's Castle while we stayed in Charlotte Amelie, so here goes. Whilst on our routine, never-ending, hunt for internet access we stopped off in Jennys Café (their spelling so no apostrophe, sorry Sue) and met the very gregarious owner who informed us that he was a part-time local historian. Long story short, he invited us on a tour to Bluebeard's Castle on the headland that evening, from where he gave a weekly talk on the history of St Thomas and Charlotte Amelie. Being at a loose end, we decided to go along. On the way back to *Spectra* we rowed over to *Right Turn* to see if Mike and Kate wanted to join us on the trip, which they did, and so we all gathered ashore at 17:00 for the walk up to the castle. It was quite a walk and we got lost a bit along the way, we also lost Mike who played the, "you must all be mad card" and went back to *Right Turn*. Not to be dissuaded, we forged ahead and eventually met up with our guide. The tour started with his friend, a local diver, talking us through his collection of artefacts gathered over more than 20 years of diving the wrecks around St Thomas. The top two floors of the small castle/watch tower were devoted to his extensive collection and the talk was quite amusing. In my opinion he was definitely more pirate/treasure hunter than history enthusiast. Finally, we went onto the roof of the tower and were given a brief potted history of the harbour before night fell and the talking had to stop. That's it for Bluebeard's Castle. By the way, the man himself, Mr Bluebeard that is, just like his piratical friend Mr Blackbeard (or is that Mr Beard?), who also has a castle named after him in Charlotte Amelie, never actually landed in St Thomas, let alone built a castle. Apparently, they turned up one day and the authorities promptly chased them away, but why let the truth ruin a good story I say.

The Spanish Virgin Islands lie about 20 miles to the North East of St Thomas making it a short, day sail over. We passed through a narrow gap in the islands and then went up behind a reef into water of less than 10 metres to follow the coast around the lee of the Isla Del Culebrita. Finally, we entered a small bay and passed behind another reef to drop our anchor in 3 metres of dead calm turquoise water. The afternoon was lightened by the sight of a small woman in a very small trimaran sailing up and down the bay with about 6 children aboard. The children were all having a whale of a time, singing and playing on the decks. Every now and then one or more of them would drop off the side for a swim as the little trimaran sailed steadily along its course. When the woman reached the end of the bay she tacked around and picked them up on the return leg, it was really great to see kids having such a simple and carefree time, well done small woman whoever you are you made us all smile. That evening Norma and Steve amused themselves by shining a bright light over the back rail of *Spectra* and watching a multitude of big fish swimming around the boat. I was less than impressed as I had been swimming earlier, and really didn't like the idea of sharing my swimming pool with those big buggers.

We were up at first light to creep out of the bay and head up to San Juan in Puerto Rico, a journey of around 50 miles. That turned out to be a bit of a roller coaster, and as it was Steve's last sail on *Spectra*, for a while at least, I was glad it was a good one. We tramped along at 5 to 7 knots all day and, apart from one 30 knot squall, the wind stayed below 20 knots giving us a pleasant last day together on the water. The only down side was the swell which did roll us onto our elbow a few times, in fact for the first time in her life Norma was sea sick!!! Even the sea sick Norma brightened up when a dare devil of a flying fish took off from our port side and flew across the deck through the gap in between our fore and stay sail before dropping back into the sea to starboard. Well done little fish, apparently next year he is going to challenge Evel Knievel's attempt to jump 13 London buses, a record never achieved in flying fish circles. Later that afternoon we turned left past the huge Spanish fort at the entrance and finally the waters calmed as we sailed into the harbour proper.

The two marinas are at the end of a 1.5 mile cut which divides the old town from the new and we were held up at the entrance for a while, as a sea plane decided to taxi out and take off right in front of us. Having seen him climb into the skies in a welter of spray we headed up the cut and dropped our anchor right under the bows of a 900ft long cruise liner creating a stirring of interest amongst the passengers lining the decks.

That's it for this one, in the next edition, marina swapping, Customs clearance again, my B@@?£^ generator and bon voyage to Steve.

I have also had it pointed out that my PS at the bottom of the blogs is incorrect, I wrote Bahamas instead of Bermuda. So; see below corrected version, and if you fancy a challenge this summer drop us a message, email or carrier pigeon.

1st Mar 2015 17:20:00

Puerto Rico and Goodbye to Steve v1.1
18:27.55N 66:05.64W
21st to 26th February 2015
6170 Miles from Ramsgate by log.

Our first night in Puerto Rico was spent at anchor in San Juan just outside of the entrances to the two marinas and alongside one of the main cruise liner docks.

Next morning, we were up and about early in order to move *Spectra* into the commercial marina, to starboard of the cut, to complete the obligatory customs clearance. The mooring in San Juan marina was stern to, with two posts set out across the current into the river which you had to lasso with your bow lines to, as you reversed by. When you factor in the 20 knot cross wind it was not an easy moor by any means and ended up with a lot of last minute fendering, heavy use of the bow thruster and frantic pulling on ropes but we did get her in (just). The US customs require you to phone them as soon as you land and so I got on with that, whilst Norma and Steve dealt with putting the boat to bed and sorting the marina office out. Customs were very friendly but wanted to visit the boat for an inspection meaning we all had to wait on board for them to turn up. They said they would be 30 minutes, it was no real surprise when 3 hours later two CBP officers turned up (complete with big guns), looked at just one passport and, after exactly 5 minutes, said thanks a lot without even stepping on board. They then added that we would all have to go to the cruise dock terminal to book in personally and pay for a cruising permit which would last for a year and be valid in all US waters. That, at least, was worth getting. The afternoon was spent trooping up to the CBP office at the cruise dock terminal and getting our cruising permit. As I said, all very friendly but we had just about kissed goodbye to the whole day by the time they had finished. Hopefully in future, with the cruising permit, all we will have to do is the initial phone call and then we will be good to go. Time will tell. At last we were free and celebrated by walking into the old town for a look around. San Juan old town is a real treat, beautiful Spanish architecture greets you at every turn and the atmosphere is both cosmopolitan and very friendly. We had a meal in a restaurant that had the coldest air con I have ever experienced; my hands were so numb by the time we had finished the first course that I was having trouble holding the knife and fork and Norma had to go outside to warm up between courses. We pointed out to the waitress that customers were eating with their coats on but apparently adjusting the aircon was beyond the realms of possibility. One highlight, though, was a large party (or party of large) American women who were having a meal in the same restaurant. At the end of their meal the leader of the pack stood up and in a very loud voice announced to the staff, to the restaurant in general, and probably to a few startled passers-by in the street outside, "Thank you very much, that was just Ab-So-Lutely Super, Duper, Duper, Duper.....Duper!" I kid you not, you just have to love the enthusiasm, don't you? By the way, the meal was OK, it certainly wasn't Super Duper etc, etc, etc.

That evening we returned to *Spectra* to find that one of the mooring posts on the dock had snapped off and was hanging down the side of the hull by what remained of my spring line. Luckily, it only left a small scratch on the rail in passing, but had it got caught up with the dockside it could have easily punched through the hull as *Spectra* was surging violently in a vicious cross current and strong gusting wind. Not impressed with the marina facilities or state of maintenance, we re-secured the boat and went to bed after finding that all of the washrooms, showers and toilets in the marina were locked. In fact, the only thing that wasn't locked was the main gate which allowed anyone to wander on to the pontoons at their leisure.

Next morning it was 'complain to the marina time'. The nice lady in the office was very apologetic and seemed to quietly agree that the facilities were not good, especially as we had investigated the yacht club on the other bank of the river which was a much posher affair and was only $1.50 per foot per night with working showers, a bar and 24-hour security, but her manager insisted that we should pay the full fee of $2 per foot per night. I then suggested that I get my boat repaired at their expense and they could then deduct the mooring fee from the bill. The manager suddenly thought $1.50 per foot per night was a very reasonable compromise offer, so I paid up and we left. The rest of our stay was spent at the yacht club Nautica pontoons across on the other side of the river which, as I have said before, were excellent and what's more the fuel worked out at only 44 cents per litre. I didn't realise just how cheap it was at first because it is sold in gallons, this being little America and all. Having brought 50 gallons just to keep us going, and after sitting down with the bill to work it out, I was galvanised into action. Calling the fuel attendant back over again, they have fuel hook up points at each berth, I squeezed another 40 gallons into our tanks which filled us to bursting. That is the first refuel since Mindelo in the Cape Verde islands back in December, so not bad going really when you consider the mileage we have covered. Another thing I managed, with the help of the Danish owner of another yacht on our pontoon, I wired a 4-pin American 120-volt, 50 amp plug up to our European 16 Amp 220-volt lead. His wiring diagram was confusing, to say the least, but we ended up with 215 volts on the boat which will give us shore power throughout the States. Having said that, I am not so sure it would pass any health and safety inspection plus the washing machine doesn't like the funny electricity and won't work with it at all, but it is certainly better than nothing and the battery charger and fridge are humming away.

And now onto Steve. We have finally said goodbye to our long-standing crew mate. Steve was with us when we left Ramsgate and helped us bring *Spectra* across Biscay along with Andy and Sarah, including spending a day on the sands on the Somme estuary, if you remember. After leaving us in Muxia, Spain he joined us again in Tenerife back in November and has been with us across the Atlantic and right up through the Windward and Leeward islands. To say he has been a help would be the understatement of the year. He has lived and breathed this adventure providing great company and great support to me in particular in solving all the niggling problems we have encountered on our travails. I will certainly miss him and so will the drinks cabinet which has had a vast array of rum cycled through its inventory along the way. Steve has promised to provide us with a list of all the different brands sampled which I am sure will be extensive. We will meet up again at the end of May, hopefully in Norfolk Virginia, for the start of the return leg back home and I am sure we will have a beer or three in the islands as we hop back over, failing that a Guinness in the Royal Cork Yacht Club is a must. From Norma, Paul and *Spectra*, "thank you for sharing the dream".

Right Turn arrived at the yacht club the day before Steve departed meaning five for the leaving dinner. We had a very nice meal out in San Juan, which was only slightly marred by the 45-minute wait for Mike's fish to be prepared (I think they had to catch the thing). Also, the lights in the restaurant were dimmed so low that you couldn't actually read the menus. It wasn't just us being old and dim of sight, other tables could be seen using the lights on their mobiles to read the menus which you would have thought the management would have taken note of. It was a good meal however and the service as always in the Americas was very attentive. The next morning Steve put on his big boy, long-legged trousers for the trip home, no more shorts for a month or two, methinks. That night we moved out to anchor again in the harbour with the expectation that we would be off early the following morning for the 345-mile trip over to Grand Turk but it was not to be. I had, on the first day in San Juan, left a stainless-steel bar, that is used to support my dinghy davits, at the local chandlers in order to get some welding done. Unfortunately, the welder had gone AWOL with my bar leaving us rather stuck until we or, in truth, the chandlers managed to track him down. Mike and Kate kindly agreed to stay for another day at anchor; a decision that was no doubt heavily influenced by the availability of free internet from the yacht club at the anchorage, and Kate needing to rearrange a party date for later this summer. Early the next morning the chandler tracked down our errant welder and my bar was restored all fixed. After clearing customs and buying a chart for the Turks and Caicos Islands we were all ready for the off.

Next time: Our trip over to Grand Turk, rough weather, a close encounter with hump back whales and an idyllic anchorage. Talk soon.................

4th Mar 2015 00:39:05
Puerto Rico to the Turks and Caicos Islands, plus a close encounter with Humpback Whales.
21:28.425N 71:09.495W
27th February to 1st March 2015
6518 Miles from Ramsgate by log.

Today is the 1st of March and a big happy birthday goes out to my sister who has once again managed to maintain her three year lead over me in the age race, well done Sue.

With my davits now fully repaired we were all set to go, and as the sun came over the horizon we pulled up our anchor. In company with *Right Turn* we headed out to sea and pointed our noses towards Grand Turk some 345 miles away. This would be the longest non-stop leg that Norma and I have completed without crew. After much discussion on watch plans, etc for the two nights and three days that we would be on passage, we finally decided not to decide and to simply suck it and see. As it turned out, this was the best policy and we fell into a natural rhythm that best suited our personal sleep patterns: Norma went to bed, and I stayed up for 48 hours!

No, just joking. As it turned out it went something like this, we were both up for most of the daylight hours but did both manage cat naps in the afternoons. After the evening meal I slept from 10 to midnight and Norma took the watch. I went on watch at midnight through to 3 in the morning, and then Norma did 3 to 5, I then went back on watch until I got tired which was usually 9 or 10 in the morning, I would then get a couple of hours sleep before lunch. This seemed to suit us very well and with a bit of slippage on the second night we managed to get enough sleep to stay the right side of grumpy on the way over. What did cause a few problems was the swell. The winds were fairly constant at 15 to 20 knots apart from a few prolonged squalls registering in the high 30's. The swell was 2 to 3 meters and had a very short period which resulted in us getting thrown about like peas in a pod at times. Once we cleared land we expected it to drop but no chance, we had the same sea conditions for the whole journey which did get a bit wearing, see previous blogs on making posh coffee at sea and or Peter's comments on using the heads (toilet) to get an idea what life is like living in a tumble dryer. Anyway, I wouldn't want you to get the impression this isn't fun so I will add that we both really enjoyed being out there on our own and, overall, it was a very relaxing and laid-back cruise.

Highlights of the trip:

Day one: As we left Puerto Rico and less than 5 miles into the journey a disturbance in the sea to starboard caught my eye. About 50 metres away a large humpback whale broke the surface and vented. I knew it was a "biggy" as its' blow hole was looked to be about the size of a dinner plate. I called Norma and she just managed to get on deck in time to see it vent again, this time about 150 metres behind us before we lost it in the swell, so no pictures I'm afraid.

Day Two: The next whale encounter was after the second night, as we approached Grand Turk. Kate on *Right Turn,* which was about 4 miles ahead of us, called up on the VHF radio to say that they had rounded the headland on the 20-metre contour and it had been pretty rough. I made the decision to give the headland a wider berth and we turned seaward on a course to keep us outside of the 50-metre contour. As I turned *Spectra* to cross the shallowest patch a huge Humpback whale surfaced right next to us. It was going the other way and I could see it in direct comparison to *Spectra* as it went by less than 20 metres away. I would estimate it to have been nearly as long as the boat so in the region of 15 metres (50ft), or in new currency, "bloody big"! Again, I called Norma up on deck with the shout "W-W-W-Whale" and she shot up and actually saw the beast this time, quick camera we both said and Norma dived below again to grab the phone. While she was below the whale turned through 180 degrees to parallel our course and I looked into its eye as it dived alongside the cockpit. Its back did a graceful arch before the whole tail, which was wider than *Spectra's* beam, rose in the air and slid gracefully below the surface. The top of the tail was black, the bottom brilliant white and it was level with the top of my head. I was completely awestruck. As the tail disappeared below the surface Norma dashed back into the cockpit with camera in hand, we now have the camera/phone in the cockpit all the time just in case. Unfortunately, that was our last sighting of the humpback whales for the day.

The Whole Trip: *Spectra* handled herself superbly throughout, even in winds of over 35 knots and being given strong side swipes from passing waves, she never once gave the impression of being anything other than perfectly safe and in control. We managed a very respectable run of 169 miles over the first 24 hours and arrived as two relatively fresh and very happy bunnies.

At 10am on the third morning we dropped our anchor into crystal clear waters opposite a small village on Grand Turk. On the final approach I noticed several small power boats surrounding a circle of white-water splashes over to starboard. Thinking it was a fishing activity I took a detour looping over that way to see what was going on and found a big group of holiday makers corralled into a circle by the support boats. They were about 50-60 strong all bobbing around splashing like mad having a wonderful time. Later more boats arrived and whisked them all back to the big cruise liner we could see several miles down the coast. All a bit too organised for me but they did seem to be enjoying themselves. The sea shelves so quickly here that I had to push in really close to the shore just to find the bottom at all. We finally dropped the anchor after a sudden dramatic reduction on the depth gauge with 1.1 metres below my keel. Putting out 30 metres of chain to hold us in the strong 25 knot offshore breeze. Luckily for me *Right Turn* had got there first and so I could use them as a confidence booster as we edged in. "Always follow a boat with a deeper keel" I say, bless them all. Thirty metres behind me, the sea dropped off to more than 50 metres, 30 metres beyond that the shelf just dropped away into the abyss literally hundreds of metres below. As always, I went for a swim to make sure that the anchor had dug in, it was like swimming in a tropical fish tank; there were brightly coloured fish everywhere and I was surrounded by coral growing along the fringes of the sand patch where we were anchored, an absolutely wonderful location.

Later that day we gained internet access via a friendly Canadian yacht anchored nearby that kindly shared his wi-fi code with us, what a star! It took some doing, but Norma and I have now managed to book our visa interviews in Nassau on the 17th March; progress indeed. Later that day the four of us took our respective dinghies ashore for a bit of an explore and discovered not a lot going on to be truthful. Grand Turk had its heyday producing salt in the giant salt pans that still run along Back Road which, you will be pleased to hear, is situated just to the rear of Front Road which runs along the beach. That's it really, the salt industry is no more and that leaves one garage, a couple of shops and as it was Sunday just about everything shut. The island survives on a few scuba diving operators, as the diving is reported to be excellent, a couple of B&Bs, and the sudden influx of several thousand tourists for a few hours when a cruise ship docks. It is so dependent on the cruise ships that not only do the few shops open on demand but pop up bars appear on the beach as well whenever a ships dock. They then tend to all close as soon as the ship leaves. Having said that, it was a pleasant break on our journey and the waters surrounding Grand Turk are truly amazing.

Tomorrow we head out for another overnight passage up to Mayaguana Island our first port of call in the Bahamas.

4th Mar 2015 14:49:00
Plana Cays position update
22:35.2N 73:37.7W
6th Mar 2015 14:50:00
Crooked Island position update
22:49.31N 74:20.89W
7th Mar 2015 14:53:54

Turks and Caicos to George Town, Bahamas
More Humpback Whales and lonely anchorages.

23:30.4380N 75:45.620W
7th March 2015
6734 Miles from Ramsgate by log.

    We've been rather busy of late island hopping up the southern Bahaman chain of islands and a very remote area of the world they are. After trying to stock up, and failing to find anything to buy in Grand Turk, we borrowed a couple of pints of milk from *Right Turn* and headed out at 9:30 on the 2nd March for an overnight passage to Muyaguana Island, which was to be our first landfall in the Bahamas. The highlight of the trip was the sight of a humpback whale breaching as we passed the Southern corner of Grand Caicos. I sighted it first about a mile away on our port side which instigated the usual rush for cameras and phones and then nothing for ten minutes or so. Just as we were about to give up he shot out of the water again straight up into the air until he was almost vertical leaving just his tail still in the water, he then crashed down with a huge splash. That was it, all about a mile away but it is a sight that I will never forget, absolutely stunning and a real privilege to witness.

    The rest of the night was pretty uneventful, the seas were quite lumpy and the winds in the high sixes so it was another rock and roll affair. We were clocking 8 knots over the ground at times which is all very well but our next stop off was an anchorage behind a reef on a not so very well charted island meaning we needed daylight to get in. I put a reef in the mainsail to slow her down and then another, away went the staysail and eventually half of the foresail had to be rolled in before we got the average speed down to below 6 knots and put ourselves back on target to arrive just after dawn. During the night we crossed the Tropic of Capricorn into Northern waters again. As we are now officially no longer in the Tropics, the woolly jumpers and socks have been put on standby for instant use, but perhaps not just yet. For some reason neither Norma nor I could sleep, leaving a very tired couple that eventually arrived at the break in the reef on the southern side of Mayaguana Island, just as the sun came up. For a change we were the first to arrive, as we had passed *Right Turn* hove too waiting for the sun to come up about an hour earlier. It turned out that the entrance was pretty easy. While I stared at the chart plotter like a myopic owl, we crept into the lagoon with Norma keeping a sharp lookout from the bows for any coral heads. By 7am we were safely into the bay behind the reef and had dropped the anchor in 3 metres of water having clocked up just over 100 miles overnight. *Right Turn* followed us in and dropped their hook 20 metres or so away from us. After a quick good morning shouted across between the boats it was straight to bed.

At 10 am I was awakened by a call on the VHF from *Right Turn* and immediately noticed that things had changed. The wind had shifted into the South just enough to allow the swell to work into our peaceful little anchorage. We were now bouncing up and down as if we were on a fairground ride and it was time to make a decision. After a quick conflab with Mike and Kate over the VHF we decided to up anchor and move over to Plana Cays some 35 miles to the North West and see what the conditions were like there. With a last look around at the miles of empty golden beaches and shoreline devoid of any sign of human life we pulled up the anchor, pointed our nose at the gap in the reef and set off again.

Once more, the journey was pretty uneventful which was good as we were pretty tired by now. It was with some relief that we finally dropped our anchor in the lee of Plana Cays at 17:00 and were in bed fast asleep before 19:00.

Once more we were awakened by the boat tugging on her anchor chain as the dreaded swell had found its way into this bay as well, making any chance of launching the dinghy if not impossible, then certainly improbable. At some point over the previous 24 hours I had managed to aggravate an old shoulder injury which left me largely one armed, the thought of another night passage did not sit very well with me. We had another conflab with Mike and Kate on the VHF and decided to move over to Crooked Island which was again some 45 miles to the North West but at least only a day sail away. By 16:00 that afternoon we were passing the huge lighthouse on Bird Island, which marked our turning point for the run in to anchor at Crooked Island. Considering the largest navigation aid we have seen in months has been the equivalent of a lamp on a stick, the sight of a light house the size of Eddystone Rock, sitting on and nearly overlapping tiny little bird island, was a bit incongruous to say the least.

We assumed our normal position and followed *Right Turn* into a lovely anchorage along a golden, tree-fringed, beach with water so crystal clear that it allowed us to clearly see the anchor hit the sand and dig in 7 metres below. As we put the boat to bed I noticed that I had forgotten to wind the fishing gear in as we came in and so now we had a mess of line and lure caught around our propeller shaft and rudder, oh well another problem for another day.

Norma had definitely been the skipper on this trip as I had been so dosed up with pain killers for my shoulder that I spent most of my time daydreaming in my happy place. The fishing line had been just one in a catalogue of simple errors that I had made during the day which was very frustrating, or would have been had I not been in my happy place (see above). Norma allowed me to pretend to be the skipper on this leg but really, she did everything, god knows where we would have ended up if I had been navigating. Now onto important matters; Norma was running out of cigarettes! This could be a calamity akin to hitting an iceberg and so drastic measures needed to be taken. With another golden sanded beach in front of us and not a shop in sight, the prospects did not look good for domestic harmony aboard *Spectra*. *Right Turn* came to the rescue again when Kate remembered that they had two packets that had been left aboard by someone about 8 years before. No sooner had this information been shared than Norma had organised a drugged-up Paul, launched the dinghy and, bad shoulder or not, got me to row across to *Right Turn*, lifting the outboard down from the rail was just not going to happen. After a very pleasant evening aboard *Right Turn* we, or should I say I, rowed back to *Spectra* in a very happy state of mind, I had added several beers to top up my own personal narcotic nirvana and Norma once again had nicotine flowing through her veins, so all was well with the world. As an aside, it was a beautiful moonlit night, almost as bright as daytime, which made the row back downwind to *Spectra* an easy affair. The moonlight was a good thing as the huge lighthouse on Bird Island wasn't working - oh well, it did look very pretty backlit by all of those stars.

We had decided the previous night to spend most of the following day at anchor in Crooked Island and then in the late afternoon head out for an overnight passage to George Town on Great Exuma which is the nearest you will get to a town in these here parts. I awoke and got on with the usual boat business: turn off the anchor lights, make a cup of tea, turn on the generator (which has been behaving itself of late), go on deck to make sure the dinghy is still there, etc, etc, etc. Halfway through this process I realised that my shoulder had stopped hurting. Happy days. It must have clicked back in during the night so, although still a bit tender, I could at least use my right arm again without drug assistance, which is a definite bonus when you are on a sailing boat. With this in mind, I decided to make the most of the day and so I sat down at the table on the aft deck, had another cup of tea while watching the day come to life. My first task of the day was to get the snorkelling gear out and cut away all of that fishing line from the rudder and prop. As I was working away under the boat cutting lumps of fishing line away from the propeller shaft I noticed two things: One; the anti-fouling that Peter and I had so laboriously painted on in Tenerife must have had fertiliser in it as the bottom of the boat is covered in muck and Two; a pair of large rays were swimming about below me. At first sight the rays made me jump and bang my head on the bottom of the boat but they were fascinating to watch. Each one had two largish fish in attendance and they were completely unconcerned by me floating 7 metres above them. I called Norma and encouraged her to come in and see the rays but, typically, by the time Norma had got herself into the water there was not a fish in sight and she had missed out again. On the bright side though, she did get to see the large coral fronds growing out of the sand over on our port side and while we were looking at them I spotted our, or should I say Steve's, fishing lure laying on the bottom. I took a big breath and dived down for it. Now I have mentioned that the water was 7 metres deep, or 23ft in old money, which is quite a way down by anyone who doesn't dive for pearls for a living standard. Going down was easy, apart from a bit of pain in my ears, you just point your nose at the bottom and keep on swimming. When I reached out and grabbed the lure I turned up and realised, one; I was quite short of breath, and two; the surface was an awful long way away. I kicked off and swam for the surface which just couldn't arrive quickly enough for my liking, as I neared the fresh air I felt a shove on my head which was Norma, who had noticed that I was about to come up under the boat and had, luckily, reached down to push me into clear water with her foot. Anyway, all's well that ends well; Steve's lure is safely back on the end of the fishing line and I now know the limits of my snorkelling depth.

That afternoon we pulled up the anchor yet again and pointed our nose North for George Town. We arrived at the cut in the reef at 9 am the following morning which allowed us plenty of light to find our way through and up to the anchorage.

We had a special greeting to the Great Exuma island range, when as our anchor bit into the sand a party of three bottlenose, ("Flipper" type), dolphins came leisurely by passing between *Right Turn* and ourselves, which is always great to see.

We arrived on Friday morning with the intention to stay until Monday at least. I will hopefully get this blog out and update on the pictures that I haven't been able to send.

I noticed in the Temple News that our enquiry for anyone interested in crewing on the trip back over in June has been pushed out by Sue Foster; don't be shy and drop us a line, it's a great adventure, I am not grumpy all of the time, and the cooking isn't half bad either. That's it for now.

GEORGE TOWN TO FORT LAUDERDALE

MARCH 2015

12th Mar 2015 11:52:11
George Town to Farmers Cay, Bahamas and I catch a big fish with big teeth.
23:57.75N 76:19.23W
7163 Miles from Ramsgate by log.

In the end we stayed in George Town until Tuesday, as we were awaiting the return of our gas cylinders from the gas plant. Unfortunately, they could only fill one of my cylinders as they did not have a fitting for the other, which leaves us a last chance in Nassau to get them all filled. This has been a constant problem on the trip and even though we carry both butane and propane cylinders, each country has its own style of cylinder leaving it a pure hassle to get any other brand filled. The reason I say Nassau is the last resort is that we will have virtually no chance of getting our gas filled in the States. The more developed a country is, the more regulated and so they will only handle proprietary brands, it's the old health and safety pixies at work again. On the bright side, we did get one of the two empty cylinders filled, so that leaves us with three full plus a small Gaz cylinder and one empty, the glass is definitely over half full.

Going ashore from the anchorage outside of George Town you pass under a small bridge to gain entry into a Salt Lake, with a purpose-built dinghy dock just to the left inside. This is the meeting place for the semi-permanent and largely North American boater population who use it and the café next door to rendezvous, fill up their jerry cans with water or fuel, get internet access and generally socialise. Just across from where we were anchored is Stocking Island which hosts a very large seasonal population of American and Canadian yachts. They come down, anchor up, stay for the season and talk incessantly on the VHF. The chatter is absolutely non-stop and is on every channel (especially 16); in the end we had to turn our radios off as the constant background noise just got too much. We had cooking recipes, happy birthday songs, detailed instructions on engine maintenance, prolonged discussions from the various beach BBQ planning committees and, of course, weather, weather, weather and yet more weather discussions. I sound grumpy, but it was actually quite amusing to listen in, especially to the kids who had a school programme running and would discuss homework assignments on air, putting out general requests for things like digital kitchen scales, after school work on other people's boats and anything else that teenagers fancy talking about. One young lady, when asked by another's mother if her Mom was around, informed the entire harbour that Mom was shaving her legs, information which Mom must have been so happy to share.

George Town is very friendly but very small and the journey into town by dinghy was extremely wet and bumpy at times. At low tide with a strong onshore wind Norma and I came out from under the bridge into breaking surf. Norma squealed and ducked down in the dinghy clearing the way for a full-blown goffer straight into my face. I was actually having trouble breathing, let alone seeing where I was going. By the time we got back aboard *Spectra* we had water up past our ankles in the dinghy and the shopping bag was half full of water, mmmm salty and soggy bread, a taste sensation. On the subject of shopping, the prices are eye watering, a standard loaf of cheap sliced white bread sells for $5.50, while a tin of baked beans will set you back $3. Needless to say, we shopped frugally, but as this is the last stock up stop before Nassau we were forced to bite the bullet and buy some of it.

After a few days and a very bumpy last night at anchor we set sail for the 40-odd mile hop up the coast to Farmers Cay early on Tuesday morning. There are two routes out of George Town bay shown on my plotter and I elected to take the easterly route, while Mike went for the westerly one. All was going well until the water disappeared from underneath us, you have to get used to sailing in less than 5 metres but I went down to 0.5 metres under the keel in a couple of boat lengths. We pulled in the sails to reduce speed and reversed the engine which was running in idle while watching the depth continue to reduce at an alarming rate. Finally, I chickened out at 0.3 metres under the keel and turned her round. Norma was looking over the side and reported clouds of sand coming up as I reversed hard to help *Spectra* in the turn by using the prop wash, the depth dropped to 0.1 metres and then we were round and retracing our steps. It was about half a mile back the way we had come before I could turn off onto the westerly route, which was still shallow in parts, but at least we kept a metre below the keel all the way out. Later when I checked against Mike's paper charts it showed my route as shoaling in parts which is always nice to know after the event. Later that day, Mike radioed up to tell us he had hooked a huge Dorado and managed to get it on deck before it jumped back over the side, how annoying must that be. Not to be out done, I deployed our fishing gear and 10 minutes later we had a strike which jumped clear out of the water and shook the hook free, so no prize there then. All went quiet for the next couple of hours as we ploughed along at a steady 6-7 knots under a reefed main, full mizzen, poled out foresail and sporting our newly repaired (by Kate) staysail until we were just lining up to shoot through Farmers Cut. Shoot through is an accurate description as the seas were breaking in the entrance which is both narrow, shallow and lined with rocks. With the wind blowing at up to 20 knots it was a matter of line her up gun the engine and ride the waves through which would be great fun in a hire boat I'm sure, not quite so thrilling when you are carrying your home with you like a tortoise.

Anyway, I digress, as I was lining up for the entrance the fishing reel started to stream out line, typical! With no time or inclination to start fighting with a fish I tightened the clutch on the reel as tight as it would go and left it to its own devices. As we manoeuvred through the cut and around the isolated coral patches on the inside the rod stayed bent nearly double. Only after about 20 minutes when everything was calm again did I managed to turn my attention to reeling the fish in. Amazingly, it was still full of fight and took a good ten minutes of further effort to bring it alongside where with a heave I got it over the rail and onto the side deck. It was a big beastie, with big teeth – a proper 1 metre plus barracuda. I could have easily got my whole hand into its mouth if I was committed to prove a point, or just completely stupid. As there was no way that was going to happen, I removed the hook with the largest and longest pair of pliers I could find.

Unfortunately, this is an area where ciguatera poisoning is reported amongst certain types of reef fish and as the symptoms range from very bad food poisoning and being ill for days, with all of the gross side effects that you would expect, right through to hospitalisation and even death it is something that you have to be very wary of. Barracuda, and in particular large ones like this chap, are the most dangerous species to eat; being at the top of the reef's food chain, they accumulate the toxin in their systems. Having already suffered from Manchineel poisoning on this trip due to "Dr Steve Crippen's" attempts on my life, the fish had to go back over the side. To his credit, even after being towed along at 7 knots for a mile or two and lying on our deck for 15 minutes while I got the hook out, he recovered very quickly and was last seen heading for open water at a rate of knots.

After another really bumpy night at anchor with the wind blowing a hooley against the tide we took the dinghies ashore for a look around Farmers Cay in the morning.

This is a lovely peaceful little community situated on a tiny island surrounded by beautiful blue waters. We tied up to the new dinghy dock and soon spotted large rays swimming on the bottom below us along with a scattering of conch shells.

Tony, a local fisherman who runs a sometimes-open conch kitchen at the pontoon's foot, was busy shelling conch at the water's edge. After a bit of negotiation, he agreed to make a conch salad for each boat which would be ready for us to take back aboard in an hour, after we had looked around.

An hour doesn't seem much but you have just about done the place in that time. We ended up with a cold beer in the Ocean Hut which is a one-stop-shop for passing yachtsmen and women with charts for sale (sometimes), cold beer and book exchange. It is run by Terry who has a keen interest in world politics and questioned us closely on the legality of fox hunting in Britain amongst other almost random things. The Ocean Hut has been in his family for generations and, although often damaged by the occasional passing hurricane, is always repaired, and manages to keep going in this very sleepy corner of the Bahamas. Terry himself travelled the world for work in his youth and was even married for a while to a woman from Hythe with the surname of Moneypenny. So, as I said, you can find out a lot about a place in an hour.

After picking up our Conch salads from Tony at the pontoon, it was back to the boats for a quick up anchor in order to clear the shallows on the 11:30 high tide and be off to Big Majors Spot, another 18 miles north, to visit the swimming pigs and spend a couple of days exploring, but that is for next time.

Update on the Conch: It was an experience and I'm glad I tried, but why bother? Really, why bother? Honestly, it's not that nice and you're better of leaving them in their shells doing their thing at the bottom of the sea. The salad was good but the finely chopped Conch tasted a bit like the eraser you used to chew on the end of your pencil at school. Looked similar as well to be honest.

I will blog again very soon, until then goodbye and happy sailing……………….

13th Mar 2015 14:45:33
Farmers Cay to Big Majors Spot - dolphins and swimming pigs
24:10.88N 76:27.76W
7182 Miles from Ramsgate by log.

When sailing along the Cays you have two choices; you can either go out into the ocean which has great depth, clear winds and uncomfortable swell or stay on the banks which has crystal clear, flat water, fluky winds and virtually no depth at all. As it turned out, we didn't have enough depth of water to get around the back of Farmers Cay and so we had to reverse our course and go back out of Farmers Cut into the ocean swell. After a bumpy 7-8 miles in 20-knot winds we turned back in again and virtually surfed through Dotham Cut in order to get back onto the Bahamas Bank.

The water immediately smoothed, turned a brilliant light blue colour and the depth dropped to around 3 metres under the keel. For the next 9 miles up to Big Majors Spot the depth hardly deviated, staying between 2.9 and 3.1 metres below our keel the whole way.

Halfway through the trip our VHF crackled into life and Mike reported that they had been joined by a dolphin. That broke us out of our lethargic state; it was cameras out and up on the foredeck deck looking for the tell-tale fins in the water. We were soon rewarded by the sight of a mother and large calf swimming towards us. The pair were properly big bottle nose dolphins (flipper types) and stayed to play for at least 15 minutes. During this time Norma used up all of the memory on her phone taking streams of pictures as the mother, in particular, crossed our bows repeatedly. Unfortunately, due to the sun on the water, most of the pictures didn't show anything more than a splash or two, but we saw them and that's enough for me.

After anchoring for the night, which was calm and settled for a change, we headed over to pig beach early the following morning. The pigs on Big Majors Spot are semi feral and wander freely through the scrub behind the beach. Over the years they have learnt a special trick for getting themselves tasty snacks from passing yachts. When you approach the beach in your dinghy, they appear out of the scrub and stand watching you closely, if you drop your dinghy anchor and rattle a bag they will swim out to the dinghy, hungrily seeking a tasty treat. It is a bit of a surreal experience to have a large pig with exceptionally large teeth swimming around you begging for food, but honestly what a great way to start a day.

Once we had fed the pigs and watched the rays swimming under the dinghy for a while, it was back to the boat to pick up the laptop and then a one-mile dinghy ride around the headland to the small marina at Staniel Cay, to try and find that ever elusive internet connection. The dinghy ride was very bumpy and very wet in our little rib, which makes hard work of choppy seas. Mike and Kate, on the other hand, shot ahead of us in their much larger dinghy, bone dry riding atop the swell as they planed along. I am sure I detected a hint of a smug expression on the back of their heads as they disappeared into the distance. A very wet and bedraggled Norma and Paul were soon reunited with a very dry and presentable Mike and Kate on the beach next to the marina and, after tying the dinghies to a tree, we headed into the marina proper. Internet was for sale at $10 per device per day which was a bit cheeky, so we declined the offer and didn't stop at the bar for a coffee either. It really should be a standard service nowadays if you want the cruising community to spend money in your establishment, provide free internet and they will flock in. We have seen it time and time again on our travels; the restaurants and bars that have free internet are packed, the ones without or who want to charge you for it are empty. You would think they would get the message, wouldn't you? Rant over. We went for a walk along the sea front to see if there was anything else in the area and soon spotted an American couple sitting on a bench under a tree tapping away on a laptop. After a quick introduction we all had internet access and settled down to connect to the outside world. It was being transmitted from a small café across the road that was closed until lunchtime but had left the router on; that's the way to do it.

After another short walk around and a trip to the local store we were heading back to the dinghy when Norma's phone rang. It was our son Tony who, by sheer luck, has called us on viber at the first time in days that we were within range of a wireless hub; what a spooky bit of good luck. While we were waiting for Norma to finish her call we wandered down to the water's edge and spotted a 4-foot sand shark swimming by in about two foot of water, which was a bit of a shocker. Sand sharks are reportedly safe to swim with, attacks or incidents extremely rare, but "who wants to be a statistic" I say, even if it is a small one!

A couple of weeks ago the fuel fitting for the large external tank on our outboard was broken by the anchor chain and so we have been using the outboard's small internal tank. I am sure from the previous sentence you know what's coming next; on the way back to *Spectra*, to my eternal shame and Kate's great amusement, we ran out of petrol and had to be towed. I am sure a very full account of this minor and frankly, quite boring, incident will be relayed in *Right Turn*'s blog, so I shall say no more.

Now, here is a chance in a million encounter: That evening we went over to *Right Turn* at sun down for a drink or three and were joined by a British couple, Andrew and Steph from Ipswich plus Chris, their American crew. They were anchored between

Spectra and *Right Turn* on their Amel Maramu, *Carousel*. As the conversation flowed I commented that we had very nearly put an offer in on an Amel Maramu in Spain but had then seen *Spectra* for sale and gone for her instead. Andrew said how strange because, likewise, he had put an unsuccessful offer in on a Vagabond like ours that was for sale in Eastbourne a few years back, but in the end had gone for the Amel. What a very small world. He hadn't recognised *Spectra* as the same boat because we have changed her colour scheme from white and blue to white and green since he had viewed her. It was interesting to hear the story of the sale from the other side and piece together the games that the broker had been up to, playing us off against each other. Anyway, Andrew and Steph are now the proud owners of *Carousel* and we are very happy with *Spectra*, so all's well that ends well.

Next time we say goodbye to Mike and Kate for a while and head of towards Nassau for our Visa interviews at the American Embassy.

16th Mar 2015 12:23:26
Thunderball Grotto, Normans Cay and Nassau
25:04.53N 77:18.72W
7258 Miles from Ramsgate by log.

The last day in Staniel Cay included a trip by dinghy over to Thunderball Grotto for a mini snorkelling safari. The grotto is a local tourist attraction, famous for its clear waters and for the multitudes of colourful fish. The grotto, and hence its name, was used for one of the scenes in the James Bond film Thunderball. You have to anchor your dinghy just outside and swim over to the entrance which is just about invisible, being no more than a small fissure in the rock face, at low water the entrance is exposed but at high tide you have to dive down and swim through the small entrance tunnel in order to get in. With this in mind we had planned our arrival for half tide, which should have given us an easy route in and still left plenty of water inside for the fish. Unfortunately, our plan went awry as the tide was running hard, causing such a huge quantity of water to rush out of the narrow entrance of the grotto that you just couldn't swim fast enough to get in through the gap. This left us hanging onto the rocks just outside wondering what to do. However, all was not lost; by simply dipping your head under the water while hanging onto the rocks an absolutely amazing display of brightly coloured fish came into view just below our feet. The water was clearer, the fish bigger, brighter, and more plentiful than any aquarium I have ever seen. What was going on just beneath the surface was, honestly, just absolutely amazing. After that great experience it was a quick dinghy ride over to Staniel Cay for an internet fix before heading back to *Spectra* and spending the rest of the day on maintenance and generally pottering about. It never stops really, but if you don't keep on top of the small stuff the gremlins will grab the opportunity to catch you out just when you least expect it. This week I checked the batteries, re-ran the VHF cable again, checked the generator starter motor (all still good, surprisingly), serviced the forward toilet (lovely job that) and planned the next two legs up to Normans Cay and Nassau. After I had finished my chores we had Mike and Kate over for sundowners and to wish them fare-thee-well for the next week until we meet up again in Exuma Park. We have set up a daily schedule on our SSB long range radios to keep tabs on progress, so if you have access to an SSB (Single Side Band High Frequency Radio) why not listen in; it is, 'Temple Net' at 12:00 UTC, frequency 2214.0, or if that fails 4003.0 at 12:15 UTC. It would be great, and frankly pretty amazing, if someone from the UK joined in on our daily chats.

Early the next morning Norma, myself and, of course, *Spectra* were off on our journeys again, but this time all alone. Thirty-five miles later we dropped anchor with 1.1 metres below our keel about 100 metres from the golden, sandy beaches of Normans Cay, a site chosen for two reasons: One, it was about half way to Nassau, and Two, it shared a name with Norma's late father. No sooner had we dropped anchor than we were joined by a couple from the only other boat in the anchorage who popped over in their dinghy for a chat. I must admit I have completely forgotten their names but he was from Manchester and she was from Belgium, they were making their way south from Florida to do a loop of the Bahamas before heading back up again. They seemed to be a very pleasant couple and we did give them our *Spectra* card with the blog details on it. So, if you read this nice couple from Normans Cay, sorry about forgetting your names (oops) and please drop us an email. Later, while Norma busied herself with painting a masterpiece of Normans Cay, I got on with carving a piece of driftwood with our boat name. Why? Well, you will have to keep reading in order to find that out. The carving is for a rendezvous in Exuma Park so see the blog next week sometime.

Today it was a 45-mile trip up to Nassau. After nearly two weeks of steady 15 to 20 knot trade wind conditions the winds have gone light on us and, as the day progressed, I had to steadily put more and more sails up in a vain attempt to keep the average speed going. Finally, we were flying the full mainsail, full mizzen sail, full foresail poled out to starboard, and our big cruising chute flying out to port. This gave us a total sail area of around 296 square meters, or in old money 3200 square feet, which is an awful lot of canvas hanging in the wind.

But, as if to thwart our efforts, the wind just kept on dropping in direct inverse proportion to the amount of canvas that I hung up. Eventually we were the only yacht left out there that was actually sailing and I had to bow to the inevitable, pull all of those sails down, turn the engine on, and motor for the last 20 miles. The upside of this was that it gave me the opportunity to run the water maker all the way and we arrived in Nassau with full water tanks and full batteries, meaning we will be all nicely showered and smelling fresh for our appointment at the US Embassy on Tuesday morning. The trip up was pretty uneventful apart from the constant sail changes and the surreal experience of always having the bottom in sight. When you are sailing on the Great Bahamas Bank you rarely find depths greater than 6 metres, in fact you usually find yourself sailing around with just 2-3 metres below the keel. This goes on for mile after mile with no land in sight and, because the water is so crystal clear, a glance over the side clearly shows every feature on the seabed, even star fish and crabs. This can be a very disconcerting experience, particularly when you come across boats in the middle of nowhere who have just dropped anchor and stopped for a while or even for the night! Later in the day, when Providence Island was growing large to our front, we were joined by a really big bottlenose dolphin as we began our final run into Nassau town. He was certainly a big fellow and as he glided along under our bowsprit he kept turning on his side to watch us watching him. It was no coincidence, there was a definite interest from both parties. Oddly enough, we were so fascinated that for once we didn't grab for the cameras but just took the time to enjoy the moment. Sorry folks no pics this time.

    We are now anchored in the centre of Nassau and have spotted our first building with more than two floors since leaving Puerto Rico. Tomorrow we go ashore to find the embassy and have a look around.

I will write again on Tuesday evening after our visa interviews as we will then know where we will be going next……. talk soon.

22nd Mar 2015 23:04:22
Nassau, Visas and back South to Oyster Cay plus a close encounter with a big shark
24:47.75N 76:49.81W
7292 Miles from Ramsgate by log.

We have them at last, our passports now contain sparkly new American Visas and so we are all legal to go to the States and meet up with Gemma, Duncan, Lily and the bump for Easter. After several months of planning, scouring the internet at every stop, taking conflicting advice from all and sundry and generally getting the run around, the trip to the embassy was amazingly easy and stress free. We got up stupidly early, just in case the dinghy had been stolen or the bus broke down or there was a natural disaster or two, subsequently arriving at the embassy over an hour before our scheduled interview time.

I was particularly uncomfortable in the heat as for the first time in months I was wearing big boy clothes: shirt, long trousers, shoes and, even, socks which finished off my spring ensemble and made me look quite the gent, if I do say so myself. The visa process was very efficient and after we killed some time by eating breakfast, (at a Macdonald's around the corner, sorry Sue) which was horrible, we presented ourselves to the nice lady at the gate. There was a long bench leading up to the first checkpoint and you had to find the person who had an interview nearest to your own interview time and then sit beside them and wait. Spot on 08:45 we were called in for the security checks, which were no more onerous than you would get at an airport, and then you were led through to the waiting room inside. Window one checked that you had all of the correct documentation, window two took your fingerprints and then 30 minutes later we were called through for our interview. After explaining why we wanted a visa and why we hadn't got one in London, we chatted to the nice man for a while about crossing the Atlantic in a small boat, and then he said he would try to get the visas processed expeditiously (his word) and we should be able to pick them up the following day. The whole interview took less than 10 minutes! As I said, it was a bit convoluted but very efficient. The next day we arrived at 15:00 and were standing back outside the embassy by 15:20 with passports in hand, which was a relief because being in a foreign land without your passport is an uncomfortable experience. The whole process was rather pleasant and very friendly without a hint of the officious attitude we have come to expect from some of the immigration services in the islands. Well done American Embassy in the Bahamas you are a credit to your profession.

Another highlight of our stay in Nassau was that we finally managed to get our last two butane gas cylinders filled and we now have a full complement of five cylinders of various makes which should get us safely back to the UK. After several failed attempts over a number of days to get the cylinders filled, due to the gas men not having the right fittings, the "nice to us but rather fierce to the gas men" lady in Browns, (which is a great chandler in Nassau that we found by sheer luck) called them repeatedly and told them to get their act together in no uncertain way (as previously mentioned, she was scary). The thoroughly chastened gas men eventually turned up in a big gas tanker and proceeded to fill our cylinders at the side of a busy road leading downtown. All I can say is that the Bahamian 'Elf and Safety Inspectors' must have been having the day off. After the second pedestrian wandered past the gas bottle filling process and through the area that now smelled very strongly of leaking gas with a cigarette in his mouth, I beat a hasty retreat and bravely watched from a safe distance the other side of the street. Having said that, given the size of the truck, the other side of Nassau probably wouldn't have been far enough not to have ended up with singed eyebrows. Anyway $30 for two cylinders and I am still alive to tell the tale so all's well that ends well.

Whilst not standing in queues for Visas or for gas refills we spent our three days in Nassau sightseeing and getting a feel for the place. Two huge bridges cross between the two islands and lead you to Paradise Island, home of the stars including Mick Jagger, Nicholas Cage and even Charlie Chaplin in years gone by.

Paradise Island has several big hotels with adjoining casinos, swimming pools, and extremely well-manicured lawns, plus lots of brand-new shops catering to the cruise liners who fill the dock over the river, and I hated it. The whole place is just an extension of the cruise ship terminal, which are all so stereotypical throughout the Caribbean that I am surprised the passengers even realise which island they are on.

What I did like was the fishermen's docks under the bridges; here you can find a fish market selling straight from the boats and the road leading to it is lined with small shack restaurants that serve amazingly fresh fish at absolutely ridiculously low prices. We ate there two days running for under $15 for the both of us including drinks. We loved sitting out the back of the shacks on the small rickety verandas hanging out over the water watching the fisherman getting on with their business while chatting to the owners.

After three nights at anchor in Nassau we headed back south again in order to meet up with Mike, Kate and *Right Turn* in Exuma Park. The first day trip back southwards started in a dead calm, with the main engine chugging along, and Norma playing her Ukulele on deck. I took the opportunity to get the water maker going and fill our freshwater tanks and also serviced the macerator pumps on the holding tanks. We will be sailing in coastal waters again soon we will certainly need to use the holding tanks when we are on the Intra Coastal Waterway. As always, just when you are halfway through a horrible job, the call comes to get on deck NOW!! I dually arrived on deck to find a large waterspout forming on our Port side about a mile away. Watching the very dark clouds and the swirling water being dragged up from the sea, we began a game of cat and mouse with the thing for the next 30 minutes or so. Luckily, it never got closer than a half mile away before dissipating but, frankly, that was quite close enough.

That was the only excitement for the 34-mile trip down to Oyster Bay. We did manage to sail for about two hours during the day, before the wind died again, and by three in the afternoon we had dropped anchor in 3 metres of crystal-clear water. As there were a lot of rocks under us I decided to go for a swim with the snorkelling gear and make sure the anchor was well dug in and hadn't hooked a rock or a clump of weed. Following our 30 metres of chain along the bottom I soon found the anchor buried up to its shackle in a patch of sand and so all was well for the night. But, and this is a big but, when I turned around to swim back to the boat, I saw a large shark on my left-hand side. I have no idea what model or make it was, but it was big and coming my way, and I am pretty sure that it had a mouth full of big teeth. As it was coming my way and didn't seem phased by me at all, I only had one option. Very calmly I assessed the situation, took a deep breath and then, squealing like a six-year-old girl who has just found a spider in her bed, swam back to the boat faster than any Olympic swimming coach could even dream of being a possibility. Please note, I was born in London and I am a city boy at heart; the only sharks I am happy to deal with all sell dodgy watches on Oxford Street. In my calm but assured blind panic I swam up the wrong side of *Spectra* (the side without the boarding ladder, that is) and was confronted with two options:

One, try to get up four foot of fibre glass with no good hand holds, cross a wooden rail and then get over a double wire safety rail, or

Two; swim around the boat in the water which contained a shark and climb the perfectly sound, purpose built, handmade, teak with rather nice brass fittings, sturdy wooden boarding ladder on the other side of the boat.

I had by now convinced myself that I was in shark infested waters and was expecting a nip on the ankle at any moment and so, as I saw it, the choice was a no brainer. I came out of the water like a prize dolphin at the safari park, put one hand on the wooden rail the other on the top safety line and literally vaulted on deck in a shower of spray. As I lay there gasping for breath the last thing I expected to hear was Norma laughing so hard that she was barely able to stand. She had watched the whole episode from the bowsprit and, apparently, the shark had spotted me, stopped, and then shot off in the other direction as soon as I squealed (roared my battle cry manfully). What's more, it had last been seen swimming away at its top speed which, according to Norma, was about half as fast as I had managed getting back to the boat. There was not a word of thanks or even a simple sign of gratitude in recognition of the fact that I had obviously rushed back to the boat in order to protect her.

You decide: funny or heroic? I know what I think. Until next time, *Spectra* out.

PS: I checked a poster at the Exuma Park Rangers' Station and I am now pretty sure it was a nurse shark.

23rd Mar 2015 18:58:12
Oyster Cay-Waderwick Wells-Cay-Boo Boo Hill–Coral reefs and Barry the Barracuda
24:22.9N 76:37.9W
7321 Miles from Ramsgate by log.

After spending the night in Oyster Cay it was a short day sail back south for our pre-arranged meet up with *Right Turn* in Waderwick Wells Cay, which also happens to be the headquarters of the Exuma Park

Authority. The SSB scheduled chats had failed miserably, the quality of the calls being so poor that we really couldn't communicate effectively, leaving us reliant on the Plan A we had made before separating. The only highlight of the journey was when we were making our final approach to the Cay we crossed a 5-metre contour line on our plotter and promptly ran aground on a sand bar. Luckily enough, we saw the depth reducing rapidly and had managed to slow down to about half a knot before we started to gently tap the bottom. A quick U turn followed, after which we headed further out to sea and then tried to head south again. This time as we came abeam of the Cays entrance we just touched bottom at the end of the sand bar, Norma at the front of the boat was standing over clear deep water while at the back we were again just tapping the bottom. With less than a boats length to negotiate, I gave the throttle a quick stab and *Spectra* slid over the sand into deep water. Phew!

No sooner had we dropped our anchor in the lovely, sheltered bay than we were joined by a large barracuda. This one was actually longer than our dinghy is wide and he seemed to enjoy hanging around the boat in the shadow of the dinghy. When Mike and Kate came over for sundowners they commented that he had been hanging around them the day before so that rather discouraged me from diving in and checking the anchor.

The next morning, we jumped aboard the *Right Turn* taxi and went over to the park HQ in order to put our driftwood carvings (remember them?) on Boo Hill. This is a tradition that is supposed to ensure that you get good winds and calm seas in the future. Not very scientific I'm sure, but who are we to buck the system. We had picked up the driftwood from the pontoon in Puerto Rico and had both been secretly carving away over the last couple of weeks. *Right Turn* went for the carved and drilled effect while we went for 3D relief. I had used the jig saw to cut out the letters, painted them different colours and then glued them to the plank. It wasn't a competition you understand, but if it had been, I would have definitely won, I think.

At the park HQ they have mounted outside the huge skeleton of a Sperm whale found washed ashore several years ago. This was apparently killed by consuming plastic waste. It is a real shame that such a large beast could be laid low by our unnecessarily discarded waste plastic bags, I really can't understand why we need so much disposable plastic in our lives it really isn't needed. The walk up to Boo Hill goes past the musical rocks, on which tunes can be played by hitting them with a stick. Of course, we hit them with a stick and I can reliably report that you can indeed play a tune, albeit badly. We then waded across a mangrove swamp and finally visited the blow holes before reaching the summit. The blow holes are small fissures in the rock through which air rushes as the ocean swell enters caves several hundred feet below, causing pressure to force its way up through the rocks. It really is a strong rush of air which moans as it shoots out, quite spooky on a silent night I would imagine. Boo Hill itself is quite an interesting place as it is part of an evolving collection of driftwood art deposits. Passing cruisers add to the pile as each season progresses, creating a living record of peoples' travels. We placed our named bits of wood amongst the huge pile, each component part of which represent someone's dreams made reality. Wow I was getting deep there!

Mike and Kate headed off up to Nassau later that day leaving Norma and me alone to do some more exploring. We took the dinghy for a ride away from our resident barracuda, who has now been named Barry, and had an enjoyable day just relaxing and motoring around. Among other local beaches we visited Loyalist Beach and several coral heads that we passed along the way.

That's it for this one, hope you enjoyed it.... next we go back to Nassau to stock up for the trip to Bimini and Florida.

24th Mar 2015 14:13:38
Waderwick Wells Cay, Allans Cay and back to Nassau and a change of plans
24:45.28N 76:50.54W
7351 Miles from Ramsgate by log.

Before I start this short blog, which is really a position update, I thought I would mention some people back home who have become avid blog readers over the last few months following our adventures on the trip. Unfortunately, they have all been dealt a blow by life at the moment and are all not well for various reasons. Debbie, Jim and Dennis, thank you for following the blog, I hope it has given you some interesting reads, and please be assured we are thinking of you and your families back home while we sail around out here.

The following day we had absolutely zero wind all day and ended up having to endure a 28-mile motor back north up to Allans Cay in sweltering heat. Encouraged by the sight of another yacht flying its spinnaker we galvanised ourselves into action and pulled our two downwind sails out of their bags. Sweating buckets under the glaring sun we pulled them up the mast, more in hope than anything else, and tweaked the control lines. For the next hour or two we flew the big asymmetric up front and the mizzen staysail at the back. To be honest, they didn't bring much to the party and we still had to run the engine albeit at lower revs in order to make even a couple of knots. What we did achieve though was lots of "wow" comments from passing cruisers which is always nice. The overnight anchorage at Allans Cay turned out to be very lumpy and bumpy because an ocean swell had managed to work its way in through the islands causing havoc amongst the yachts gathered in the roads. Even the two 130 ft+ motorboats were pitching and rolling on their anchors and so it was with some relief that we pulled up the hook first thing in the morning and headed over to Nassau for another meet up with *Right Turn*.

Update: I have just had a conflab with Mike re weather and there appears to be a low-pressure system coming out of Georgia on Friday. The ramifications are that after Friday morning there will be strong northerly winds in the Florida straits which will be against the gulf stream therefore making it a rough and nasty crossing. We have therefore decided to leave Nassau early tomorrow morning and cross directly over to Fort Lauderdale. This should take 30 hours or so and means that we have to bypass Bimini. Missing Bimini is a bit of a bugger but if we go there the chances are we will get weather bound until sometime next week and then miss our meet up with Gemma, Duncan, Lily and the bump in Palm Beach which is not an option, so tomorrow it is then. From Fort Lauderdale we will be able to travel up the Intra Coastal Waterway to Palm Beach, no matter what the weather is doing in the gulf stream.

The next blog will be from the land of the free and I will have to change my spell checker to keep the text colourful.

FORT LAUDERDALE TO WILMINGTON

APRIL & MAY 2015

30th Mar 2015 23:33:13
Position Update Chubb Cay
25:24.58N 77:54.62W

Position update Fort Lauderdale
26:07.144N 80:06.605W
31st Mar 2015 02:13:34

Nassau, Chubb Cay, overnight to Fort Lauderdale and we start up the ICW.
26:34.9N 80:02.88W
30th March 2015
7578 Miles from Ramsgate by log.

As promised this blog is from the land of the free, we made it!

Leaving Nassau early doors, we motored all day in absolutely zero wind to get up to Chub Cay which was our jump off point for the crossing to Fort Lauderdale.

Chub Cay was a fitting last anchorage in the Bahamas: white sandy beaches, water that was so crystal clear that I could see the anchor dug into the sand on the end of 30 metres of chain, and a glorious sunset to boot. We had a swim around the boat and found the sea bed covered in really big star fish but the swim was cut a bit short when I spotted a 3ft remora attached to our hull, they are probably harmless but after the shark and barracuda I am still a bit twitchy when it comes to big fish. Even the thought of a bag of fish and chips brings me out in a cold sweat.

Early next morning, we pulled the anchor up and headed out across the banks for the 120-mile jaunt to America. All went well during the day, and we made reasonable progress averaging about 6 knots passing Bimini as the sun went down. After that it was out into the Gulf Stream for the crossing. The wind soon whipped up to over 20 knots from the North East and with the stream running at 3-4 knots our leeway was absolutely shocking, if I pointed the nose at Fort Lauderdale I am sure our predicted land fall would have been New York. It ended up being a slow crab across the stream with our nose pointing somewhere down below Miami, while being buffeted by a confused sea all the way. It was a very tired Paul and Norma that eventually sailed into Fort Lauderdale at 9 am the following morning. Norma is now sporting a black eye as a particularly vicious wave slammed us at one point stopping the boat dead in the water and throwing Norma into the wheel; she is not a happy camper. The sensible thing to do would have been to free up and go with the stream up towards St Augustine but sailing to a schedule forced our decision again.

Typically, we had to wait for a cruise liner to exit Port Everglades before we could come in which caused us to just miss the bridge opening, the result of which was us sailing around in circles for half an hour waiting for the next scheduled lift. Our meandering track while we waited brought us into contact with the local sheriff who shot up in a high-speed rib and moved us over to the other side of the river to wait on the opening. He was very nice about it though and said, and I quote "The guy in the bridge should have told you not to stray into this side of the river but they're not very bright". With that little drama out of the way, the bridge opened on time and we motored through thereby completing our first mile of the Intra Coastal Waterway (ICW). We completed the journey from the Bahamas when we tied up to our mooring buoy in the Los Olas Marina, $45 dollars a night, ouch! While mooring up we discovered that the Gulf Stream had also claimed our boat hook at some point in the night, which will need to be replaced as mooring to buoys without it is not easy and we will be doing a lot of that in the next few weeks. *Spectra* has quite high bows and free board meaning that without a boat hook we have to bring the buoy alongside midships and connect it there before dropping back again; achievable but more difficult than it needs be.

The boat on the buoy next to us was a sister ship of *Spectra* from Galveston Texas but unfortunately the owners were away and so we couldn't swap notes. Norma did, however, give it a thorough scrutinizing down to almost the cellular level and found it wanting in several aspects and so she was happy.

We spent two days in Fort Lauderdale with Mike and Kate, sharing the culture shock of being back in the big wide world.

The customs clearance process after all those months of chasing new visas consisted of a telephone conversation and a welcome to America from the Border Protection Officer. I almost insisted that he should jolly well come down to the boat and look at my visa but decided not to push it. The only thing that marred the stay was our generator finally going bang, big cloud of smoke and it is no more which, oddly enough, is almost a relief as it has been a thorn in my side since the Cape Verde Islands and now I can put it behind me. Not having a generator is not such a big issue at the moment as we have nearly 1000 miles of motoring ahead of us on the ICW so plenty of wiggly amps for the batteries there. The problem will be the crossing back to the UK in June, as I really do not want to be running the main engine for battery charging and so I will purchase a small portable petrol generator which will provide battery charging for that trip and then sort out a wind generator and solar panels for the future.

Mike and Kate have parked up for a couple of weeks in Los Olas, at great expense I must add, (sorry Kate I know you wanted to break that to Mike gently) to travel over to the West coast for a family birthday get-together for Kate who is 21 again. We plan to meet up with them in St Augustine in a few weeks' time, from where Mike will be heading back single handed to the UK in *Right Turn* while Kate proves the theory that nothing goes to windward as well as a 747 jumbo jet and flies back. We said a fond farewell to them both at the marina and collected 1½ packets of cheese for storage in our fridge while they are away, we are a strange lot doing this cruising lark you know.

We have now completed two days on the ICW. Last night we dropped anchor in Roco Baton Lake amongst a hundred speed boats, swimmers and girls woo wooing at the tops of their voices, it was absolute carnage. Two hours later, at the first hint of night descending, there was a mass exodus which left a grand total of five yachts and one motor cruiser on the lake. This morning, after a chat with the neighbours, we found out what direction the shops were and went ashore in the dinghy to find a Target shop to complain about Norma's new American phone, purchased in Fort Lauderdale, which worked for exactly six hours. With no idea on how to find the shop Norma asked inside a travel agent's that we were walking past. The girl looked it up on the internet and then called us a cab. Brilliant, but it gets better. The cab took us to the store, which was about 10 miles away, and we explained the problem. No hassles, the shop assistant said he would contact the provider and get it sorted while we went and had breakfast. All good so far. After breakfast, while I took advantage of the free Wi-Fi, Norma went outside to feed her smoking habit and, as is Norma's want, got into a conversation with a lady called Cindy. Cindy was having a day away from the family doing a bit of shopping and was fascinated by our adventures. Long story short, she happily offered to drive us back to the dinghy dock. She even waited while we picked up our repaired, and now working, phone and then we drove away in her Lincoln Continental enjoying the air-conditioned luxury. Cindy had only recently moved to Florida from California with her husband and, as we entered the freeway, she admitted to having absolutely no idea where the dinghy dock was but with a smile assured us that we would be able to find it. And we did, albeit in a rather circuitous way but what a star she is. If all Americans are half as nice as Cindy this will be a great trip. We gave her our *Spectra* card and she said she would look up the blog and so if you do Cindy, thanks a million.

Whilst on the subject of the blog, I had an email from "Yachting Monthly" asking if they could link it to their website as it was, in their words, "a very good read". I agreed of course and I must admit that I was pretty chuffed to be asked, even though there was no money on offer. I have also been contacted by "Sailing Today" who have asked me to contribute articles for their "dispatches" column, so doubly chuffed about that too. The first article has been written and accepted and so will go to print in the next edition. I have asked them to mail a courtesy copy of the magazine to the RTYC so that any members back there who are still following our blog can have a read when it turns up.

That's it for now, we have motored another 15 miles this afternoon and requested seven bridge openings, which only leaves a cool beer to drink in the waterfront bar that is literally 50 metres from where we are anchored by the Lantana Bridge, and my day will be complete.

Gemma, Duncan, Lily and the bump flew into America yesterday and after they have visited Mickey Mouse and friends will be meeting up with us at Riviera Beach Marina the day after tomorrow so happy days...

10th Apr 2015 20:29:29
Riviera Beach to Fort Pierce, Gemma, Duncan, Lily, and the bump gets a name.
26:46.4N 80:03.1W
7600 Miles from Ramsgate by log.

After a very pleasant evening at anchor by the Lantana Bridge, we motored up to the Riviera Beach

Marina area near to the Fort Worth inlet, as this was the agreed meet up point with Gemma and family. Our plan was to save some money and anchor off for the first night before going into the marina the next morning, aiming to be settled in by the time Gemma arrived, all fresh from a relaxing day at Disneyland with Lily. One of the suggested anchorages in "Captain Bobs ICW Guide" was just to the North West of Peanut Island which, being the closest anchorage to the marina, became our first choice. As we pulled out of the main ICW channel the depth below the keel went from 3 metres to 1 in half a boat length and half a boat's length later we were aground. Bugger! Luckily, Norma shouted no depth from the front and I slammed *Spectra* into reverse resulting in us only doing about 0.2 knots when we ran up the bank. Lots of reversing and twisting later we popped back out into the channel and decided to go for the anchorage on the other side of Peanut Island which turned out to be a gem. So, all's well that ends well. As an aside, we have seen another two Vagabonds on the way up, one at anchor which was absolutely pristine and looked brand new, the other one, which was painted very similarly to *Spectra*, was coming the other way and both crews grabbed pictures of each other as we went by.

The following morning, we moored up in the Riviera Beach Municipal Marina and waited for the family to turn up. The marina was a bit of a disappointment to tell you the truth, as it has just started a major rebuild leaving all the facilities in a rather patchy state of repair. But we were committed to stay and so we did. Gemma, Duncan, Lily and the bump all turned up later that afternoon and after the usual kisses and cuddles we discovered that the bump now has a name. The newest addition to the Macdonald family, and therefore to the Russell clan by default, will be little Martha who will grace the world with a first appearance sometime in July. The other thing Gemma brought with her from the UK was the last stages of a cold but more of that later. Over the next couple of days we visited Peanut Island, snorkelled, bought a new generator and Duncan took Lily paddle boarding. That didn't go too well. Duncan was just getting the hang of it and had moved about 30 metres away from Lily when she drifted very gently into the side of a moored boat. Lily, deciding that this was far more dangerous than it actually was, let out an incredibly high pitched scream followed by "DUNCAN, I THINK I'MMM GO-ING TOOOO DIE-YI-IIIII" at the very top of her voice, which is approaching the audio pain level and caused much concern to a passing group of American fisherman. As they tried, and failed miserably to reassure a panicked Lily, Duncan, in a shower of spray, valiantly paddled across to the rescue under the disapproving scrutiny of half of the residents of Florida. As soon as he got there, Lily jumped onto the pontoon and came running back to *Spectra* with her bottom lip all of a-quiver for a cuddle from Mum. This left Duncan (who for some reason was being blamed for the whole incident) the job of bringing both boards back to the hire station; a paddle of shame which was no mean feat in itself. We all had a day trip over to Peanut Island, a state nature reserve, which involved negotiating 100 metres of river with a very pregnant Gemma in our little dinghy. Gemma was fine, Lilly was fine, Duncan and myself were a picture of serene calmness itself. Norma, however, flapped around like a hyperventilating budgie until Gemma was safely back ashore.

A trip to Home Depot followed to solve our generator problem. Unfortunately, America just does not cater for 240 Volts, but I had a cunning plan. With the 50-amp shore power plug fix that I had wired up in Puerto Rico in mind, I purchased a generator that had a 30-amp 120/230 Volt output. This is an odd outlet as it uses 4 pins and a 5-core cable as the casing is also wired-up. What it actually provides is two separate 120 Volt phases. Confused yet? Trust me, it doesn't get any better. All I had to do was work out how to get the electricity from 5 wires (2 separate 120 Volt Phases) into three wires single 230 Volt Phase without making something go bang. After a very prolonged wiring session I had a cable made up, I put it all together, started the generator and switched the power on..... Yes, no bang so all good, so far. Now the big one, water heater on.... generator working a bit harder but, yes, we have heat. Next, battery charger on, eyes shut, flick switch, wait ....Yes, 25 amps above the drain flowing into the batteries, happy days again. I did, at this point, do a little jig in the cabin and the family came out from under cover. This is by no means a permanent solution, and it doesn't produce as much power as the old generator, but it is a damn fine back up and will get us back to the UK with our electric tooth brushes still buzzing away. All I have to do now is work out the fuel consumption and then estimate how much petrol I will have to bring on board to keep the batteries charged for the next Atlantic trip back home. One thing I have learnt on this trip is that I need wind, solar and/or prop shaft power generation for the next one. Relying on one system has been the biggest black mark on the whole expedition and caused me endless grief, not to mention the fact that I have been one grumpy bugger at times when the generator has been playing up. Next job is to position the generator in-between the aft deck seats which will be its new home for the next month or so. I can't put it below due to the exhaust which would require a bit of an internal rebuild. Aren't boats fun, eh?

As I have mentioned, the Marina was not up to grade and rather expensive. Isn't it odd, marinas remove facilities but the berthing prices stay the same? Perhaps we should remove a couple of days from the working week but still get paid the same, sounds like a plan to me. After a great night out in Palm Beach, which included street food and an open-air concert, we elected to move the boat 50 miles up to

Fort Pierce which seemed to be a much better proposition. Another thing we decided was to keep the hire car for the duration of Gemma's stay as everything in America is 'only a short car drive away'. After a bit of a family conflab it was decided that Duncan, Gemma and Lily would drive down to Miami and the Florida Cays for a visit and stay overnight, while Norma and I took *Spectra* out of the Fort Worth Inlet and travel up the outside to the Fort Pierce inlet in one day. The trip up was a baking hot, windless, motor sail, dodging fast trawling fishing boats all the way, as it was Easter Bank Holiday and the American pleasure boat fishermen were out in force. We did do a 'man overboard drill' to recover, what we thought was, a funny fishing lure. Norma didn't want to bother but we decided Steve would probably like it and so around we went. Norma snatched it out of the water with the boat hook (we have a new one) and then said, "I'm not sure this is a lure, it looks alive". Sure enough, we had a Portuguese Man-O-War on the end of the pole. Fascinating though it was, it had to go back in, and quickly.

We arrived in Fort Pierce, as planned, at low tide and passed under the fixed bridge. By my calculations we should have had 66 feet of clearance at low water and our mast measures 61.5feet from the water line so it should have been fine. I kept repeating that to myself like a mantra as we went under and I wouldn't look up. Honestly, what's the point? If you're gonna hit, you're gonna hit and, guess what, we didn't, so the calculations were correct; smiles all round. The final approach to the marina was pretty tricky - 0.5 metres below the keel in a narrow channel with a 3-knot cross current. "What fun this is" I said as we crabbed in at a 45-degree angle to our course, staring at the depth sounder like myopic owls. The marina wanted me to drive into the berth but I don't like doing that if I can avoid it; my theory being if I can reverse in then I know I can drive out. The dockmaster seemed a bit perturbed when I backed away and said I was going to come in backwards, but I three-point-turned her and slotted in amongst the power boats first time. I am not sure what standard of parking he was used to but he was embarrassingly full of praise, even to the point of high fiving me, for crying out loud, and when Norma went around to the office to pay they all commented on "what a fine piece of ship handling that was". I am not one to brag, as you know, so I will only mention it here, in Yachting Monthly, Sailing Today, and to everyone I meet for the next week or two and, of course, I am having it tattooed on my fore head for future reference.

I did mention that Gemma brought the remnants of a bug with her to the New World. Well it jumped ship and infected me big style. I have spent four days, starting with the trip up to Fort Pierce, feeling like a deep boiled cabbage. Once or twice I have surfaced to perform my family duties, but I have been more or less sleeping non-stop and so I will write of our Fort Pierce experiences, which are all amazingly good, the next time.

Next exciting edition: Air boat rides, Alligator encounters, Racoons, Bald Eagles, Manatees, and the Kennedy Space Centre.

12th Apr 2015 01:05:55
Fort Pierce, Air boats, Alligators, Manatees, Racoons and Spacemen
27:27.017N 80:19.380W
7656 Miles from Ramsgate by log.

We wished Gemma and family goodbye this morning, and now the boat seems very empty without Lily running around. The bug from the UK finally gave me a break and jumped over to create havoc with Norma's well-being, resulting in her being bedridden for a couple of days, which has been a real shame, but we did make the best of it. Whilst I was still feeling sorry for myself, we all jumped into the hire car and drove down to the Everglades to take a swamp tour on an air boat. When I say "we", I slept while Duncan drove the three hours each way. Everyone should own an airboat; they are great fun! It was an absolutely brilliant experience, the boat itself was like a fun fair ride and the Everglades are a real gem. We saw Alligators and Terrapins on the trip, while Lily very nearly lost her packed lunch to a very cheeky Racoon.

On the way back to *Spectra,* we stopped off at a local nature spot and found a river full of Alligators; any thoughts of me going into the Florida waters are now officially cancelled for the duration. Adjacent to our mooring in Fort Pierce is a "Manatee Information Centre" which must attract the Manatees because on our return we found one lolloping about in the harbour. 'Lolloping about' covers it really; they are a very strange beast, 1000 lbs of blubber that hangs in the water, moving in slow motion. I studied the one near the boat and even breathing seemed to be an effort for it. Trust me, those things have a face even a mother couldn't love. All I can say is that if the ancient mariners mistook those for mermaids then they had been at sea far too long. Anyway, from the Manatee Centre is useful Manatee factoid number one, their closest living relative is the cow, so now you know.

Norma was bed ridden for a couple of days and so we tucked her up with a good book and went to the Kennedy Space Centre, loving family that we are. Now that is a good day out, I was like a big kid, it was great. What more could a young lad like myself ask for, rockets, outer space and modern-day heroes? I was in my element, much to the amusement of Gemma and Duncan. They have lots of different displays and film centres covering the early days, Apollo, the space shuttle, Mars and things to come. Each and every one of them is really well presented, and the time just flew by. Before we knew it, it was seven o'clock and we had not nearly covered it all, but we had to go and check on Norma, so into the car it was. When we got back Norma was feeling well enough to worry and had been about to call the FBI, CIA, CHIPS and probably my Mother as we were well overdue.

As I said at the beginning, Gemma and family are now flying back, which left Norma and myself to get *Spectra* back into sailboat mode again. After about an hour moping about, feeling quite down in the dumps because basically we both wanted to be on the flight with them, we gave ourselves a shake and got on with things. We plan to be back in time for the birth of young Martha in July and so, for now, it is full steam ahead. We spent the morning cleaning decks and then topped the tanks up for the expected long days of motoring ahead along the intra-coastal waterway. One hundred US gallons for $326 which is pretty cheap, at 86 cents per litre. We pulled out of Fort Pierce at 16:00 that afternoon and travelled a grand total of 1 mile, which included going under the 65ft bridge again, (like an elephant, I still can't look up when I go under bridges), before dropping anchor just south of the first Bascule bridge going North. Tomorrow we head on up towards St Augustine where we have an appointment to meet up again with *Right Turn* on the 20th, and so the adventure goes on. But tonight, we are sitting in the cockpit watching the lightning all around.

14th Apr 2015 23:53:05
Arrived Titusville
28:37.11N 80:48.33W

As we have just reconnected to the outside world and I have sent my latest blog, I thought I would send a very quick position update. We have been travelling for two days now. Last night was spent at anchor at Dragons Point inlet which included an amazing display by the local dolphins, five of whom were rolling over and over each other just in front of our bows, like a giant sushi ball. Today we sailed past the Kennedy Space Centre and were lucky enough to catch the launch of a space station re-supply rocket. We thought we had missed it, but it was delayed by 24 hours probably because of the violent electrical storms yesterday. We are now on a mooring buoy for $20 per night at Titusville and intend to stay for two days and have a proper look around. The only excitement so far is finding that KFC do a chicken pie and gravy, and when I nearly ran over a manatee in the dinghy; a quick right-hand turn and we glided by.

That's it for now, I will blog when we get going again.

20th Apr 2015 18:06:16
Arrived in St Augustine, aground again and anchored under the guns of a fort.
29:53.732N 81:18.389W

7836 Miles from Ramsgate by log.

This is a more detailed update of our latest travels and covers Fort Pierce all the way up to St Augustine and so overlaps a bit with the quick update I sent from Titusville earlier.

The Intra Coastal Waterway is not the 'carefree, cruise up an inland waterway' that I expected. The water depth is planned at a minimum of 12 feet for the 900 odd miles from Fort Lauderdale to Norfolk, Virginia which, considering Spectra's 6-foot draft, should present no problems. That's the theory, anyway. Day one found us motor sailing along with a couple of metres below the keel in a very nice wide channel heading to Dragons Point some 43 miles north. The dolphins and manatees were regular sights, along with a whole smorgasbord of feathered friends; we lost count of the hawks and eagles that flew by with fish in their talons.

In fact, it was a good day "what could possibly go wrong" I thought as I continued to do my on-watch cycle: plotter, depth sounder, visual check on buoys; plotter, depth sounder, visual check on buoys etc, etc, etc. Point to note, the ICW is not a canal, it has short canal type sections that connect the lakes and inland waterways together. Most of the days' travel on this section is on wide expanses of water that have buoyed channels denoting the deeper dredged water meandering through them. A small island appeared and the plotter showed the channel turning a sharp right around the back of it. On the turn we drifted all of 10 metres away from centre channel. Crunch! Hard aground. No amount of reversing would move her and, as there is virtually no tide on the Indian River section of the ICW, it was a frantic search for the Sea Tow insurance policy and telephone number. Mike and Kate had suggested this as a good idea, and what good advice it was. For $169 we are covered for everything up to a full-on salvage operation and that is where our normal insurance cuts in. A quick call and 1 hour later a very nice man turned up in a powerful RIB. He circled us and found 7 feet of water an arm's length away on our starboard side – so close and yet so far. With a quick rev of his very powerful engines he pulled the nose around and off we popped, none the worse for wear but a little red in the face. His advice was rather pragmatic "stay in the middle, and if you run aground in the middle just give us a call". Thirty seconds later, whilst he was still behind us filling in the paperwork, we ran aground again – this time smack bang in the middle of the channel. Luckily, it was only just aground and we managed to get ourselves free before he caught up with us again. When we signed his paperwork it showed that, without the insurance, the bill would have been over $1,300, which is a definite 'ouch' and I suspect we will certainly touch bottom again before we arrive in Norfolk.

    The original plan had been to try and get as far as Titusville on the first day, as that is the nearest town to the Canaveral Space Centre and a launch was scheduled. Unfortunately, with the grounding we ran out of time and interest to be honest. The launch was at 16:00 and at our current pace we would have missed it anyway. That night we pulled out of the channel after passing under the Indian Harbour Bridge and headed a half mile to starboard into the mouth of the Banana River. Dragons Point is so named (I think) because of a 20-ton metal dragon that stands on the headland. Or it did stand on the headland until it collapsed several years ago and now it lies slumped rather dejectedly into the water. Anyway, this was a lovely little spot: mosquito free and frequented by a family of dolphins. I think it must be breeding season because they were definitely being a bit damned familiar with each other. They rolled over and over each other like a giant dolphin sushi ball right in front of the boat, even bumping into the anchor chain a few times in their excitement. After watching dolphin porn until the sun went down we went to bed with the, now familiar, crack and bang of the nightly thunderstorms ringing in our ears.

The next day was pretty uneventful apart from the internal flood as we continued north passing under five bridges on the 36-mile trip up to Titusville. The flood happened two hours into the day's journey when Norma suddenly shouted from below "there is water pouring in down here!". Now that's a statement straight from a skipper's nightmares. With a view to not running aground, I got Norma into the cockpit to take over the wheel and dashed below. I was met by water pouring into the galley from the ceiling. Yes, that was the ceiling/deck head that I said. I had a bit of a brain freeze and just looked at it for a moment as the water poured in, I even looked out of the window to make sure it wasn't raining and then tasted it. Now the penny dropped – it was fresh water and I could now hear the water pump buzzing over the engine noise. I switched off the fresh water pump and the flow stopped. We have good showers on *Spectra* with a stinging spray; the downside of a big pump, and the clue's in the title, is that it pumps a lot and at high pressure. The hose leading to the deck outlet had popped off the fitting above the galley and filled the cavity with water in no time at all, before literally cascading through the deck lining into the galley, causing havoc below. It was an easy fix once I got the deck lining down. I tightened the hose back onto the fitting and all was well with the world, but it did take two days for the lining and lights to dry out properly. On the bright side, it did give the galley floor and the engine bilge a damn good wash down; every cloud has a silver lining, I suppose.

    On arrival at Titusville we grabbed an available mooring buoy outside of the municipal marina and launched the dinghy for a trip ashore. Narrowly missing a manatee on the way into the harbour, we tied up and met the really helpful and friendly staff at the Titusville Municipal Marina. Halfway through our conversation the ground began to vibrate and a loud rumble could be heard. "Sounds like the launch", said the man behind the counter and then dashed outside, along with everyone else in the shop, leaving our card in the machine. We followed just in time to see the rocket climbing into the clouds; the launch had been delayed by 24 hours and we did manage to catch it. One more tick on the 'bucket list' for me. Titusville was very nice but seemed pretty devoid of people as does much of America so far; big wide spaces and not many people, is the impression we have.

After two nights we headed north again, this time for Daytona Beach 47 miles away. Trying to get into the unmarked anchorage here was an experience, twice I had to reverse quickly as the bottom rushed up to meet us but, eventually, we found our way round the back of the sand bar and dropped the hook with one metre below the keel. We shared the anchorage with the local rowing team who, rather pragmatically, cheerily changed their course to make us the finish line, as soon as we dropped anchor, and carried on with their practice session. Daytona Beach was memorable for the chocolate factory which had a free tour advertised, and so in we went. Now, if you run a small chocolate factory and you want to be different, you have to push the boundaries and this place had – chilli chocolate (not too radical), chocolate covered crisps (sounds strange but surprisingly tasty) and, the step too far, chocolate covered bacon, (oh my God why would you do that!!). We did actually buy a box of chocolates, minus the bacon, and very nice they were too.

One night in Daytona Beach and then we headed, yes you guessed it, north again, 39 miles up to Fort Matanzas. This was a great day, deep water for 37 miles and no hassles at all right up to the last corner. Captain Bobs Guide to the ICW says that shoaling occurs near the Matanzas river inlet and to obey local buoyage. With Fort Matanzas temptingly in sight and 3 metres under our keel we were steaming along doing 7 knots with the current in our favour when I saw a seemingly impenetrable line of green markers right across the channel. I slowed right down and turned left towards the shore as the depth reduced rapidly. Eventually, with 0.5 metres below the keel, and about a boat's length from the beach, we squeezed passed the last green buoy and found a very shallow channel parallel to the beach which ran for half a mile around a huge sand bar. When the channel finally opened out again we found ourselves in the mouth of the Matanzas River, where Captain Bob suggested turning to Starboard out of the ICW and going up the river to find an anchorage in 8 to 11 feet, and 100ft below the Fort. With no other yachts in sight it was a rather tentative approach at under 1 knot as we crept up the river, eyes glued to the depth sounder. Long story short, after a very nervous approach we dropped anchor under the guns of Fort Matanzas with a healthy 1.5 metres below our keel and settled in for the obligatory thunderstorm as night approached.

Three other yachts joined us as it got dark and a very pleasant night was had, once the local sports fishermen had stopped buzzing around, woo wooing, in their high-speed RIBs.

Sunday morning dawned bright and sunny and, after summoning the crew onto the foredeck for Sunday service, (which they rather pointedly refused to do), I shattered the tranquillity of the day with my shiny, new, bright red, two-stroke, petrol generator. It is noisier than the old one and doesn't give the same amps, but it works, so I love it, thank-you Gemma and Duncan. We had a debate about going ashore but, as it was very isolated and Norma was keen to get on up to St Augustine, so we decided to up anchor and head north again. This decision, I discovered later, was heavily influenced by the fact that Norma's cigarette packet was nearly empty, although she denies that this was a contributory factor, and the fact we were nearly out of milk for my tea in no way influenced my vote. The trip was a mere 14 miles and we found the deepest water so far - 10 metres under the keel, wow, but that didn't last for long. As the St Augustine Municipal Marina was full, including the large mooring buoy field along the river, we had to go through the Bridge of Lions and anchor up on the other side for the night. No great hardship but I had no milk and Norma had no cigarettes, the situation was tense. I was not happy with either the depth, which was dropping fast, and the holding which, although it seemed good, had a strong current making the anchor work for a living. Because of the strong current I would not launch the dinghy to go ashore, which did not help with marital harmony; a tense situation became tenser. The scheduled thunderstorm came through as always, but this time with a change in the direction of the current flow, combined with 30 knot gusty wind, our anchor tripped out and reset slowly. The problem was it took a boat length to reset and was still dragging slightly, leaving us far too close to the shore side pontoons for my peace of mind. Norma gallantly donned waterproofs and went out into the deluge to get the anchor up while I motored out into deeper water. With the anchor reset and 35 metres of chain on the bottom, we settled down under our full cockpit canopy and watched the rain lashing the windows, it was quite nice really.

That's it for now, we are waiting for the call from the marina to let us know our mooring ball is free and then we will go ashore for nicotine and milk, what more could I ask for?

25th Apr 2015 01:37:54
Tourists in St Augustine, Flying dolphins and transformers.
29:53.732N 81:18.389W
7836 Miles from Ramsgate by log.

Here we are, still in St Augustine and having a very enjoyable time, thank you very much. The weather has been kind to us but unfortunately Mike and Kate were caught in a 50-knot-plus squall on their way up here from Fort Lauderdale. It was a very tired couple with a ripped spinnaker and a tale to tell, that we met at the fuel pontoon on Tuesday morning. After a quick catch-up, we left them to find their mooring buoy which, as it turned out, is the one in front of ours, (or behind, depends on which way the tide is running, really) and grab some much-needed sleep. Meanwhile, we got on with the mundane things in life like washing clothes and ordering new bits for the boat online. I realised that I still hadn't bought charts for the Azores and Bermuda. Unlike Columbus, who didn't bother with that sort of thing and made his own as he went along, I do like a paper chart to back up the plotter. They are now on order courtesy of book harbour and will be delivered to the RTYC in Ramsgate next week, from where, hopefully, our support team, Tommy and Sue, will pick them up and bring them out with them to Wilmington next month. I have also had a bit of a brainwave (well, Norma did really) regarding the new generator, which either gives out 120 volts or my lashed up 200ish volts from the 30-amp plug, and is not providing enough power to the batteries for my liking. I have brought a 120v to 240v step up transformer, which is now installed and provides and allows a clean 120v to come out of the generator as designed which is then stepped up to 200

Volts cleanly, This not only provides enough power for the battery charger but also the fridge and water heater, happy days indeed. As an added bonus the washing machine likes the frequency of the power provided via this route and so we now have all the comforts of home.

St Augustine is one of the oldest settlements in America and definitely has a bit of history about it. The locals as always are very friendly and just can't do enough for you. As it has been a while since we stocked up on groceries we jumped in a cab and headed out to Walmart; the big shops are always a car ride away. The taxi driver who was very chatty, decided to take a short cut down a narrow side road and promptly bumped into the one-way sign knocking it over at a crazy angle. His first reaction was, "wow and it's not like I have even been smoking any weed today" and his second was, "hey you guys, do you want a souvenir sign for back in the UK?" Thus, filled with confidence we declined the souvenir and carried on to Walmart where he dropped us off with a cheery wave. Our plans for the next few days include a ghost tour of old colonial St Augustine and a trolley bus trip around the town taking in the freedom marches of Dr Martin Luther King fame, many of which came through here in the 60's.

As it was St Georges Day, Norma and I decided to visit The Prince of Wales, an English themed pub, for lunch. I had fish and chips washed down with an ice cold Magners, whilst Norma had a steak and ale pie. What can I say? It was delicious and St George would have been proud of us, even though the very nice lady in the Prince of Wales had no idea that it was St Georges Day.

Last night we had Mike and Kate over for a meal aboard *Spectra*, ocean pie made with my own fair hand and not too shabby, even if I say so myself. Today was a pre-planned shopping trip ashore for the girls, which turned into a marathon, as these things tend to do when Norma and shops are involved. Having seen how the shopping trip was panning out, Mike and I bailed out of the girls' shop-athon and walked to the edge of town where there was a warehouse full of boat bits to peruse at our leisure, while walking we of course put the world to rights.

We then managed to meet up with the girls again through the powers of our dirt cheap American mobile phones, which have been amazingly useful, and had a very nice meal in a courtyard restaurant in town. After that it was back to the marina, courtesy of a water taxi, and our respective boats followed by an early evening punctuated by the healthy hum of my new generator. I know I go on about it but it is my new toy and I do like it, thanks again Gemma and Duncan.

Finally, the flying dolphins: As we settled down to relax a large splash was heard next to the cockpit. I looked over the edge to find a really big bottle nosed dolphin leisurely swimming by, slapping his tail on the water each time he dived. We watched for a while and then he was joined by another adult and a youngster in tow. The young dolphin, which was about half the size of the adults, was in a serious play time mood. He swam along between the two adults on his back slapping his tail on the surface and then dived out of sight repeatedly. While we scrambled for the camera, as is always the way, he dived down for a minute or two and we thought we had lost him. Suddenly he erupted out of the water between us and the boat behind in a whole series of jumps and acrobatics which carried on for a good five to ten minutes (flying dolphin, get it?) Finally, one of the adults slapped the water with its tail three times which must be dolphin for playtime is over as young Flipper re-joined the group and they were last seen heading towards the inlet under the bridge; now that's the way to end a day.

We are here until Monday morning and then we are heading north again so I will write soon.

30th Apr 2015 02:10:33

Goodbye to Right Turn, Lovely St Marys, shallow water, No-See-Ums and Otters

30:42.97N 81:33.19W

7903 Miles from Ramsgate by log.

We decided to do the full-on tourist thing in St Augustine over the weekend. After the girls had completed a thorough pamper session (pedicures and

Champagne, by all accounts), we dragged Mike onto a trolley bus tour of St Augustine old town. From my perspective the tour was actually pretty good, the driver or drivers - we had four of them - were all very enthusiastic and the tour took in the whole of the town. Stop-offs included the old town jail - site of two official executions and a number of lynching's, by all accounts. Before that, we had only managed to go half way around the town square when Norma and Kate spotted a children's string band in the park and so off we all trooped to listen for a while; they were actually very good. We then went on to a distillery that has only been running since 2012 situated in an old ice factory at the edge of town. Their product range included, Gin, Vodka, Rum and Whisky, all of which were on sale apart from the whisky which has another year or two in the barrels before it is ready. After a speech from the MD and part owner, the sampling began; very nice it was too and I gave it a thorough sampling. All of their raw materials are sourced from local farmers, making for a really close-knit, community-based company. I hope that they do well in the future; if there is one thing this world is short of it is purveyors of alcohol in all of its many wonderful varieties and brands.

After a last sundowners aboard *Right Turn,* we bade Mike and Kate a fond farewell and headed back to *Spectra*, completely forgetting that we would be sailing right by them again the following morning. Next morning bright and early as we sailed by, we bade Mike and Kate a fonder and heartier farewell. They have been great company as our paths have criss-crossed over the last few months and an absolute fountain of good advice on this cruising lark. The final communication was a good luck and steady winds to Mike for his solo Atlantic crossing which will start in the next week. Our plan is to all meet up again at Kate's birthday bash in Hythe in July, can't wait.

We topped up two containers with petrol, or should I say 'gas', at the ever-helpful marina to keep the generator fed while we travel and then, having requested a bridge opening for 9:30, motored under the Bridge of Lions and departed St Augustine. I liked that place, we will return one day, methinks. Our next leg up the intra-coastal was, I must admit, a bit drab. Miles and miles of empty marshland as far as the eye can see, but as always, we did have a bit of excitement on occasion. Two hours into the trip a bright yellow sea plane suddenly dropped out of the clouds and landed on the lake next to us, he gave a quick wave before accelerating into the air again. Well, I thought, that was very sociable of him, but the penny dropped as he completed a big circle and did it again, he was practising. I looked for the L plates but couldn't see them anywhere.

All morning the depth had been a healthy 4 metres below the keel and then it changed! Suddenly, the depth reduced rapidly until we had less than 0.5 metres of wriggle room and were struggling to find any deep water in the narrowing channel. We got through one shoal patch, but the second one got us and we gently touched bottom. I managed to reverse out but it took nearly 20 minutes to find a channel deep enough for us, which was no fun at all. Likewise, later in the day the plotter didn't line up with reality. It was showing us on dry land for about 3 miles when we had more than 4 metres below the keel, which hardly fills you with confidence, but I suppose I must quote Peter again, "It's not a holiday, it's an adventure"!

Having avoided a proper grounding, the rest of the day passed without incident and we even added a new species to our list of sightings, White Pelicans. We spent the night anchored just north of Sister Creek Bridge in a small pool to the right of the main channel, just after you go under the bridge, which is just about all there is to say about that place and so I shall move on.

Bright and early next morning we found the weather outside to be grey and miserable, and for the first time we kept all of the cockpit covers on as we continued our motor up the river. Leaving the covers on means that driving *Spectra* is a bit like being in command of a Tiger Tank, the whole world is viewed through a slot in front of you, absolutely horrible. But it was dry and the rain was bouncing so it would be churlish to complain too loudly.

That evening we crossed St Mary's inlet, again struggling to find deep water, and turning left away from the ICW worked our way up the St Mary's river to drop anchor 100 metres from the dinghy dock on the national park of St Mary's Island. It was getting dark and the designated anchorage was absolutely littered with grapefruit-sized crab pot marker buoys; the inevitable happened. Just after we dropped anchor and began to reverse up I felt a thump from behind, the prop had caught a buoy. I peered over the side with some trepidation but was relieved to see two halves of a buoy pop to the surface and float away. I checked below and thankfully the stern gland sump was still nice and dry. A 24" prop with 90 horses behind it and a very sharp rope cutter had saved the day, I did however hide my face in shame when we passed the fishing fleet on our way over in the dinghy the next morning.

    The next morning, we visited St Mary's by dinghy and it proved to be a real delight. This is our first stop over in Georgia and the greeting was amazing. As we walked up the pontoon we were warmly welcomed to the "Great State of Georgia" by the first group of people we met sitting at the top of the pontoon. We were then ushered into Knuckleheads, the local water front hangout, by Paul, the owner, sat down, given coffee and free wi-fi connection, whilst being interrogated on everything we had ever done and informed of everything all of the locals had ever done. Paul was an ex US Marshal and pathologist who had also sailed his boat around the Pacific and even gone into Russia single-handed. He was now settled in St Mary's, running

Knuckleheads and actually just enjoying life. One of the local hire boat skippers was also an ex-marine biologist from the National Park Service and we were soon discussing every fish we had nearly caught on the way over. He informed us that Bull Sharks were known to come this far up river on a regular basis and so, not willing to be a part of the Bull Shark-Alligator tug-of-war spectacular, I have kept swimming off my list of things to do this week. Two hours into our trip ashore we hadn't managed to get beyond the first house, but it was a well spent morning, the wi-fi connection was fast and five coffees cost the grand total of $2. We had also met some remarkably interesting people plus a dog called Bubba who stopped off at Knuckleheads every morning for a biscuit. For the rest of the day we walked around St Mary's which is just what you would expect from a southern town, picture perfect wooden homes with Spanish moss drooping from every tree out front and the locals are just SO friendly. We visited the local museum next, where we learnt all about the dastardly British who had attacked the 80 troops based here in 1812 with a force of 1,500 and, unsurprisingly, won a rather convincing victory only to loot the place, free the slaves, and sail away again taking the freed slaves with them to Trinidad to start a new life. As it turned, out communications being what they were in the 1800s, the war had actually finished before this invasion and no one had told the combatants, so the dastardly British were indeed very dastardly indeed. I offered my sincerest apologies to the curator for my ancestors' boorish behaviour which she accepted with both grace and southern charm.

Later that afternoon we had a look around the local cemetery which may sound a bit ghoulish but it was fascinating. In the oldest section there were lots of graves marked as 'a soldier of the revolutionary war' and slightly later a lot of graves from the American Civil War, many of these had small notices attached saying this grave is maintained by an organisation called, 'The daughters of the South'. One downside was that the cemetery was located pretty close to a patch of marsh land resulting in us both being eaten alive by No-See-Ums as we walked around.

> I would like to describe a No-See-Um,
> but I can't as you just cannot See Um,
> We tried and failed to Find-Um,
> Although we for sure did Feel-Um.

The final highlight of the day was, after walking through the perfectly manicured town park, we were blocked from getting to our dingy by a bi dog Otter busily having a scratch by rolling around on the pontoon. He was a big boy and seeing him made a perfect end to the day.

6th May 2015 15:48:45

We are in Savannah I do declare...Forest Gump, lovely people, and new crew
32:25.81N 80:40.57W
6th May 2015
8077 Miles from Ramsgate by log.

After leaving St Mary's Island the next morning we travelled on northwards for 45 miles crossing St Simon's inlet and finally dropped anchor just south of the Golden Isles Marina on Lanier Island. The next morning, we took the dinghy ashore to see what we could find and tied up onto the marina office pontoon. As I scrambled ashore, I noticed another Vagabond 47, *Live Now II,* moored in the marina. Making a beeline for it I introduced myself to John, the owner, who was on deck doing a bit of varnishing (when do you not do a bit of varnishing on a Vagabond?), and we compared notes on our boats as you do. We were soon joined by Norma and then John's wife, Pat, came on deck and invited us aboard. They have owned *Live Now II* for 12 years and she is in a very good state of repair. The layout was slightly different from *Spectra* with two single bunks up front and the side cabin converted into a walk-in wardrobe. She also sported a very large shower accessed from the aft master cabin which also took up a portion of the side cabin; the original owners liked to shower together apparently!!! All Vagabonds are different and I think most were semi bespoke at the time of building which only goes to make them more interesting in my humble, and definitely biased, opinion. We swapped war stories of our travels and then took our leave, saying that we were going to walk over the bridge to Lanier Island. John and Pat looked aghast and would not hear of us walking insisting that we borrow their car. Yes, they were quite happy to lend their car to two complete strangers. What an amazingly generous gesture which we, of course, accepted. In our new transport, (a Mazda MX5 or Miata in America) we arrived at the little touristy town on Lanier Island in some style, but very slowly, as this was the first time I had driven a car in nearly a year. I am sure they drove on the other side the last time I tried. The island was very picturesque and had lots of arts and crafts shops along the waterfront which kept Norma busy all afternoon. We did buy Martha a handmade dress which the lady in the shop adjusted for size as we waited. That night, after we had safely returned their car, and given them an apple pie in thanks, we invited John and Pat aboard for Sundowners which turned out to be a very pleasant evening for all; a few beers shared with new friends as the sun goes down is a good way to end a day in my book.

Up early the following morning it was engine on and into the northerly wind again for another 47 miles jaunt up to the Wahoo River and an overnight stay under a full moon on a deserted side river. The trip up was notable for its shallow patches, which had me twitching and forced me to slam the boat into reverse several times when the depth gauge dropped into the 0.2's and below, but we got through the day without touching bottom which is a good thing.

Much to Norma's amusement, I gave a very confident wave to a man standing waving from his lawn as we sailed by. I think I may need my eyes tested as, when we drew level, I realised that he was a cardboard cut-out in a baseball player's uniform.

After a very pleasant and peaceful night we were again up early and yes, you've guessed it, heading north into the wind for a 45 mile hop up to Savannah. We didn't actually moor in Savannah as getting into the city by boat is a bit of a mission in itself. Instead we dropped the hook in Turners Creek about five miles outside of the city centre. Again, the approach to the anchoring pool in Turners Creek was a tortuous trip with tight bends and very shallow water. We did touch bottom once, but only just, and the old girl slid off into a very healthy 0.5 metres after a bit of a rev on the engine. The journey involved passing along stretches of the Wahoo River, Johnsons Creek, North Newport River, Bear River, Big Tom Creek, Ogeechee River, Burnside River, Skidaway River, through Hells Pass (very, very, shallow), Crooked River and finally into Turners Creek to anchor in 4 metres below the small boat yard. As we came into the anchorage, passing shrimp boats moored along the dock, we were hailed by David, aboard a trimaran, who was moored on the shrimp boat dock.

He got on the radio and advised us on the best spot to drop the hook or hooks as we were advised to anchor fore and aft to avoid the boat swinging in the narrow channel. As it was getting late, we jumped into the dinghy and went straight ashore, stopping to thank David on the way. David was full of good advice and so we found a dinghy dock that was free for guests, they welcome all travellers as guests, directions into Savannah for the next day and, most importantly, directions to the local watering hole, Cheers, which was on the waterfront right next to the little working marina. The bar and dock would probably be best described as rustic, but everyone was welcoming and it literaly buzzed with life, both human and insect, as the locals enjoyed their Sunday evening. We met up with Kevin, Chris and Graham, fellow Brits, aboard the catamaran *Sweet Sensation* who were doing the great loop all the way north and then masts out for the trip back down to the Gulf. We also got chatting to Aileen and her husband who hail from Scotland and Manchester respectively and who, having lived in Georgia for several years now, gave us some top tips on places to go to in Savannah. Much later, and now thoroughly lubricated, it was off to bed in anticipation of an early start the next day to catch the bus into Savannah.

      Our day started with a row ashore in order to catch the local bus to Savannah and of course we stood on the wrong side of the road. That problem was eventually corrected by two ladies who joined our queue and gave us some advice on both buses and places to eat in town. We thanked them and then crossed over and caught the right bus. Of course, we had missed two buses while standing on the wrong side of the road, but ho hum, that's life. As all buses do, it meandered all over the place and took us through several suburbs of Savannah, some of which didn't encourage getting off for sure, taking about 10 miles to cover the five into town. The bus driver dropped us off at a large tourist information office come library which is always a good start. Following the advice of the tourist information lady, we had a really interesting day out in Savannah. To start with, we followed the street map provided for us by the nice lady and took a walking tour of most of the squares in the old city centre before meandering along the river front boardwalk in the afternoon, and then heading back to the boat before dark. Savannah was lucky enough to have been surrendered without a fight in the civil war and which saved its architecture and well worth the saving it was. The city is simply beautiful, each square has its own character, much more so than I can do justice to or write here. If you want to know more, get on the internet or even better visit if you can, it is an interesting place and steeped in history. We did stop for lunch at Chippewa Square where the bus stop bench scene from Forest Gump was filmed; no bench in sight as that was a prop for the film but we took a picture of the empty spot anyway along with the church tower that the feather floated over at the beginning, if you remember the film that is

The day ended with a bus ride back, right bus first time this way, and a bit of a marathon shopping trip in the Publix supermarket by the dock, as we are beginning to stock up for the trip back. On that subject we are now all crewed up: Steve is re-joining us, glutton for punishment that he is, and we have a new crew member Adamant from Sweden joining us in Wilmington at the same time. We have also been contacted by Jen who is in the US and has had problems with her planned trip back on another boat, as the skipper walked off refusing to take the boat to sea; must be a story to tell there, methinks. Jen has crewed aboard *Stiletto* in Ramsgate in the past (small world) and was recommended to us through the Ramsgate grapevine. She has still not confirmed, but we plan to meet up soon to discuss options. That covers us as far as the Azores, hopefully with a stop of in Bermuda, where we will pick up Willem for the final trip back to Ireland or the UK mainland, depending on wind and waves. We are now all good to go crew wise. All we need now is about two tonnes of foodstuff stowed away and a tonne or so of fuel.

The final chapter in this epic dialogue is our latest hop up to Beaufort, South Carolina. Again, I was up early trying to get the boat ready before waking Norma with an idea of going out to sea and travelling up the outside to Port Royal Inlet. Two things wrong with that plan;

1. The promised steady force 4 easterly wind ended up a very light North Easterly.
2. My thumping about on deck and general cursing my lot in life as I was being eaten alive by the No See Ums woke a very grumpy Norma from her beauty sleep.

The problem was the stern anchor had got itself well and truly stuck in the mud. I tried pulling it over the stern using a cockpit winch, which usually works, but not an inch of movement could I get. Next, I ran a line along the length of the boat and through the bow roller allowing me to harness the power of the windlass, all to no avail. Eventually I dropped the boat back until the anchor was amidships and connected the chain to the main halyard. With Norma holding the chain away from my varnished rails I winched the Halyard in creating a direct vertical and continuous pull on the beast. After a lot of sweat and the boat leaning at a good angle the suction finally gave way against the steady pressure and, with a cloud of glutinous muck, the fisherman style stern anchor reluctantly pulled out of the river ooze. Covered in mud, eaten alive by insects, pretty well exhausted and still in our PJ's we started the day's journey at 7:30 in the morning with two Krispy Kreme doughnuts each for breakfast and well deserved they were. Giving up all thoughts of the outside passage due to the lack of wind speed and direction, 49 miles of lovely deep-water river motoring later, Norma manoeuvred *Spectra* perfectly alongside our mooring buoy just outside of the Downtown Marina in Beaufort and I passed a line through the loop, settling us in for the next couple of days.

Watch this space for the next exciting episode from the adventures of *Spectra*.........

9th May 2015 04:06:42
Beaufort North Carolina to Charlestown. Rain, Wind and we meet Jen
32:46.43N 79:56.83W
9th May 2015
8144 Miles from Ramsgate by log.

We ended up on the anchor ball adjacent to the catamaran *Sweet Sensation* who we had previously met at Turner Creek near Savannah, two days before. I would say small world but as we are all heading in the same direction bumping into each other is kind of inevitable. While I'm on the subject of bumping into each other, no doubt to maximise revenue the anchor balls here have been placed very close together and it was not a comfortable first night as the two boats moved about with the changes in wind and tide. No contact was made, although it was inches of separation at times. *Sweet Sensation* left the following morning, leaving us with plenty of swinging room. On the first night in Beaufort, Norma and I headed ashore for a bit of a walk about and to book into the marina.

At the marina desk, Norma was mortified to find out that the husky voice on the radio who she had been calling Sir belonged to a Southern Belle, who was very polite, but obviously less than impressed. After taking advantage of the marina's showers and washing machines we sat on the waterfront drinking a glass of wine as the sun went down over the bayou, lovely.

Early(ish) the next morning we walked around the old town and liked what we found. The historical landmark district of the town is jam packed with antebellum mansions all oozing southern charm. Norma has now officially banned me from using the phrases "I do declare honey bunch" and "Oh my, Lordy, Lordy, sweet lemon pie" as I have rather over used them at every opportunity every day ever since leaving Savannah.

Potted history of Beaufort (from what I can remember from our walk): Founded in the earliest colonial times, Beaufort became one of the richest cities in America on the backs of the plantation slaves and took a leading role in the War of Independence. At the time of the Civil War it had a population of 6,000 whites to 11,000 slaves. Emancipation changed all of that, and the city became one of the largest centres of freed slaves for many years. Beaufort's wealth declined rapidly after the cotton industry collapsed and 38% of the population moved away, starting a period of steady decline. It eventually became one of the poorest regions in the United States. With the approach of the second world war the Parris Island

Marine basic training camp and nearby military airfield were established and the defence contracts poured in creating a local renaissance. The last single race school was only closed in 1971 bringing Beaufort into the modern world and it has enjoyed a steady economic growth founded on the defence industry, farming and tourism ever since. That's it, all I can remember anyway; it is a beautiful city living with an uncomfortable past that is well worth the visit, if you are in these here parts.

On the evening of day two in Beaufort, Jen, one of our potential Atlantic crew. came up from Florida to meet us, along with the skipper who had resigned from her previous yacht. Of course, we questioned them both closely on the reasons for abandoning ship before even leaving port. Apparently, the yacht had just been purchased after sitting on the hard standing for four and a half years, and the new owner wanted to more or less drop it in and sail it back across the Atlantic. Having experienced the teething problems when taking a well-maintained yacht blue water cruising, the drop in the water and go approach would have sent me running for the hills as well. I think the hired Skipper made a wise choice standing by his judgement and saying to the owner no the yacht is not ready for an ocean crossing and, when the owner would not delay, voting with his feet. All went well with the meet up and I think Jen is a keeper, so we are now all set for the trip back. The last leg will be a bit crowded with 6 on board but, after all it's not a holiday, it is an adventure. We are just waiting on Jen to get all of her ducks in a row and then confirm that she is coming and, if she is, she will meet up with us again at our jumping off point for the trip back.

Our trip up towards Charleston started late, as we had a bit of a lie in and then the weather closed in. The day started well enough, with the local American military jets buzzing overhead under the cloudy sky giving us something to watch, as we chugged along under staysail and engine making pretty good time. Our peaceful progress was broken by a large, low-pressure system which had settled in over the Jacksonville area, and we were soon feeling its effects. With the wind regularly into the 30+ knot bracket and due to the narrow, winding channels that we were steering along, we could do nothing but follow our track, taking the wind and rain on whatever quarter it decided to batter us from next. Rather inevitably something had to give and one of the shackles on the staysail turning block gave up the ghost in a 40-knot gust. No real drama, we simply furled the sail away and decided to call it a day earlier than expected. Norma studied the charts for a likely anchorage, while I continued to steer us through the twisty little channels (50feet wide) whilst peering myopically into the driving rain. By this stage I was wearing my full waterproofs for crying out loud, and it was freezing! However, I was still bare foot; you have to maintain standards after all. Norma found us a spot 5-miles ahead just at the end of the narrow channel and I happily called it a day, gratefully turning left out of the ICW into a subsidiary river called Rock Creek, where we dropped the hook in the lee of some trees and dived below for hot tea and warm towels.

Sitting in a completely isolated anchorage, with nothing around except for miles of empty marshland and with the wind howling outside we decided to have a film night and what better film to watch considering our present location, than Forrest Gump. I don't care what anyone else thinks, it is a good movie and we both had a no-see-um in our eye by the end of it. The weather report next morning was full of dire warnings to small craft of high winds and higher seas. The low-pressure system that has kept us on the inside track (ICW), has developed into Tropical Storm Mona and stalled itself 20 miles or so offshore, smack bang between Jacksonville and Charleston or, in other words, just about on top of us. I thought it was blowing a bit last night! With that in mind, we set off early and motored, yes you guessed it, north into the grey and windy dawn. As it turned out the day wasn't too bad at all. At least the rain kept away and we made very good time to cover the 47 miles up to Charleston through some pretty deep water for a change. The depth sounder even went into double figures on one occasion. In fact, as we approached a cut between two rivers we met a mini liner head on as it came up river from the sea. I checked his vital statistics on the AIS system and he came in at 180 feet and only 2.1 metres deep, so I guess he was made with these waters in mind. I rather graciously radioed the skipper and said I would hold back and allow him through the cut first, the net result being I got to follow a deeper keeled boat for a couple of completely stress-free hours, happy days indeed.

With thoughts of the trip back now beginning to dominate our thinking, we have begun to convert the boat from a travelling home to blue water yacht again. We have started stocking up on foodstuffs, the long-life milk store is filling nicely again, as is the canned goods cupboard. I have decided to replace the domestic battery bank as it is not holding its charge to my liking, even though the batteries are only three years old, 4 x 220 amps an hour is going to cost a bit. I suspect the erratic charging while I was having generator problems did them no good at all. Norma spent the day cleaning the accumulated grime and suntan cream from our lifelines and I have stripped the water maker down and finally given up on the salinity probe. I have a bag of those things, each one costs £100 and lasts 6 months at the most, before giving out incorrect readings (totally over-sensitive and a complete rip off, please note *Spectra* water makers, if you are reading). With the probe sitting in a glass of fresh water it still says, 'high salinity' and rejects the produced water. I have taken advice from other cruisers who run similar systems and followed the emergency advice in the manual. I now run the produced water straight into the bilge for a few minutes and then taste it; salinity probe says bad, my taste buds say good so divert into the water tanks, check every 15-20 minutes, job done. I only fill one tank at a time as a safety measure and it all seems to work fine to make 50 litres an hour of good drinking water, and we will not be a thirsty or smelly bunch when we hit the UK. The staysail sheets have nice new shackles and I am making enquiries about either getting the old girl lifted for a bottom clean and anode change or contracting a diver to do the job in Wilmington. You wouldn't believe the growth that has attached to the bottom since we started up the ICW; this water is a veritable organic soup. The colour of the water is a dark murky brown and all the boats, us included, soon sport what is known as a Chesapeake moustache from the bow wave, staining the sides. An interesting point is that the dolphins, of which there are many, all stay grey and sleek looking; there must be a special dolphin brand anti-foul out there somewhere.

Anyway, long story short, we dropped anchor in Charleston this evening and are now sitting listening to the wind howl outside again. Tomorrow we go ashore to see what we can see.

Watch this space for the next exciting episode from the adventures of *Spectra*.........

Georgetown North Carolina, Mosquitoes, More No-See-Ums and other things that go bite in the night.

33:21.95N 79:17.06W
13th May 2015
8210 Miles from Ramsgate by log.

After arriving in Charleston, we anchored outside of the big marina on the north shore, finding a tight spot just out of the main shipping channel and quite close to the Coast Guard Depot; at least *Spectra* would have some guardians while we were ashore. No sooner had we dropped anchor than a local artist/live-aboard came over and introduced himself. He turned out to be a mine of useful information and after I had done a bit of maintenance on the water maker, we went ashore with at least an idea where we were heading, a novel experience indeed.

As it was Sunday, Charleston was very much closed but what we saw was very nice. We had a Mexican-style lunch, then checked up on the weather and were soon hurrying back to *Spectra*. Tropical Storm Mona turned out to be Tropical Storm Anna once I checked on the internet. The Coast Guards seemed to be having a, 'who can talk the fastest competition', on the VHF radio, making them very hard to understand at times. What I discerned now, was that Anna was lying offshore from Jacksonville and would move up to the Charleston area by midnight with winds of up to 60 knots predicted for Charleston harbour. Our anchorage was nowhere near secure enough for those conditions and, as I mentioned earlier, quite tight, so we could not lay out the amount of chain that we were going to need. In short, we had to move! Charleston Marina has a mega dock which is about a mile long, but when we asked for a berth at the marina office, even with that huge pontoon along the river, there was no room at the inn. Apparently, boats for miles around were heading for shelter and had pre-booked every available slot that could possibly have held *Spectra*. Forced back onto our own resources, we decided the safest option was to move across the river to get into the lee of an island and find a bit more swinging room. On the way back to *Spectra* in our dinghy we were hailed by another live-aboard as we passed. The young lady on board the small sail boat was having anchor problems and, having dragged two of them on deck, could not get the rusted shackles open. Knight in Shining Waterproofs that I am, I wrestled the shackles open for her while standing in my dinghy alongside (it was a small boat) and then her friend arrived in a borrowed dinghy to help lay her extra anchors for the night, leaving us free to get on with sorting out *Spectra*. Having up anchored and crossed the river, I found a likely spot tucked in reasonably close to the shore in 4 metres of water. Norma worked the windlass as I carefully reversed back laying out all 80 metres of chain on the main anchor, and then dropped the second bow anchor and motored forward back along the same path laying an additional 20 metres of anchor chain back the way we had come, whilst pulling in 20 metres of the main anchor chain. This is called a Bahamian Moor, and allows you to get a lot of chain down but reduce your swinging circle. As both anchors had dug in well we set the anchor strop on the main chain to take the pressure away from the bowsprit and onto the Samson post. Then, as confident as we could be, we settled down to watch the end of series 1 of Downton Abbey on the television, to which we have become addicted this week. I would like to enliven your day now with a tale of us battling hurricane force winds all night with an heroic deed or two saving a dusky maiden or three chucked in for good measure but no, nothing untoward happened. I had left the instruments on as we can record wind speed and direction for up to 24 hours and the wind peaked at 20 knots around 0100 in the morning or, in other words, it would have been a boisterous day sail. To be honest I am not complaining at all, a peaceful night's sleep was had by all, apart from the cast of Downton Abbey of course, who are in a right old pickle and no mistaking it.

The next day turned into a marathon shopathon with Norma, which was so much fun that it has all blurred into one joyous memory for me, and so I shall write no more on the subject.

As a rule, America does not seem to be very pedestrian-friendly; in Charleston the solution is to supply orange warning flags to carry as you cross the road - you return them to the holders on the post after crossing. Norma was slightly perturbed (and very embarrassed) as I insisted on waving the flag vigorously above my head as we crossed every street.

We also met up with the crew of the catamaran *Sweet Sensation* again, who were moored on the end of the mega dock. After a beer or two in their lovely, spacious cockpit we bid them fare thee well and headed back over to *Spectra* for our final night in Charleston, and the start of series 2 of Downton Abbey. I have serious concerns about Mr Bates the Valet and Thomas the Footman's working relationship, I can see no happy ending there.

With the Mr Bates and Thomas situation still unresolved by the next morning, we picked up our anchors and headed out of Charleston harbour. Point to note, remember all the ironmongery that we laid on the bottom while awaiting the arrival of the storm Anna non-event, well it all had to come back aboard again! The main came up on the windlass fine, but the second bow anchor had to be hand hauled in, leaving a very tired Paul star fished on the foredeck as Norma steered us away from Charleston. When Fort Sumter, (where the first shots of the American Civil war were fired), came into view ahead we turned left just astern of a large Coast Guard Cutter and re-joined the ICW. Our first day out from Charleston turned into a bit of a marathon and we ended up covering 54 miles before dropping anchor for the night in Minim Creek. The journey started late, due to the first bridge not opening until after 9 am and involved some fairly shallow water and commercial traffic at first, which always keeps you on your toes. The anchorage was calm, isolated, scenic and absolutely jam packed with every stinging, biting and generally annoying flying insect known to man. Even with all the hatches closed and the insect repellent sprayed liberally around, my evening of Downton Abbey was not a pleasant one at all.

After a horrible night, and sporting a new collection of little red lumps, we got up early to catch the tide for the 12-mile final leg of this journey into Georgetown. With the tide helping us along we touched 8 knots at one point and our anchor splashed down in the little creek near Georgetown just after breakfast. We had decided to only stay here for the one night and push on tomorrow, so we launched the dinghy and headed ashore as soon as the anchor had settled on the bottom. Georgetown is a small place with a big history, the docks were a hive of activity during the 19th and 20th century as it was a centre for the exportation of lumber and cotton in the Carolinas, but that has now all passed. The old docks have been very nicely converted into a riverside walkway with an array of bars, restaurants and arty shops supporting the town's new industry of tourism. Rather sadly, a whole chunk of the riverside frontage was burnt down a few years back which has left a 100-metre hole in the centre of the town, but I am sure it will be rebuilt soon.

Jen has confirmed that she is going to join us, we are now all set crew wise for the trip back. We are now awaiting an email confirming our mooring at Cape Fear Marina, Wilmington, as we hope to get there a day or two earlier than expected, which will give us a bit of extra time to start prepping the old girl for the trip back, before Tommy and Sue arrive. The other reason we need confirmation of the marina slot is that the price they quoted, at $8 per foot for the entire stay, is so cheap that we are convinced it must be wrong, or maybe the price was per foot per day, in which case it is ridiculously high and we will be going elsewhere. The email was not as clear as it could have been, so time will tell.

It is a planned late start today, as we have to wait until after low water at 11 am which will give us a rising tide for the next stretch. Having taken the time to write to update all of our latest travails, I am now going on deck to try and borrow a share of the internet from the nearest bar, Big Tuna, before we head on up to the next anchorage. I am not sure where that will be yet as Norma is doing the navigation on the ICW and going by the noises coming out of the aft cabin she is still fast asleep, but it will be 30 odd miles north from here that's for sure.

PS; Mr Bates has returned, much to Anna's delight; the other housemaid has been a naughty girl and gotten herself pregnant to the dashing Major while Mr Bates and Thomas are still not getting along at all, I can see nothing but trouble ahead and as for Lady Mary, well who knows what's going on there?

We need series 3 and 4 as a matter of urgency, this is at the very least a Pan situation.

Keep reading there's more to come from the exciting adventures of *Spectra*.........

17th May 2015 17:04:00
Georgetown to Wilmington and we finish with the ICW.
34:15.37N 79:56.87W
8329 Miles from Ramsgate by log.

Well that is it for the Intra Coastal Waterway. We are now moored alongside a very peaceful pontoon in Cape Fear Marina, 12 miles upriver from the ICW and this is as far North as we plan to go, our next port of call is planned to be Bermuda. After leaving Georgetown, we did, as predicted, go north for about 30 miles (26 to be precise) and then dropped anchor in a little side pool just upriver from the Bucksport Marina. This turned out to be a bit of a bonus stopover, as when we went ashore in the dinghy, we found that this little out of the way place had been invaded by the Harley Davidson brigade for American bike week. It is estimated that 25,000 Harley Davidsons arrive for Bike Week in South Carolina every year, not all of them at Bucksport I hasten to add. There was a very local live band singing away and biker people everywhere, looking like extras from

Sons of Anarchy and having a good old time. To cut a long story short, we joined in and had a good old time too. The evening ended with us sharing a table with the barmaid, Sarah, whose father came from Coventry, but we didn't hold that against her. Sarah introduced herself as follows, "High my names Sarah, I'm working here because I divorced my military husband as he was a cheating S.O.B and I suffer from ADHT, here's a big dragon fly isn't it pretty?". That's more information in the first 10 seconds that I have found about from some close friends who I have known for years. The marina manager, Jeff also joined our table to finish the night off. Oh, and we were the last ones to leave, I did rather expect more from the Harley boys and girls but they are all middle-aged stockbrokers in the daytime, I suspect. Jeff was telling the tale of the American yachtsman who was in the news recently for surviving 60-odd days in a dismasted yacht after being hit by a storm in the Gulf Stream. He kept his small yacht at Bucksport and worked at the marina in exchange for mooring fees. From what Jeff told us he definitely seemed to have had a few personal issues going on which culminated in him upping and leaving one day, turning up a couple of months later on the television having been rescued by the Coast Guard.

Bucksport is a great little stop over, soooo friendly and super helpful. Jeff walked us back to the dinghy, opening his office on the way as he had stored in his fridge some homemade sausages that we had bought earlier and left in the office while we had a beer or two. As we got into the dinghy, the trees and swampland around us was echoing with a strange whooo-ump noise, Jeff made a casual comment of, "don't worry about that it is just the gators' mating call, they sound pretty frisky tonight". And so, with that reassuring note ringing in our ears, we set off into the dark rowing our <u>rubber</u> dinghy back to *Spectra*, which was out there somewhere, invisible to the human eye because we had forgotten to turn the anchor lights on before going ashore. Once back on board, we shone our big spot light along the shoreline and picked up a whole series of twinkling reflections from the alligators' eyes in the reeds. I must point out here that this was a bit of a worry for me, I am a city boy at heart and anything more ferocious than a Trafalgar Square pigeon needs to be in a cage, in my opinion.

With last night's over-sexed alligators in mind *Spectra* Cruise Management cancelled the water aerobics session scheduled for the morning and replaced it with callisthenics on the fore deck, (unfortunately no one turned up).

Before leaving Bucksport, we decided to fill up on water and diesel. I have been deliberately running the tanks down to get an accurate estimate of fuel consumption and I am now confident that with full tanks we could motor 24 hours non-stop for over 5 days which, hopefully, will never happen. Our destination for the day was a little river and fishing community called Calabash, 36 miles north east from Bucksport. The journey was actually pretty good, the depths stayed fairly constant at around 2 metres below the keel and we held the tide all of the way, going at nearly 8 knots at one stage. The only tricky part was at the Shallotte Inlet where temporary buoyage had been set up, because of shoaling. It involved a really tight set of short dog legs which took us almost back on ourselves at one point and the depth under the keel dropped to 0.3 metres which is always a worry. Anyway, what doesn't kill you and all that, we got through and the rest was plain sailing apart from the final entry to the anchorage. Again, as we turned to port off the ICW the depth disappeared and we had to very tentatively edge our way back and forth until we found enough water to get into the Calabash River. As soon as we were over the bar the depth went to 5 metres and we finally dropped the anchor just behind another British yacht that we later discovered was heading south for Florida. Calabash itself was about a mile further up the river from our anchorage and so it was out with the trusty dinghy and off we went. A small collection of shrimp boats came into sight moored to Port and alongside one of them was the catamaran *Sweet Sensation* last seen in Charlestown, who we later found out had overtaken us while we were anchored in Bucksport. After a few hellos, the Captain of the shrimp boat kindly said that we could tie up behind him and use his dock. We tried to buy some shrimps from him but the Carolina shrimp season doesn't start until this weekend and so our great plan for cheap seafood was scuppered. With, what is now, typical American hospitality, the boat's engineer offered (insisted) to drive us into town for groceries. With Norma in the cab busily engaged in conversation with Jay, her new best friend, I jumped into the back of his pickup along with the fishing nets and welding gear and we headed for the bright lights of Calabash. Actually, the lights were not very bright, but we did stock up with the essentials of life, beer and bread while Jay waited to run us back; they are really so helpful to complete strangers here.

Later that evening we ate in a waterside restaurant suggested by Jay (I am pretty sure it is family) with the crew of *Sweet Sensation*. Kevin, Chris and Graeme were great company and we tucked into a fried seafood meal and swapped sailing war stories. They come from Brightlingsea and as previously mentioned, are doing the great loop so will be on the ICW for some time yet. One interesting point was that after we separated in Charlestown, they had been boarded by the Coast Guard and told that they had to check in every time that they moved the boat. Like us, they hadn't been doing that every day, just calling up when they crossed state lines. They were given a written warning and the threat of a $5,000 fine for infringing a law that was not clearly stated anywhere that we could find. Our last call to the Coast Guard had been from St Augustine so we decided that we had better get our act together. On arrival at Wilmington I gave them a call only to be met with little interest and the statement that "if I hadn't been outside of the US I didn't need to call at all". I told the story of *Sweet Sensation* and the threat of a hefty fine to which he said, "yeah right, that's not going to happen". Anyway, I insisted he took our US cruising license number and got his name as a reference just in case we hit problems later. There is a problem here in that each Coast Guard sector and even each Coast Guard officer seem to interpret the rules differently with the result that you just have to keep smiling and get a reference for each conversation to cover yourself. While on the phone to the Wilmington Coast Guard I got myself transferred to Immigration to check on the procedure for departing the US. The answer is there is none, they do not issue departure paperwork and you just go. As I said, it can be confusing. I questioned them quite closely and said the crew were flying in on commercial airlines, but no, the answer stayed the same, you can just go and so we will. On the bright side, we do have exit papers from Puerto Rico which we can use if we really need anything on arrival at a Bermuda.

    You have probably guessed from the above that we have arrived in Wilmington therefore bringing our 775 mile Intra Coastal Waterway odyssey to an end. I wouldn't say it has been all fun but it has certainly been a great part of the adventure and we are both very happy that we decided to do it. I took advantage of the Cape Fear inlet area to test the water maker as the water was salty, and the water maker has been playing up recently. I have now rigged it to bypass the salinity sensors as mentioned before. The output now flows either into the tanks or the bilge and so by using the manual override I can get it going and then simply taste the water. Once we have good water flowing into the bilges decided by my taste buds, I divert the flow into the water tanks and check it at intervals. The forward shower drains into the forward bilge along with the waste output from this test phase and will get pumped over the side whenever we have a shower so all is good. I am happy to report that it all worked fine and that is one worry bead put to bed. After passing through downtown Wilmington and the permanently moored battleship USS North Carolina, we arrived at Cape Fear Marina which is possibly the friendliest place we have been to so far and that's saying something. Three boat owners, including Anthony the live-aboard dock master, who was actually off duty, helped moor us up and all got involved with sorting out our power connection. Dan and Paula lent us a domestic power cable which saved the day and we now have 240v of lovely power flowing through the boat, the batteries are fully charged, the fridge is on and the beer is cold, happy days indeed.

The first night we were invited aboard Dan and Paula's lovely 1960's wooden motorboat for sundowners and we met up with Sport, the ship's hound. With the sun going down, good company and a dog to stroke we had a very pleasant first night in

Wilmington. The next morning, I was up early with the pressure washer cleaning the accumulated muck from the ICW from our decks and the sides. Dan offered to take Norma to the local store for groceries which was really helpful, and we now have a fully stocked fridge complete with a bottle of fizzy stuff ready for Tommy and Sue's arrival on Sunday. Dan has also offered us the use of his Jeep any time he isn't using it. As I said, amazingly helpful and friendly.

Spectra is looking a lot more respectable after a day of non-stop cleaning and she is looking quite good, if I say so myself. We have put on clean underwear, brushed our hair and cleaned under our nails; we are now figuratively speaking standing by our beds ready for Tommy's inspection of the yacht. If you remember way back to the Florida blogs, we passed a beautiful black Vagabond anchored outside of a boat show. It is now moored just down the pontoon from us and so we have competition. There is also a rather nice, and very recently painted, Formosa 52 here which is bigger than *Spectra* at over 60ft but of a similar design. I have, of course, been over chatting to the owners, as you do. Last night we had Dan, Paula and Sport aboard for some reciprocal sundowners and later we were joined by Billy who lives on the boat next door across the pontoon. A good night, which actually ended early on Sunday morning, was had by all.

The adventures of *Spectra* and crew go on, keep reading...............

Wilmington area with Tommy and Sue.
34:15.37N 79:56.87W
21st May 2015
8383 Miles from Ramsgate by log.

I have had to rush this edition out as, according to Sue, Piers will be worrying about his Mummy, so here goes.

Tommy and Sue have been with us for a few days now and we have had exciting adventures indeed. There was the 'find our way into Wilmington trek' – half a mile by river, 4 miles by road, trying to avoid walking along the Interstate and a short cut through a pretty dodgy neighbourhood. A completely riveting 'trip to Walmart' enjoyed by all and of course lots of beer aboard *Spectra* as the sun goes down. To be honest, the first few days were dominated by my need to get *Spectra's* mini refit underway ready for the crossing. We are now booked in for a lift, clean and anode check on Thursday the 28th, a new 80-amp hour battery charger is on order and I am awaiting prices on my 4 new batteries. The stern gland needs a bit of a repack and so I will do that while we are in the slings. All in all, everything is going to schedule and we have had no dramas, so far, I hasten to add. Everyone has been very helpful; the marina has agreed to let us use their wholesaler discount card for supplies and offered to give us a lift there and back which should be a real boon. The staff at the local boatyard are extremely helpful and competent, which has given me a warm fluffy feeling about the trip preparations. Also, as previously mentioned, we have the use of our mooring neighbour Dan's jeep, anytime they aren't using it. Which is a bit above and beyond in my book.

With all of that set-in motion we decided to head back down the Cape Fear River with Tommy and Sue for a couple of days of well-earned R&R and visit Southport. We tried to stop of there on the way up but there was no room at the Inn. The 20-mile trip down the river was a bit extended as we had to punch the tide for the first two hours. The lifting bridge at Wilmington will only open for pleasure craft at 10am and 2pm which leaves you a bit limited on tidal options. Having said that, it was a very pleasant trip down the river motoring gently past the USS North Carolina in Wilmington town centre and we even managed to sail for a mile or two when the wind picked up.

The bridge crossing the river at the entrance to Wilmington has a 65 feet clearance giving us at least 3.5 feet at the full height of the tide but, unused to going under bridges, both Tommy and Sue developed worried expressions and even ducked a bit as we slipped below. Looking up you could see cars crossing through the open grid of the metal road surface, a bit disconcerting to say the least. Norma and myself were calm and full of confidence, not mentioning the fact that we had crept under that bridge very slowly going the other way just a couple of days before.

We arrived at Safe Haven harbour, Southport, just before low water and made an attempt to squeeze into a 'free - patrons only' berth at the Provision Company shoreside restaurant. As I reversed in all was going exceptionally well until *Spectra* gently ran aground and stopped with over half of her length sticking out beyond the finger berth. The rather keen dockside helper/waiter from the restaurant gallantly kept pulling on the stern line encouraging me to keep her coming until I told him we are hard aground and all of the pulling in the world wasn't going to shift her any further backwards. Not to be put off by such a minor setback, I pulled out and went into the next berth over forwards. With *Spectra's* underwater shape being considerably shallower up front, we managed to get the bows all of the way in and everything tied up without touching the mud again. It actually wasn't quite that easy as the pontoon was a bit on the rickety side (sinking) and the young lad helping was a bit too keen. The mid ships line was thrown and I pointed to the cleat I wanted it attached to. He fastened the line on and I gently applied throttle to spring us in, going ahead at about 0.01 knots with no effort at all, caused a splintering of wood as the cleat ripped clean out of the rotten dock. In a flash the young lad tied it off to another cleat and then rushed forward to take the bow line from Sue. Having got his hands on the bow line he started to haul on it manfully swinging our bows inwards toward the dock alarmingly and making his hastily tied mid ships line slip on the cleat. At this point I had to shout stop and get him to calm it down a bit. We got Tommy ashore and his wise old head soon brought some order to the situation. Ten minutes later we were all snugly tied up with our pulpit rail sitting about three feet away from the nearest table on the open deck of the restaurant while the diners carried on eating with slightly forced smiles and a few nervous twitches. If Norma had leant over the rail, I am pretty sure she could have stolen a chip, sorry French fry. Later that night, at high tide, our bowsprit was actually above the roof of the restaurant which was an interesting if slightly unusual view.

Southport is a real microcosm of an all-American town. Lovely little houses lead on to main street which is wide and lined with small family businesses catering to the passing trade. We had a good walk about and then ate out at the restaurant behind the one we had docked at, the Frying Pan. No social boundaries were trespassed upon as both restaurants are owned by the same family, as is half the town by all accounts.

The next morning, we were up and about early for a short trip up the river to the Federal Point Yacht Club at Carolina beach. We had a warm welcome at the yacht club and were soon all tied up with the shore power attached and the fridge busily cooling the beer down. The yacht club boasts its own swimming pool for guests and all for $1.25 per foot per night. Added to that, the nice lady in the office gave us a discount for being Sea Tow members and only billed us for 45 feet so, all in all, it was $50 for the night. After a day around the pool listening to a man continuously telling his well-behaved children to play quietly at the top of his voice we put our glad rags on (clean pair of shorts) and headed into town for the night. In town we found a bar called, the "Fat Pelican Shack", which strangely enough was, a "shack and had some plastic Pelicans in the beer garden". Above the door of the "Fat Pelican Shack" was a sign that said, "Women in low cut dresses will be looked down upon" which titillated Tommy no end, and we went in! Passing the bar, a door at the back of the "shack", opened into a refrigerated lorry container, yes it was that posh, which had over four hundred varieties of bottled beer, plus wine and I am sure there was a single can of Coke in there somewhere but I didn't look too hard. The idea was that you make your selection and then take the bottles to the bar, pay for them and then find a quiet corner of the bar or large outside area to drink them in. Unfortunately, a squall had come through that afternoon along with absolutely torrential rain which had soaked the outside area making everything a bit drab and soggy but not to be deterred we found a corner and had a pleasant beer or two in very strange surroundings.

After a meal ashore and a singing contest as we walked back to *Spectra*, (say a word and everyone has to sing a line from a song containing that word), we settled in for the night with the wind howling outside and all was well with the world. This morning we awoke bright and early to a blustery old kind of day which turned out to be a very slow start for the crew of *Spectra*. After many false starts which included Sue cancelling her hair regime until later, we finally cast off and headed back. A passing motorboat skipper called over to Tommy "nice ride you have there fella, where you from?" To which Tommy replied "England, Europe". "Get outta here, well done you guys" was the response. That kept us smiling for most of the morning. Norma used the trip back to itemise our medical supplies and finish one of her paintings and we three got on with sailing the boat and, of course, putting the world to rights. If anyone out there had burning ears today now you know the reason why. For the second day running our GPS lost contact as we went up the river which was a bit of a worry with the big crossing pending. Later that day I asked in Bennett Brothers Boat Yard if it was common to lose GPS on the river, to which Al, the technical manager, said that the huge military logistics base was known to block the signal in the local area, which is a new one on me, but as it happened in the same place on two separate days you have to suspect foul play don't you? The GPS has worked faultlessly for weeks, by the way.

We are now moored back in Cape Fear Marina and I have just put my 4 new 8D batteries on order at $260 each plus tax, so all is set for next week. Norma is getting a lift to the wholesalers on Tuesday and we are borrowing Dan's Jeep tomorrow to grab some supplies at Walmart. I think the cunning plan is to take advantage of having the Jeep and drive over to the USS North Carolina in the afternoon, but as it only has front seats that will be an interesting exercise, (I bet Sue bags a front seat). Monday is Memorial Day and to show willing we are going to dress *Spectra* overall, or all over, I can never remember which one it is, but it will show a bit of solidarity with our American hosts and, of course, it will make *Spectra* a nice backdrop for the marina BBQ to which we have all been invited on Sunday.

PS: Piers, Sue says Mummy loves you.

The adventure goes on ………

28th May 2015 13:24:47
Wilmington: Shopping & Shopping, New batteries, Alligators, Snakes & shopping.
34:15.37N 79:56.87W
Still 8383 Miles from Ramsgate by log.

Today is Tommy's birthday and we have decided to eat out in Wilmington tonight at a restaurant that serves Alligator satay for starters. An unusual choice but Tommy and Sue found the restaurant a few days ago and it looks like a good one, so more on how that went in the next edition, my guess is that Alligator will taste like Chicken as these things tend to do.

This week has been a busy one, the boat preparations are going full steam ahead, so even though Tommy and Sue are out here on holiday we have managed to do boat work each morning. Last Monday was Memorial Day and to show a bit of solidarity with our cousins across the ocean we dressed *Spectra* all over and I put up my RAF Yacht Club flag, very pretty she looked too and earned a lot of praise from those passing by. I also took the opportunity of finally getting around to replacing my Rear Commodore's Pennant with a standard RTYC one. Stan officially replaced me in January so it really was about time I took it down. Truth be told it had just about frayed away and was a very sad looking scrap of cloth when it reached the deck. Tommy commented that now I definitely had no balls which just about summed it up (yachty joke). As I never explain humour, even pretty poor humour, look up flags and pennants in Wikipedia.

Anthony, the dockmaster of Cape Fear Marina, and his wife ran an all-welcome BBQ on the office veranda on Sunday afternoon, so we loaded up with a case or two of beer and went along to join in. It turned out to be a great day out. There was another British couple there who are getting their yacht fixed up by Bennett Brothers yard for a trip down to the Bahamas, so we discussed bilge pumps, toilets and general electrical things as the meat cooked. The food was very good, full credit to Anthony and partner. We relaxed and the conversation flowed. I got talking to Butch who is an ex US Marine Captain from the Vietnam era and served through the Tet offensive which, if you know your history, was very bloody indeed. Butch is in the process of buying a boat on the marina and is bringing to market a new sailing dinghy/tender, very like a Sailfish, manufactured by his son Pat which looks very nice. He will be living aboard at the marina once the boat purchase goes through as, even at the age of 74, he is still busy working at the nearby power plant project, managing a major environmental clean-up. His friend Loretta, who originally hailed from New York, proved to be a real find. Her sense of humour was great and she got my mark pretty quickly. Loretta kindly offered to drive us down to Wrightsville Beach one day in the week, which is another example of the amazing generosity Americans show to complete strangers.

  Monday morning Tommy and I borrowed Dan's Jeep and found a local garage in order to fill up all of our deck containers with petrol for the generator, including the full tank on the generator. We now have 130 litres of petrol stored on deck which has seriously reduced Norma's smoking area. Once that little job was completed and everything tied down we headed into Wilmington for the day. After a lunch ashore, we ended the day with sundowners in the cockpit zapping any mosquito that dared to come close with our new toy, an electric tennis racquet fly zapper. Small things please small minds I suppose, but it is extremely satisfying getting one back on the mozzies for a change.

Tuesday was spent shopping, shopping, shopping, and then we did a bit more shopping. First thing, the Marina manager, Robert, took Norma and me, along with the biggest shopping list I have seen in a while, to Sam's wholesalers so that we could benefit from his corporate card discount. I am not sure he realised quite what he was letting himself in for but he seemed more than happy to join in with the marathon shopping expedition as we dashed backwards and forwards around the warehouse-sized building. A couple of hours later, as he dropped us back at the marina, his pickup was groaning under the weight of our food stuffs. Tommy and Sue headed into town to do the holiday thang as *Spectra* was inundated with stores and the process of finding a place for everything began. Once that lot was away, we borrowed Dan's Jeep and headed for Walmart for round two. Again, two trolley loads were stuffed into the back of the Jeep, along with a new American gas bottle as we can't get our UK bottles filled here. On the way back, we passed Tommy and Sue walking up the road in the North Carolina heat, but could not offer them a lift as the Jeep was filled to the rafters with shopping. I did stop and grin at them though as they trudged along in the heat, just to show solidarity you understand. Back at the marina we quickly unloaded the Jeep into the carts and then I decided it would be politic to go and pick up the wanderers. They must have had a final spurt of energy because, as I approached the marina gates, they were already there. I say "they were there" but they were actually standing on the other side of the road staring at something on the ground. Suspecting early onset of senile dementia or maybe just heat exhaustion, I approached with caution so as not to spook the old folk. What had happened was that Tommy had spotted a snake on the path and shouted to Sue to watch out. With the instant reaction to a clear and concise command that one would expect from an independent woman, Sue carried on and stepped on the snake's tail. Luckily, the snake's reaction was to go stiff and play possum as opposed to having a bite, and all was well, but it could have been very different! When I arrived on the other side of the gate they were busily taking pictures of one seriously disgruntled, and slightly flattened, snake as it went on its way.

Back on the dockside with another pile of shopping piled high, I was sure that *Spectra* would be in danger of sinking if we put the second load of food on board, but it all found a place and the waterline is still visible, in fact it has hardly moved to be honest; it is amazing just how much stuff you can store on this boat. All that is needed now is the final shop for fresh food over the weekend and we are good to go.

The next morning over coffee, as Tommy and Norma were putting the world to rights again, an alligator swam along the river about 20ft from the side of the boat, which is always a nice way to start the day. With swimming in Cape Fear River still firmly off the agenda we gave Loretta (from the BBQ in case you haven't been keeping up) a call to take her up on her kind offer of a lift to the beach. Loretta was more than happy to give us a lift, and at 12 o'clock, spot on time, she turned up in her nice new Corolla and we all piled in. Above and beyond the call of duty is all I can say about Loretta. Not only did she give us a lift, but she also gave us a guided tour of the area and proved to be great company along the way. After dropping us off at a pier on the beach, Loretta headed back home and we had a walk along the beach for about a mile to the next pier down, taking the opportunity for an alligator-free swim along the way. Although alligator-free, the swim was not without incident as the surf was pretty lively and we were all tumbled over at some point; I suppose the surfers riding the waves should have been a giveaway. Norma took several spectacular tumbles and later, when drying off in the restaurant's changing rooms, found that she had stolen half of the beach and bought it back inside of her bikini. Having reached the second pier, we gave Loretta a call and invited her for lunch. Once we were all dried off and Loretta had arrived, we had a very pleasant meal on the pier overlooking the sea swapping pictures of families and tales of our adventures. On the way back to *Spectra*, Loretta again gave us another guided tour of the area, large parts of which I rather rudely missed as I just couldn't keep my eyes open. Swimming, sun, and beer make Paul a sleepy boy. My sleepiness was noted by Loretta, and I was given a thorough mocking along the way, all very tongue-in-cheek, of course.

On our return I discovered that our batteries had been delivered and the new battery charger had also turned up, happy days, new toys to play with. Next day, Norma got on with cooking our much-delayed Sunday lunch (it was Wednesday), while Tommy and I rigged a block and tackle to haul the old batteries up out of the bowels of the boat. Finally, with them all in the cockpit, it was all hands-on deck to swing them over the side onto the dock using the main boom as a crane. That was a hard afternoon's work and by the end of it I was stinging with both sweat and the effects of battery acid and I needed a hose down. The old batteries are now up at the boat yard and we will bring the new ones down in the morning. As the sun went down, I fitted the new battery charger after having to take it apart to remove a jumper so that it will work on 220 volts; nothing is ever simple, is it?

That's about it for now really, the Sunday Lunch on Wednesday was a culinary triumph as expected and we spent the evening zapping mosquitoes and partaking of a glass or two of red wine.

Today, to celebrate Tommy's birthday, we will fit the new batteries, tighten up the stern gland, test the battery charger, get the boat lifted, cleaned and re-anoded (if that is even a word?) and then re-launched. Oh, and after that it is off downtown for a taste of alligator as mentioned at the beginning of my musings, and the waitress had better make it snappy (sorry couldn't resist that one).

Watch this space for the next exciting episode from the adventures of *Spectra*.........

WILMINGTON TO BERMUDA

MAY AND JUNE 2015

30th May 2015
Wilmington: Final update, goodbye Sue and Tommy - Hello new crew
34:15.37N 79:56.87W
Still 8383 Miles from Ramsgate by log.

Once again, we have said a fond farewell to Tommy and Sue who have now headed back to the UK, we will see them sometime in July, I expect. The alligator did indeed taste like chicken and the last meal out with our intrepid support team was a good one. Tommy and I sweated blood getting the batteries into *Spectra* because, as you might expect, they didn't fit. Same model, measurements taken and double checked but these had a slightly different design of handle which increased the overall length very slightly. End result, I had to break the end of my battery box apart in order to get them to sit flat. All of that bent double in a tiny space in 25-degrees heat was not a nice experience. Anyway, they are now all in, secure and fully charged. The lift out and bottom scrub went without incident. A small army of worker bees descended and *Spectra's* bottom was scrubbed clean in no time. Everything was in good order down below, including the anodes and there was no need to fit the new ones so they were put in storage for next time. Finally, we were re-launched the following morning bright and early. After helping us to bring *Spectra* back onto her berth Tommy and Sue departed for the airport, hopefully we have given them a few good memories for the future. The owner of Bennett Brothers boat yard came down to say goodbye to Tommy. Small world that it is; after hearing Tommy's Liverpudlian accent they got chatting and it turned out that they had worked for the same company in Liverpool back in the 1970's; now that was a coincidence.

Two hours later a taxi pulled up and Steve arrived and within the hour both Adamant and Jen had also turned up. The rest of the day was a blur. We got them settled in and did a tour of the boat. Safety, boat rules, plans for the next few weeks and generally getting to know each other took up the rest of the day. Adamant, who we hadn't met before as he had come to us via 'Crew Seekers', seemed to be a competent and likeable chap. One potential fly in the ointment was that, being a Muslim and Ramadan starting soon, his eating arrangements were going to be out of synch with the rest of us. I had a frank and open conversation with him as I have serious concerns about handling a boat in the cold and wet with no food inside of you. Ramadan is due to start on the Bermuda to Azores stage of the journey and we decided that we would give it a go for that leg. If that works out, we would carry on. Let's see how it goes, at the moment I have a gut feeling all will be fine as he has fitted in very well. Jen is like an excited puppy, virtually jumping up and down with enthusiasm to get going and volunteering to do absolutely everything. Of course, Steve is Steve and, should I fall over the side or go missing, I have no worries that between him and Norma the rest will be ok, come what may.

Last night we had a meal ashore to get to know each other a bit more, and to swap some war stories of course, before early to bed. The last day in Wilmington will be spent getting the new crew better acquainted with *Spectra* and her foibles before completing any final shopping, yes really. Then we are ready for the big off.

1st Jun 2015 11:34:00
Wilmington to Bermuda Day 2
32:52.70N 73:55.6W
260 Miles from Wilmington
8643 Miles from Ramsgate by log.

The bridge opened spot on time and at 10 am on the 31st of May we departed Wilmington heading south towards the Cape Fear inlet. A small crowd had gathered on the pontoon to wish us well. There were a few tears I will be honest; Wilmington has been a wonderful final stopover, which will be added to our memories of America and help to remind us, in years to come, of the open armed and friendly reception that we have had, almost without exception, whilst we have been in America.

Three hours of steady motoring with the outgoing tide brought us into Southport Marina, our last stop in America. The stopover lasted exactly 45 minutes, just enough time to top-up our fuel tanks, squeezing in every last litre of diesel that we could manage, and then fill the water tanks to the top of the filler tube. The weather report shows a low-pressure system developing down south that will be on us up here by Thursday; we plan to get out ahead of that and be across the Gulf Stream before it hits. Unfortunately, that will leave us with light East to South East winds for nearly the entire trip over to Bermuda, hence the need for every drop of fuel.

Jen and Adamant, have settled in well and Steve is like part of the furniture around here anyway so he slotted in straight away. Jen was on Mother Watch for 24 hours starting from 1400 on the first day and the first meal at sea was down to her. A full Sunday roast was duly served up – she is definitely a keeper. As Jen was on Mother Watch she got to sleep through the first night, and Adamant went straight into the watch system. For his first night, Steve and I did an extra hour each so that he had company for his first shift cycle. Tomorrow Adamant will go onto Mother Watch and Steve and I can shadow Jen on her first shift cycle. Third night out I will be Mother and so I will sleep in the cockpit, and be available if they need me and Steve will fall back into the normal 2 hours on, 6 hours off routine that we run at sea. Norma, while all of this has been going on, has been shadowing both Jen and Adamant in the galley, to get them used to the intricacies of our domestic life and to show them all the little pokey holes that we have used to squirrel away our mountain of supplies. All is well so far, apart from a total lack of wind. Looking through the log, Force 2 has been the strongest and that was smack on the nose so it has been a non-stop motor sail so far.

This morning we had a big take on our fishing gear. The line screamed out and it must have been a big one because the blighter pulled the hook straight and got away. We have seen three dolphins, none of which came to play, unfortunately. We also sighted the fin of a really large shark swimming by and have sighted several Portuguese Man-o-Wars. Perhaps the strangest sighting was a dog bowl floating on a block of polystyrene, no sign of any dog fish though (get it, Dog Fish? Honestly, this stuff is priceless).

Night two went peacefully with Adamant creating a very nice curry in the galley and Jen completing her first night watch monitored by me, for the first hour, and then Steve for the second. The winds remained stubbornly light throughout the night until we got a mini break at 0400. The wind climbed to the dizzying heights of 9 knots and we actually managed to switch the engine off for two whole hours before the wind went light again. This morning we have played with the cruising chute, which again pulled us along for 30 minutes, before the wind died and it was back under engine again.

That's it for now motoring, motoring, and more motoring, but all in the right direction so it would be churlish to complain too loudly. The fishing gear has been deployed and I, for one, can't think of a single reason why we won't be eating Dorado for dinner tonight.

The next blog will be on Thursday by which time we should be very close to Bermuda.

3rd Jun 2015 11:37:00
Wilmington to Bermuda Day 4
32:48.85N 69:54.96W
4th June 2015
412 Miles from Wilmington
8795 Miles from Ramsgate by log.

Well, the Dorado dinner never happened which was a surprise to me, as I was sure we would catch the big one. Needless to say, the lures are still out and there must be a fish out there somewhere with our name on it.

Night three went without incident, and both Jen and Adamant have now completed their first solo night shifts. Well, nearly solo; I slept in the cockpit but was not needed so all is good on that front. With thoughts of Willem joining us in the Azores, I thought it best to get the sextant out and make sure it was all ok. That turned into a teaching session with Jen and Norma, who both managed to take a Sun sight. That evening I took a sight from the moon and from Venus, so all is well with the sextant. Adamant has turned out to be a bit of a sailing guru – he showed us all up with his knowledge of sound signals and obscure lights when we were playing with the flash cards for Jen's benefit, and he adjusted the sextant for errors before we had a go with it. We did try to take a sight from the pole star but it was too small and the boat too jumpy to keep it in the sights long enough, eventually I gave up on the effort and called it a day. The wind finally arrived yesterday and we managed 7 hours of sailing with the wind on the beam at a steady force 3 which was a real tonic. Unfortunately, all good things come to an end, and as the sun went down the wind went with it, so it was on with the engine again. In the early hours the wind picked up again and we sailed for the rest of the third night making steady progress.

This morning I was called with the most scary call a skipper can hear at sea … "Paul the toilet has blocked". I must admit I ignored the problem until I had finished my breakfast and then I did a bit more ignoring while I had a cup of tea until, eventually, even I had to admit that I had really delayed the job for as long as I could. I girded my loins and after fetching a bundle of tools and a torch from the locker I was joined by Adamant who wanted to see how to fix a toilet (????????), which is a skill I wished I had never mastered. Joy of joys it was just the inlet/outlet switch that was stuck, so ten minutes later we have a working forward heads. To celebrate I went and sat on our all singing and all dancing electric throne in the aft cabin which promptly refused to flush. Have I ever mentioned just how much I hate toilets? I suspect the problem is that the pump is getting old and will not spin fast enough without full power and we were sailing at the time so I will try it again this afternoon when we do a generator run.

That afternoon after a tack, the aft heads decided it liked that angle and flushed perfectly so it must have been air locked, phew. Two toilets fixed and I didn't even get my hands dirty, all is definitely well with the world. The wind has stayed with us and is now blowing a steady 14-15 knots from the South East. Unfortunately, Bermuda is to the South East which means the best course that we can presently steer will take us about 60 miles north of Bermuda at best, and onto a point somewhere in the middle of the Azores. My present plan is still to try to make Bermuda, as it would be nice to fill the fuel tanks again in anticipation of the Azores high and its fluky winds.

Last night and yesterday was pretty busy with the wind jumping about the compass and constantly changing in strength keeping everyone on their toes as we tried to get as much south into our heading as we could.

What happened on the good ship *Spectra*: Norma managed to complete her painting of Grenada for Paula and Andrew, and she is slowly catching up on her self- induced backlog. A flurry of excitement met the sighting of our first whales of this trip even though they were a long way off and all that we really saw were the water spouts. Adamant won the chocolate bar challenge for the predicted log and this morning we were greeted by our first flying fish on deck, they really are smelly, you know.

That's it for now, next blog on Saturday by which time we should either be in Bermuda or we will have bypassed it and be sailing directly for the Azores.

6th Jun 2015 11:39:00
Wilmington to Bermuda Day 6 Saturday
32:22.51N 67:04.42W
550 Miles from Wilmington
9345 Miles from Ramsgate by log.

I honestly expected to be in Bermuda today but we are still slogging our way to windward. It has been a 48-hour motor with no wind followed by a 400-mile upwind beat so far, which is not exactly the pleasant cruising I had hoped for. On Thursday afternoon the wind and leeway was forcing us ever higher northward of our desired track. When we expanded the plotter display we were actually laying a course for somewhere near Belfast, and I decided enough was enough and put in a tack to drop us south in order to position ourselves for the predicted wind shift later in the day. After 8 hours of heading directly for Cuba the shift came and we tacked again, only to have the wind shift back almost immediately. Our course was now for the Azores again and, with my bottom lip sticking out, I decided that we would press on and see what happened. As the day and night progressed the wind moved from SE through S and eventually, we were seeing a bit of SW occasionally and our course dropped accordingly as we followed the wind. At first, we were pointing at Portugal, then the Canaries and finally at some point in Sub Saharan Africa. The point is, though, we are now tracking just to the south of Bermuda, hard on the wind and bowling along at 6-7 knots in a force 5-6. Living life at a 20-degree angle is not pleasant and when combined with a whole series of squalls, heavy prolonged showers, and five crew moving around in wet gear, *Spectra* is now almost as wet inside as out, or as I like to say all 'yukky'. As of 8 o'clock this morning, we find ourselves some 115 miles from Bermuda and should be there tomorrow. *Spectra* has held up well, as have the crew who have all gelled in a remarkably short space of time. Our predicted daily run competition, for the coveted prize of a chocolate bar, has now been won by Adamant twice, myself and Steve once and the girls not at all, meaning that they are without chocolate which, in my experience, can be a dangerous situation.

All of the systems have been working well apart from the wind indicator which must have been knocked or come loose as, on Port tack, it shows us sailing at up to 30 degrees from the wind (I wish) and on Starboard at 65 degrees at best. Someone will have to go up the mast in Bermuda and realign it me thinks, but who, I wonder, while sitting here looking at Steve! The other problem has been water forcing its way into the anchor lockers via the chain holes which has never been a problem before. Then again, I have never buried the bows under the waves every 5 minutes for three days before. The chain lockers sit below the waterline, which is nice as it keeps the weight low, but bad as they drain internally into the forward bilge. The accumulated muck and the odd bit of weed collected as we anchored along the ICW have found their way into the forward bilge and blocked the pump. I cleared it with a bucket and got the pump working again and then, as a temporary measure, stuffed the chain holes with rags and taped it all down to make a watertight seal. We are now all good to go again.

Wildlife: we haven't been fishing for the last couple of days, in order to conserve the Atlantic fish stock you understand, but we were visited by our first dolphins on Thursday night and a large shark was seen below the stern yesterday. The synchronised swimming practise has been cancelled for the foreseeable future. Two flying fish have now attempted Kamikaze attacks on *Spectra* and were both found dead on deck in the morning.

That's it, Bermuda is squarely in our sights and we are tracking directly on target for an arrival on Sunday. Next blog from there…….. or if not, from somewhere else; I always like to keep my options open.

7th Jun 2015 20:57:22
Wilmington to Bermuda Day 7 Arrived
32:22.689N 64:40.938W
720 Miles from Wilmington
9515 Miles from Ramsgate by log.

Norma had the privilege of catching the first glimpse of Bermuda when she sighted the Gibbs Hill lighthouse at 03:10 on Sunday morning. By 07:30 we were close enough to see the land and to contact Bermuda radio on VHF. It was really nice to hear the cool calm BBC English coming back to me on the radio; it has been a while. The reintroduction to British bureaucracy was another thing and they soon had me dashing around the boat gathering the required information:

- Type and capacity of the life raft
- SSB Radio details including call sign

- VHF Radio details including MMSI number
- EPIRB details including hexadecimal registration number
- Small Ships Register number
- Home port and country
- Departure port
- Next destination port
- Crew and nationality
- Boat type
- Length in feet
- Depth in feet
- Name of vessel phonetically
- Do we carry in date electronic charts of Bermuda?
- Do we carry in date paper charts of Bermuda?

I think that was about it – the most information ever requested but all done very calmly and professionally.

The morning passed as we sailed the length of Bermuda in a gentle South Westerly breeze finally arriving at the Customs Office in St Georges just after lunch. We are now moored stern to at Captain Smokes Marina which consists of a wall with enough space for five yachts. It has one shower, wi-fi, a really happy pair of old gents running it and all for $2 per foot which is extortionate but then everyone had warned us that Bermuda was expensive.

The journey over took a day longer than expected and two days longer than I had hoped for but, considering two days of no wind followed by two days of heavy headwinds, we are lucky to have made it at all. We will catch our breath here and restock. The plan is to head out again on the 9th, which incidentally is also my birthday, so I will blog again before we head for the Azores and our meet with our final crew member, Willem.

Tale of the tape:
720 miles run – 668 by Rhumb line.
Average Miles run 120 NM per day.

Eng hours		56	
Generator Hours		15	
Water	maker	Hours	6

BERMUDA TO FLORES, AZORES

JUNE 2015

9th Jun 2015 14:16:29
Bermuda Departure day and my Birthday
32:22.689N 64:40.938W
9515 Miles from Ramsgate by log.

Bermuda is one of the nicest places we have visited. The people are friendly and polite, the officials efficient and welcoming and the island itself a real jewel in the ocean. I haven't seen a single bit of graffiti anywhere and less litter than anywhere I can think of. In fact, the whole place has a feeling of honest civic pride about it. As you can tell I, am impressed and it has been more than worth the upwind slog and days of motoring to get here.

Day two, AM, was spent sorting out the boat. We had a few minor sail repairs to attend to and I swapped my battery chargers around so that the new 80-amp unit is now going into the domestic bank and the old 40-amp unit is now connected to the engine batteries and switched off, as it is not usually needed as the engine batteries are isolated as soon as the main engine is switched off. That should not only reduce our generator run time but also allow me to run the water maker for the whole period that the generator is on. Norma and Jen talked the dockmaster into driving them into town with a mountain of washing and also our gas bottles to attempt to get them filled. We all finally met up again at lunchtime with the plan to go into Hamilton. Typically, just as we were about to leave, Norma gave the deck wash outlet a quick test and the pipe under the galley ceiling burst again flooding the place, Bugger! It really wasn't that much of a drama, we had it all fixed within half an hour and were again ready to go. The scorching hot weather was described by the dockmaster as a 'real Sally Bassett day' which stopped me in my tracks and got me questioning him on the terminology.

The story goes:
In 1730 Sarah (or Sally or Sary) Bassett, a slave valued at 1 pound, was burnt at the stake having been found guilty, under dubious evidence, of poisoning her owner. It was an exceptionally hot day when she was executed and now, on the Island, really hot days are sometimes referred to as, "a real Sally Bassett day".

The bus ride into Hamilton was a scenic delight with azure seas and brightly painted houses around every bend. Hamilton itself was a bit busy as a cruise liner had docked but, not to be put off, Norma went into shopping mode and I dutifully tagged along, showing the required level of interest in each and every trinket that she discovered. The others, mutinous bunch that they are, abandoned me and went sightseeing on their own. We all met up again at 5 pm and jumped on the bus to go back to *Spectra*. After a quick pit stop on the boat, the early evening found the 'Famous Five' walking through Georgetown on their way to Tobacco Bay for a swim.

More History:

Tobacco Bay was the scene of the Bermuda Gunpowder Plot. During the American War of Independence (or the First Civil War as I like to call it), the Americans were rather short of gunpowder. A group of intrepid Bermudan entrepreneurs, who were sympathetic to the American, (or treacherous dogs, depending on your stance, I suppose) stole 100 barrels of gunpowder from the Royal Arsenal in Georgetown and gave it to a group of passing American ships in return for trading rights. Tobacco Bay was where the transfer of goods took place.

That's it for the history of the bay, as for the present day it was a lovely little beach, the sea was warm and the snorkelling good. Later we walked up to Fort St Katherine on the headland and had a very good meal in the restaurant as the sun went down. No green flash but a fitting final night in this lovely island. Before the meal, Norma and Jen went through the female gymnastics required to change out of swimwear and into evening clothes while hiding behind a towel in the car park, classy bunch that we are. Steve was all dry as he had decided not to take to the waters that day, whilst Adamant and myself just drip dried whilst we ate.

Today is my birthday and we are setting off again. At the grand old age of 52 I must say that life has been very kind. Unfortunately, it's the weekends that are killing me. The morning is given over to personal choice but we have planned to all meet up at the boat again by three o'clock and so we should be good to go by 4. The fuel dock is only 100 metres or so around the corner and Customs a short walk from there. The plan is that, while the guys get *Spectra* all topped up, I will clear Customs and we should be out of the cut by 17:00 if all goes well. Due to bad planning on my part, I am on Mother Watch tonight and will have to make my own birthday dinner. Don't feel too sorry for me though, I am, after all, sailing on a blue ocean in a lovely boat, with a great group of people, and a wife I love, so life ain't half bad, is it?

On that note, without her kind permission , I have reproduced Sue Foster's article about Norma from the Royal Temple Yacht Club's 'Temple Newsletter'...see below.

IN PRAISE OF MRS RUSSELL

Now, here's the challenge – plan menus and shop for supplies to feed and water 5-6 people for 5-6 weeks. You cannot pop out to Waitrose if you have missed something in the middle of the Atlantic.

It's tricky enough to plan for two for a few days. Norma compiled the meal plans and shopping lists to take care of their crew on the return leg of their cruise. Being a shopper of Olympic standard does have its advantages, especially when shopping in the USA – we are, after all, divided by a common language!

Tommy and I have just returned from North Carolina where Norma and Paul were preparing for the journey home to Ramsgate. *Spectra* was lifted out and scrubbed down and all mechanical/technical items were checked/replaced/mended in readiness. No doubt you have read Paul's very entertaining blog, so I will not elaborate.

However, it is the logistics of feeding and caring for a crew for an extended voyage that has left me in awe of Norma's organisation skills. Catering is one of the most important aspects of a long trip that keeps the crew's morale high. Norma has a freezer full of meat and fish and cupboards full of tins (their record for catching their dinner on the trip is pretty poor so could not be relied upon to supplement the larder!). Also included are umpteen cartons of long-life milk, dozens of eggs and large bags of flour for baking fresh bread. Apparently, the smell of a freshly baked loaf is very uplifting in mid-ocean. I can only imagine that and have no plans to find out!

Also brought on board was a huge box of wet wipes to prevent smelly bodies in the event the water-maker breaks down and showers are taken off the agenda.

Norma has used her time on this trip to great effect, having decided to teach herself the ukulele (we have noticed a vast improvement since Barbados at Christmas when we were treated to numerous renditions of 'Jingle Bells') and her painting has come on in leaps and bounds and she has produced some very creditable impressions of their journey.

We now look forward to seeing them back in the Royal Harbour. They departed America on 31 May and hope to arrive early-mid July, planning to pitch up on a Saturday. We hope to have a party at the club to welcome them so, as soon as we have a firm date, will let everyone know. In the meantime, we wish them a safe journey with kind weather.

Sue Foster

PS: For Sue and Tommy, Thanks for the T shirt but I'm keeping my old faithful there are years of life in that yet.

PPS: That's it for this one next blog in a couple of days hopefully while heading Eastwards at 7 knots.

11th June 2015 20:10:49
Bermuda to Flores, Azores 1

33:17.72N 61:01.66W

190 miles from Bermuda

9705 Miles from Ramsgate by log.

Two nights out and all is well. The clearance from Bermuda went without a hitch and having topped up on diesel and petrol we are now on our way to Flores in the Azores. The island was in turmoil as we departed as there had been a bank raid in the capitol Hamilton. Not the brightest of moves I would have thought on an island 14 miles long , the Police were busily tracking the gang of blaggers down as we sailed away, (note to self, check bilges for stowaway, masked men). After calling up for permission to go through St George's narrow cut and out to sea, a final farewell from Bermuda radio came through wishing us a safe and pleasant journey and inviting us to come again. That really summed up just how pleasant and friendly a place Bermuda is, but oh so expensive. Norma was really ill for the first 24 hours having, we suspect, picked up a dose of food poisoning on our last day and so she was confined to bed for the first night and I covered her watch pattern. I decided that we would keep going for 4 hours and if her condition began to deteriorate, we would head back in. Fortunately for the passage planning, once tucked up in bed she was fairly content (if sick, and miserable) and on we went. Back up again now she is busily organising my daily life, I really can't understand how

I managed to get through the last 24 hours without her help.

My birthday kind of slipped by lost in the activities of getting us to sea again, but it was nice to get emails from family and friends in the morning and, of course, a card, kiss and present from Norma. A highlight of the day was that I got the opportunity to duck a gossipy and shrewish woman in the harbour, so here is the story of that little side show. As Norma and myself walked through the town on the final morning a historical re-enactment of a public ducking was getting underway and I was asked to help operate the ducking stool. Always willing to lend a hand, I spent a happy 20 minutes ducking a 17th century woman in the harbour who had been found guilty of gossiping and acting in a shrewish manor. The historical re-enactment members really got into their roles with lots of rushing around, cries for clemency and appeals to the crowd's better nature. The evidence was clear, she was definitely of a shrewish temperament and so into the ducking stool she went for three good ducks in the harbour which cooled her ardour. My civic duty complete, we left a repentant and very wet woman behind us as we walked back to *Spectra*; I loved it, and I think it made a lasting impression on Norma as she has been very attentive and not at all shrewish ever since. What really made my day was, after the first evening meal at sea, Jen and the guys gave me a card and present from the crew. I am now the proud owner of a bright white Pith helmet that Tommy Foster will just hate on sight but, I must say, it is my best hat everrrr, and I love it.

The wind was predicted to be very light for a few days but we got lucky over the first 24 hours and were soon scooting along heading North East at 5 to 7 knots in a steady(ish) North West force 3-4. The only downside has been a counter-current of about 1 knot which has slowed us a bit. On the second day out, the predicted light winds arrived and we had to turn on the engine twice when it went dead calm. The upside of motoring for a few hours has been that the diesel smell down below has now dissipated. When I went to clear Customs leaving *Spectra* on the fuel jetty, I asked the guys to "fill her right up" and they took me at my word, filling the tanks up to deck level. As the fuel level has now dropped back into the tanks the smell has gone which is a very, very good thing indeed. Even with the wind dropping, overall progress has been good and I am more than pleased so far.

This morning I managed to get a weather report on the SSB and, amongst other things, the Tropical Storm Centre (Center) in America reports no storms predicted in the next five days which always gives you a warm fluffy feeling.

That's about it; Steve managed to catch a seagull on the fishing line today (not on the hook, I hasten to add) and it was one seriously peeved bird by the time we had reeled him in and set him free. Adamant has taken up Astro-navigation with a will and is plotting all over my charts while I still cheat by taking the sights and then punching the results into an App on my cell phone. Jen is sooo keen and enthusiastic about everything that she wears me out just watching her and, of course, a fully recovered Norma continues to keep us all on the straight and narrow, well fed, rested and sane.

PS: That's it for this one, next blog in a couple of days will be from Jen. Yes, you guessed it, she volunteered!!

13th Jun 2015 14:58:08
Bermuda to Flores, Azores 2, Jen has her say!
36:01.76N 57:29.768W
426 Miles from Bermuda
9529 Miles from Ramsgate by log.

Captain's bit:
Progress has been frustratingly slow so far. We had a good first 24 hour run and then sailed into a big hole of nothingness. After downloading a GRIB file (weather report) I found wind developing to the north of us and so we turned our nose towards Greenland and motored for 24 hours to get us up above 35 degrees of latitude. We did indeed pick up a light westerly wind but it was not to last. After 18 hours of slow sailing to the North East the wind died again and on went the engine. On the bright side, now that we are above 36 degrees the contra-current has switched

in our favour, the crew are all disgustingly happy, well fed, and healthy, there have even been reports of people enjoying themselves, which is a worry!! I will, from today, instigate a routine of meaningless tasks, hard tack and regular beatings in order to bring morale down to a level that makes me look like the happy one.

That's it from Paul, now onto Jen's bit:

Jens First Ever Blog! Day 3 of our journey from Bermuda to Azores.

Firstly 'Hello' from me! I was a stray that was rescued by Norma and Paul. Actually, to be more precise, I'm an escapee from another sailing yacht in Florida that wasn't at all ready for her planned voyage across the Atlantic. Luckily my friend Georgina (with whom I studied my Day Skipper Theory) put me in touch with Norma and Paul. By pure fluke I found that they were sailing right near me, and I managed to get my previous skipper to give me a lift to meet them. Now I find myself about a month later surrounded by a Ramsgate crowd (except Adamant). I can sail with *Spectra* all the way home and have a drink in the Royal Temple Yacht Club! How amazing is life sometimes!

As I'm a beginner, I have learnt so much already and still much to learn. Norma, Paul, Steve and Adamant all have a weighty bag of knowledge and experience, so I couldn't have wished for a better crew. My favourite shifts are the night ones, after doing my first checks for other vessels, check all gadget readings, check sails and then inspect the sky for clouds that may cause us a problem. I then find the stars Steve taught me such as Venus, Jupiter, Saturn; he hasn't shown me Uranus yet! Following the Plough to find the Northern star. There's nothing better than admiring the vast array of stars in the sky, watching *Spectra* glide through the water, and then seeing the waves we created sparkle with plankton. It is magical.

Last night I saw, what looked like, a burning red light on the horizon... it seemed so close I wasn't sure how I missed it. I was so concerned I changed our course 20 degrees N and ran to wake Paul from his deep sleep and comfortable bed. As I came up on deck again, I saw that the red light had grown in size very rapidly and now made the shape of a sail. Once Paul was on deck, I calmed and looked at the shape again... and to my embarrassment I realised what it really was! I turned to Paul and said 'oh no! it's the moon isn't it!..I'm so sorry!!!' He laughed it off and went back to sleep. Phew!

During the last few days we have been playing with the sextant... later Paul is going to help me plot my reading on the chart. Adamant is working it out the hard way whereas Paul is using his app!!! Haha! Adamant seems to know so much information and it turns out he taught himself, he seems very dedicated to learning. Puts me to shame.

At the moment we are heading NE with the engine on (to our dismay) as we found ourselves in the middle of a high-pressure system with no wind, and the weather forecast informed us that we would have been stuck for 5 days until some wind came to us. Going 100 nautical miles NE should help us pick up the westerly winds and then we can put all the sails back up. Four is normal, foresail, staysail, mainsail and mizzen! We put the cruising sail up for a bit this morning when we still had a breeze, but it didn't last long.

We still have not caught any fish! I joked that we should write to the manufacturer of the lures (the colourful things we have on the end of the fishing line, for people like me, that have no idea about fishing terms!) and tell them to rebrand it for birds. So far, we have caught 3 birds and 0 fish. My heart sunk every time a bird got caught in the line, and then I was so relieved when Steve and I managed to set them free with no damage done. Poor things...sore wings and Steve telling them that they are stupid!

We usually make bets on the ETA of our next landfall, and also how many miles we have achieved over the last 24 hours. Paul seems to have won twice in a row...do you suspect anything?!? I was accused of being a pessimist when I guessed that we would arrive in Bermuda at 3pm on Sunday 7th June.... But again, by a bit of a fluke I won (I should have lied and told you I spent many hours working it out!), we didn't plan for the fact that Bermuda is one hour forward from American time (so that helped me out)! Snickers bar for me! Yay! Our next landfall is the Azores... again we made our bets… We have all guessed around the 21st - 22nd except for Adamant who guessed the 27th! And he would have been right if we had stayed on our previous course and not acted on the weather report. If you are reading this blog why don't you make a bet for when we arrive and treat yourself to a special drink or a chocolate bar if you guess right?

  Norma has now fully recovered from her tummy bug/food poisoning you'll be glad to hear, and her spirits are high again. I'm looking forward to seeing Norma's next piece of artwork, the last one was lovely and I'm trying to coax her out of the cabin when she practises her ukulele, so that I can listen to her on my shift. She is a very talented person and inspiring to be around.

  Day 4- What a fab day! We have wind! Whoo! We put up some sails I've never seen on *Spectra* which were the cruising chute (asymmetric) and the mizzen stay sail. These two sails are brightly coloured with purple, green and white and are made from a lighter weight fabric, than the main. They look stunning! I just wished we had some other boats to make jealous, but we don't! We have seen three tankers over the last few days, but in the far distance. We managed to get up to 6.5 knots, which was a great sense of achievement considering our last few days.

  At 2pm I started my Mother Watch and started preparing fishcakes for dinner. I came up for some fresh air and with perfect timing, 6 dolphins came swimming next to us, two made a small jump out of the water by the bow, showing their light grey smooth bodies with speckles on their heads. It made my day! Paul commented that they were different to the others he had seen as they were usually dark slate grey.

I just found out that I missed the 24 hour mileage competition by 2 nautical miles! Steve guessed 115 and I guessed 114, the correct answer was 116!!! Damn it! Tomorrow... I'll try again!

P.S I was reminded by Paul before writing my piece how to spell two things correctly.... 'Russell' and 'Brilliant' and he commented both have two 'l's' so I thought I had best make sure everyone else knows how to spell those two words too, as they seem very important!

I'm being warned by Steve that I'm going to block up the system with my essay... so I better stop now. It was nice writing my first blog and I hope I didn't bore you

15th Jun 2015 10:16:00
Bermuda to Flores, Azores 3, Strong winds and wet decks
36:20.21N 50:43.50W
759 Miles from Bermuda
9862 Miles from Ramsgate by log.

The crew remain disgustingly happy with their lot, despite my best efforts, and so I am considering a long, slow, keel hauling - that should sort them out. Adamant has attacked our brass work with a bottle of lemon juice and a scouring pad and the results are, frankly, amazing. He seems keen to get everything all shiny so we will probably have to wear sunglasses below decks before long. Jen is busily completing her Yachtmaster theory course and you wander through the saloon at your peril... "Paul? Adamant? Steve? Norma? could you just have a look at this secondary port calculation for me?" It's so much easier in the UK, www.easytide.com is the way forward, I think. Knot tying practise, explanations on the intricacies of bilge pumps, sea cocks, winches and spinnaker launching are all par for the course if you are careless enough to wander within Jen's learning bubble. I was even cajoled into giving a 10-minute lecture on that most dangerous of beasts, the marine toilet and all of its internal machinations. Norma has completed another picture and is busily sewing the flags of all nations onto a halyard for our return, whilst Steve continues to fish...............and fish............and... .Not Catch Much.

I, on the other hand, when not sleeping or being all "Master and Commanderish", spend my days trying to think of something to put in these blogs.

The weather has turned in our favour. We have now been barrelling along for over 24 hours with a steady force 5-6 from the west. According to the GRIB files, we should have good winds for the next three days, four if we can keep the speed up and stay in the low-pressure zone for longer. Last night I was awakened at midnight by Jen as the wind was up, it was pouring with rain and she thought we needed a reef. Typically, just as I came on deck, the wind reduced and so I made us both a nice cup of tea and awaited developments. I was just explaining to Jen my theory that all skipper decisions come better after a nice cup of tea when the wind suddenly blew up to 30 knots and *Spectra* responded with 9.5 knots through the water. Half-finished tea or not, it was time to reef and we quickly rolled half of the foresail away. That reduced our speed back into the 7-8 knot bracket and all was well with the world. Apart from the torrential rain, of course. On the next shift, not to be beaten, Steve hit 9.7 knots even with a reef in the main and half of the foresail away; as you can tell, we have been making good progress at last.

Here are our daily 24 hour runs so far:
- Day 1   74 miles (15 hours)
- Day 2   115 miles (Part motoring)
- Day 3   141 miles (All motoring)
- Day 4   116 miles (Part Motoring)
- Day 5   161 miles (All sailing)
- Day 6   172 miles (All sailing)

We reached somewhat of a milestone last night when, for the first time since the crossing of Biscay last year, I pulled on a pair of socks to keep my tootsies warm. Ah, the Caribbean sun is already a fading memory. This morning, I am glad to report that my feet are once again naked and out in the open for both the edification and delight of all who survey them as the sun is up and the skies are blue once more.

Wildlife: apart from a multitude of sea birds, animal life has been a bit on the scarce side, to be honest. Adamant sighted a whale breaching in the far distance yesterday and we have had pods of spotted dolphin playing around the boat for very short periods on two occasions and that's it really. The most prolific wildlife has been Portuguese Man-O-Wars which have been continuously floating by in sizes ranging from a 5 pence piece up to monsters that would fill a dinner plate.

Later in the day, and not to be beaten by Steve, I had a mini squall come through whilst I was on watch which launched all 20 tonnes of *Spectra* down the face of a wave in a shower of foam. After the old girl had settled herself down and got back on course I prised my fingers from the wheel and checked the speed dial which now had a new maximum speed registered of 10.7 knots! Needless to say, the second reef is now in the main and the crew have been absolutely forbidden to try and beat the new top speed while the Skipper had a sit down with a nice cup of tea to steady his nerves.

Last night the wind increased to force 8 for a few hours with heavy, squally showers which was, let us say, less than pleasant for the on-watch crew and not very nice for the off-watch sleepers either. The wind has now settled into a steady force 7 Westerly with constant driving rain but still the crew remain all chipper and upbeat. There has even been laughter reported in the early hours, for crying out loud. *Spectra* has handled the weather with her usual good grace and has carried us through with calm, safe, assurance; this boat is really made to be out here, you know. Yesterday, in a mid-Atlantic force 7, I made a full Sunday roast for four, plus a breaded salmon fillet for Adamant, with all of the trimmings - Yorkshire puddings and a hollandaise sauce. For dessert I made a bread and butter pudding with custard. What's more, we all managed to sit around the table to eat it without any ending up on the floor; try that in a lightweight, modern cruiser.

That's it for now, we are all safe, well and, even if a bit on the moist side, finally making excellent progress towards Flores in the Azores.

17th Jun 2015 17:02:00
Bermuda to Flores, Azores 4...Norma has her say.
36:27.21N 45:32.93W
735 Miles to the Azores

10,132 Miles from Ramsgate by log.

Captain's bit: We have completed over 10,000 miles since leaving Ramsgate, happy days.

All going well, with no breakages to speak of. After the last blog we had another 24 hours of F7 with 6 hours of F8 in the middle which Norma will, no doubt, mention in her dispatches below. We crossed the half way to the Azores mark on Tuesday morning and, hopefully, it will be all downhill from here. The 24-hour run, tale of the tape, so far, is:

Day 1	74 miles (15 hours)
Day 2	115 miles (Part motoring)
Day 3	141 miles (All motoring)
Day 4	116 miles (Part Motoring)
Day 5	161 miles (All sailing)
Day 6	172 miles (All sailing)
Day 7	149 miles (All sailing)
Day 8	121 miles (Part Motoring)

Waves, Wind & Rain (lots of all)

While sitting down below in the warm and dry, the urge to feed that old monkey that I carry around on my back grew ever stronger. (Smoking, yuk...PR)

With waves as high as houses and rain falling so hard it could cut through you like a knife I had no other choice than to go outside and join a very wet Steve and Jen at the wheel. I wasn't officially on watch but that monkey was needing to be fed, so up I went.

On opening the hatch, I was greeted with an almighty barrage of swear words that I thought were from Steve, (he can be a big girl sometimes) but no, (sorry Jen's mum and dad), it was Jen. She did have good reason though, when I popped my head out, *Spectra's* side rails were completely under a very large wave which, in turn, was filling up the cockpit with crystal clear water up to above her knees. I asked myself "why am I doing this?" But then quickly talked myself out of retreating as the urge to feed that monkey grew stronger than the fear of the soaking I was about to receive.

Later, with the monkey fed and my watch officially started, Jen and Steve started slipping away to the warmth below to dry out before their next watch. Left alone, I mused over the fury around me. OMG what a sight, with 3 reefs in the main; 2 reefs in the mizzen; 1 reef in the stay sail and no foresail at all, good old girl *Spectra* was holding her own in a force 8 gale. As for me, I was strapped to the cockpit with two harnesses for that extra comfort and, of course safety, which is something I will later regret. Body contortions were something I didn't envisage at my age but, to get out of the knots that I managed to tie myself into, they are a must. Being on watch means exactly that, eyes everywhere which involves doing a full 360° every 5-10 minutes to check for other things that are like us, mad enough to be out here.

At one point during my watch my heart was in my mouth as Paul and Steve had to go forward on deck to secure the spinnaker pole which was shaking itself to death. As they got themselves into position a very large wave picked up *Spectra*, her bow rising in the air almost vertically and I, of course, knew what had to come next. Yes, she would have to come back down. In my mind's eye I could just see two little men, (did I say little, I meant men, although they did look very small with those huge waves as a backdrop), being thrown over either side. Although they were strapped on it would not have been pretty or easy to retrieve them both at the same time and quickly, a choice would have to be made; (sorry Paul) Steve is just that little bit smaller. No need to worry, all was well; they stuck fast to the deck, riding the waves and did not even feel what I had just seen.

Whilst all this furore was going on above, Adamant still maintained his work ethic and continued polishing our brass clocks to within an inch of their lives and, as Jen would say, "with amazing" results.

Two hours later, when my watch had come to an end and my heart was back in my chest, my thoughts went straight to drying out and feeding my crew as I was now on Mummy Watch. Oh, for some well-earned hot food and sleep.

The gale wasn't all bad though, during one of my 360's in the cockpit, I spotted dolphins surfing the waves right next to me or, should I say, above me. The happily playing dolphins looked as if they could land on the aft deck at any moment. I did another quick spin in the opposite direction to retrieve my phone and started snapping, not sure of the results. Later, to my amazement, on reviewing the pictures I had managed to get a shot, but I am afraid you will have to wait for that one until we are in port and have decent internet access and it will be accompanied by many more of Mother Nature's Fury. (By the way my next painting will be named Fury) so you can sort of guess what it will be about.

PS: Note for Kate: those trans-Atlantic flights are now, more than ever, looking really inviting.

19th Jun 2015 14:27:12
Bermuda to Flores, Azores 5 ... just bob-bob-bobbing along
37:35.81N 40:11.41W
423 Miles to the Azores
10,380 Miles from Ramsgate by log.

Day 1	74 miles (15 hours)
Day 2	115 miles (Part motoring)
Day 3	141 miles (All motoring)
Day 4	116 miles (Part Motoring)
Day 5	161 miles (All sailing)
Day 6	172 miles (All sailing)
Day 7	149 miles (All sailing)
Day 8	121 miles (Part Motoring)
Day 9	129 miles (All sailing)

Day 10   119 miles (All sailing)

The arrival lottery stands at:

Paul 21st AM – almost definitely missed.

Norma 21st PM – probably missed.

Jen 22nd AM – outside chance

Steve 22nd PM – Still in with a shout

Willem – 25th. A late bet by email, could be a winner if the winds go light.

Adamant 27th – Now that is just being a bloody pessimist!

Why not have a guess yourself it is a great game for all the family (Guess the ETA © Spectra 2015, 1 or more players aged 5 to 80, sorry Roger)

Day 10 completed and all is going well apart from the fact that we have run out of eggs. That makes sixty that we have eaten since leaving Wilmington! On a brighter note, we have hardly used any toilet paper and the heads remain in pristine condition, perhaps there is a connection that I am missing? On a more serious note, we are just about finished with the fresh food. Apart from potatoes and onions, which always last a long time, we are down to a couple of carrots, half a cabbage and a squash. After that it will be tins, packets, dried fruit and the contents of the freezer until the Azores.

Ramadan has started and Adamant has gone all nocturnal with his eating habits but, apart from that, the normal routines continue apace. Yesterday, to break the monotony and as the wind had died, I offered the chance for a mid-Atlantic swim, we only had one taker. So here are the stats, Latitude 36.36.39N, Longitude 44.47.82W in an area near the Corner Seamounts and with a depth of 5,000 metres Jen dived over the side. I would like to say she surfaced in a shower of translucent bubbles and glided through the water like a sea nymph but the reality was a lot splashier and had a certain "OK, done it, now get me back on board"-ishness about it. But credit where credit is due, Jen is now a fully paid up member of the 'Mid-Atlantic Swimming Club'. Whilst on the subject of things that swim, we have been joined on several occasions by pods of spotted dolphins and have also sighted two turtles drifting by busily chowing down on Portuguese Man-O-Wars. It is quite surprising that the dolphins can survive in this barren ocean as evidenced by the results of our fishing, there are, in my humble opinion, NO FISH OUT HERE!

After a very light wind day, the wind finally settled into the South around midnight on the 17/18th and has blown a fairly consistent force 3-4 ever since, which means we are trotting along happily at between 6 and 7 knots without any fuss at all. That is until the wind drops to force 2-3 when we slog along at 4 knots. The all-natural polishing of the brass work down below is steaming ahead, with Adamant determined to keep his mind off food during daylight hours he is like a man possessed - if it is metal it gets a squirt of lemon juice and an attack with the polishing pad. I am doing my part by eating his share of the Snickers bar stash and keeping him honest by reminding him, on a regular basis, that lemon is a food so he can't lick his fingers or take a tea break until the moon comes up. The flags of all nations have been sewn onto the bunting lines by Norma and just need the addition of the Azores and Portuguese flags to be a complete set of all of the countries that we have visited on our little trip. Steve and I have repaired the latest ravages to my stay sail, spending a happy hour yesterday morning on the fore deck gently bouncing up and down whilst sewing a section of ripped sacrificial strip. I made the mistake of mentioning, in casual conversation as you do, the internal workings of a yacht winch while standing within Jens learning bubble, and so now we have added servicing all of the winches to our 'jobs to do' list. So far, Jen and I have stripped and serviced two single-speed and one double-speed winch on the mainmast; so, just 8 to go then!

Last night was the calmest yet and we all had a good night's sleep as *Spectra* ghosted along at 5 knots on a smooth ocean. That's it for now, I am Mummy from 2pm onwards today and I have made the bread up this morning. After sending this it should have risen and be ready for the oven. Calm seas, the smell of baking bread and the sound of Adamant scraping away at the latest bit of tarnished brass as we gently close down the distance to the Azores – life is sweet aboard the good ship *Spectra*.

21st Jun 2015 12:52:24
Bermuda to Flores, Azores 6 ... Nearly lost the mast by Jen
38:30.172N 34:54.966W
180 Miles to The Azores
10,380 Miles from Ramsgate by log.

Due to bad weather and violent bumping, my old silver laptop has finally died. Unfortunately, it took 4 or 5 unread emails with it which we cannot now recover. If you sent *Spectra* an email between PM on the 19th and PM on the 20th would you resend them please?

The last two days have been altogether too eventful by far. Firstly, we were in line for breaking our daily run record of 187 miles when the forestay broke away from the bowsprit and caused several hours of mayhem in the dark. While sailing at 8 knots with the foresail poled out to starboard the 12mm thick bar that holds the forestay and furling gear in place sheared along the weld line and set the beast flying in the breeze. How we tamed it is covered by Jen below, but we now have three halyards running to the bowsprit end and cranked in hard so everything is solid again. Providing that we don't do anything silly like pulling up the full mainsail, the main mast is now in no immediate danger of falling down. The following morning, I repaired the beaten-up starboard navigation light that had been torn from the rail in the night and later Steve reattached it. Surprise, surprise it lit up first try. We do have a secondary attachment position for a forestay so, if we can't find a welder in Flores, all is not lost but there is no way we can get it connected in the conditions we are presently under – very short lumpy seas and 20+ knots of wind. It will have to wait. In the meantime, we are still managing 4-5 knots average under stay sail and Mizzen (jib and jigger), which is our storm rig, so I am pretty impressed with that. Occasionally, I also put the main up with 3 reefs, this brings the head in line with the staysail head and lower spreaders which keeps it securely stayed. Our present ETA from the plotter is in the PM of the 22nd so fingers crossed we will be drinking cold beer in a day or two. All is well with the gallant crew in our little green boat except for my little finger that got itself caught while wrestling with the forestay and rather hammered into the deck splitting the pad wide open, which is just about as painful as it sounds. Norma has told me that I am a brave little sailor and assures me that my dancing career is not over so all is well with the world. The light at the end of the tunnel has dimmed but remains on. Now here are some stats and then Jen can have her say.

Day 1   74 miles (15 hours)
Day 2   115 miles (Part motoring)
Day 3   141 miles (All motoring)
Day 4   116 miles (Part Motoring)
Day 5   161 miles (All sailing)
Day 6   172 miles (All sailing)
Day 7   149 miles (All sailing)
Day 8   121 miles (Part Motoring)
Day 9   129 miles (All sailing)
Day 10 119 miles (All sailing)
Day 11 157 miles (All sailing) ½ under reduced rig
Day 12 121 miles (All sailing under reduced rig)

The arrival lottery now stands at:

Paul 21st AM – missed by a mile

Norma 21st PM – No chance now

Jen 22nd AM – 100/1 shot

Steve 22nd PM – On target for the chocolate bar

Willem 25th – Could be a winner if the winds go very light or something breaks.

Adamant 27th – Still being a bloody pessimist.

Hello to you all, it's Jen again!

Not much happened yesterday daytime, the water was calm and the wind was soft and, despite that, we had been doing a steady 8 knots. We kept referring to the Chart plotter (that had been temperamental since the gale) and talking about our bets. It was looking like a very close competition between Steve and I. By the close of the day Norma was looking like she may actually be the winner.

It feels so good to think we are only 2 or 3 days away from land. A place where I can dig my feet into the sand and watch it fall through. Where I can sit at a table and eat my dinner without worrying about it rolling away or landing onto someone else's plate. Where I can take a shower and not have to turn it off between washing and best of all I can stand up straight, rather than doing my own version of yoga in the bathroom, to stop falling over. All these little things I have started to cherish and wish for. As edible things go, a glass of wine and a bite of dark chocolate is on my list. Steve told me not to get my hopes up, it is an island, but how could any place not have these two things? I have my fingers crossed!

I went to bed to get some kip before my shift 12-2am......went into a sweet sleep...

AARRRGGGHHHH!!!!!! MAYHEM OCCURRED!

I was woken by Norma shouting 'JEN.. we need you on deck NOW!' Waking from my sleep, I hurriedly put on my life jacket and rushed up. I heard some awful noises and tried not to overreact to my imagination.

I went up on deck, it was dark already, but the deck was flooded with a strong white light. To my surprise I saw Paul, swamped by a sail on the foredeck. It took me a few seconds to absorb the carnage. The forestay had ripped out of the deck and was now swinging in the wind, Steve and Adamant were trying to hold it in place. I was requested to stay in the cockpit and look out for ships while everyone else could concentrate on the mess. Norma pulled the foresail down the port side of *Spectra* and tied it down with sail straps. Paul and Steve continued to try to fix the forestay to the foredeck. We undid the sheets and other bits of ropes unneeded so Paul, Steve and Adamant could rig something up to make this lump of metal stop moving. I was so worried that it would land on someone's foot the way it kept lifting in the wind and clunking down. Paul made a yelp, and Norma rushed to attend to him (pretty useful having a first-aider as a wife). He had crushed his little finger and it was bleeding badly. Ouch!!! Now he is all bandaged up, poor little finger.

Luckily the men managed to secure the stay down, not in its original place but to starboard foredeck and shrouds. The next thing was to take the strain of the main sail from the mast, as the forestay is a support for the main mast. We took the main sail down and packed it away, and then released the boom so it rested on the deck. We secured this down too. We looked at what was left to sail us to the Azores for a further 3 days... we still have the staysail and the mizzen. The deck looked much more organised than the hour before. We put the kettle on and had a cup of tea. Yes, sooo English!

We have managed to continue at a speed of 4-5 knots. We do have enough fuel to engine us into safety if need be. Now we will have to find a welder in the Azores to fix up *Spectra*. I could see a cloud over Norma and Paul today as they woke to the horrible reality, I do feel so sad for them. Their beautiful bird has damaged wings, but I know it will get fixed and it will just add to the many amazing crazy stories of their adventure.

Jen's take on her latest experiences with *Spectra*

Well, there I was on my shift, staring into the mass of sea trying to think of things to write about; as all the exciting events had happened earlier in the week and had been written about already; this was before the dramatic events of the night such as the gale force winds we endured. Firstly, I'd like to stick up for myself. Anyone who was in my position would have sworn if they had been sitting on *Spectra* as she tumbled down the 10 foot waves, which pushed her completely on her side for a good amount of seconds, meaning the water came too close for comfort. The wind was so strong it was picking up the top layer of the sea, making visibility poor, the rain hit my face with such force it felt like little needles. My fingers were all shrivelled after being on deck for 5 hours (out of choice), I looked like I'd been in the bath way too long, if only that had been the case! I'd rather see what's going on than be taunted by the noises of creaking and water splashing against the side with great force. I have too much of a wild imagination, not the best thing at sea! I managed to bite my tongue for the rest of Steve's shift. Thankfully, there was no one to listen to my language when I was on my own shift. Strangely enough I wasn't scared, I felt quite safe, which was to the contrary of what I expected of myself.

My Atlantic swim, or 'dip' as Paul put it, surprised me greatly as the sea was so warm! I did a little scream on entering the water and I thought I would scream again with hitting the coldness too, but all that came was surprised pleasure. Even though *Spectra* had all sails down and her motor off, she still pressed though the water faster than I could swim. So, I quickly put the life ring around me and promptly got out before a Portuguese Man-O-War came to sting me; they worried me more than the 3 miles of water under my feet.

Well that's all for now. We are all a bit tired of the current motion of the boat, as we have big waves coming right on our starboard side, making it difficult to do anything, even sleeping. Thank God only two more days to a three-course meal! And yes, I'll treat myself to all the trimmings!

Over and out.

22nd Jun 2015 11:49:18
Bermuda to Flores, Azores 7 … The final run in
39:09.56N 32:10.74W

60 Miles to The Azores
10,918 Miles from Ramsgate by log.

    We have aboard *Spectra* an old Singer sewing machine that was kindly gifted to us by Peter Duke. It is the type your mother would have had, black with gold trimmings, a crank handle on one side and it all comes in its original Singer dome-shaped, wooded box. Oh, and in case you have never tried to lift one of those machines, they are very, very heavy. Do you get the picture? It is a lovely piece of engineering and lives on a shelf at the bottom of my bed securely restrained by a 4" high rail. I was awakened this morning when our Singer sewing machine leapt over its 4" high retaining bar and landed on my feet, lovely start to the day and a fitting end to a really s"£$""# night. On the bright side, it's a good job I wasn't sleeping the other way around or I would have a Singer sewing machine hat. The wind died at about 17:00 yesterday for a couple of hours, leaving us rolling like a dog and so on went the engine. Finally, the wind started to come back but it was extremely gusty and changeable. By midnight it had gone from SE into the West and by dawn it was a Northerly. The result of this is that the confused lumpy seas that we were travelling through have become even more confused and lumpy which I didn't imagine was possible. So much so that navigating down below is akin to a day out at monkey world, for the residents.

I have decided to keep motoring as the changing winds and lumpy seas are putting too much strain on our rig which, if you remember, is now minus a forestay. Our ETA in Flores is between 17:00 and 19:00 UTC this afternoon, and it can't come soon enough to be honest.

Moaning aside, all is well, the crew are all tired as the horrible motion over the last three days has made sleep very difficult, but I am sure by the time they reach the end of the jetty and have a bar in sight morale will be fully restored. The chefs, and that is all of us, have worked wonders in the conditions and we have had good, hot and hearty meals delivered on time every day. We have even been baking bread which is a real morale booster, particularly for Adamant on his night time eating routine.

Here are the stats up to date:

Day 1   74 miles (15 hours)
Day 2   115 miles (Part motoring)
Day 3   141 miles (All motoring)
Day 4   116 miles (Part Motoring)
Day 5   161 miles (All sailing)
Day 6   172 miles (All sailing)
Day 7   149 miles (All sailing)
Day 8   121 miles (Part Motoring)
Day 9   129 miles (All sailing)
Day 10   119 miles (All sailing)
Day 11   157 miles (All sailing) ½ under reduced rig

Day 12 121 miles (All sailing) All under reduced rig
Day 13 141 miles (Part motoring)

The arrival lottery now stands at:
Paul 21st AM - missed by less than mile.
Norma 21st PM - No chance now
Jen 22nd AM – missed by a nose.
Steve 22nd PM - On target for the chocolate bar
Willem 25th - Could be a winner if the winds go very light or something breaks.
Adamant 27th - Still being a bloody pessimist.

Watch this space for the next rip-roaring adventure as the 'Famous Five' become the 'Splendiferous Six'

23rd Jun 2015 10:32:55
Bermuda to Flores, Azores 8
39:22.82N 31:09.96W
Porto Das Lajes Flores The Azores
10,968 Miles from Ramsgate by log.

Arrived safe and sound at 18:00 on the 22nd June 2015.

Here are the final stats for this leg of our journey:

Day 1   74 miles (15 hours)
Day 2   115 miles (Part motoring)
Day 3   141 miles (All motoring)
Day 4   116 miles (Part Motoring)
Day 5   161 miles (All sailing)
Day 6   172 miles (All sailing)
Day 7   149 miles (All sailing)
Day 8   121 miles (Part Motoring)
Day 9   129 miles (All sailing)
Day 10 119 miles (All sailing)
Day 11 157 miles (All sailing) ½ under reduced rig
Day 12 121 miles (All sailing) All under reduced rig
Day 13 141 miles (Part motoring) under reduced rig
Day 14 50 miles to end (all motoring) under reduced rig.

The arrival lottery results = A win for Steve!!!!!

FLORES & HORTA, AZORES

JUNE 2015

26th Jun 2015 15:05:32

Flores to Horta…Willem arrives and we have a great stay on a lovely island.

38:31.53N 28:37.30W

26th June 2015

Lajes, Flores to Horta, Faial.

11,108 Miles Since leaving Ramsgate by log.

Before I start this blog, I have to mention that Steve has been given two penalty points in the daily distance run competition due to receiving outside assistance. Unknown to us, he has been getting moral support from his sisters or as they are also known 'the Devonian cheerleaders' while the rest of us carry on without any hint of a supporters' club to provide moral support. Having said that, he actually stands no chance of getting fat on the amount of chocolate bars that he has won so far.

On day one in Flores and it was all-hands-on-deck to fix the old girl up again after her experiences on the crossing from Bermuda. Now that we had a stable platform we could slacken off the backstays and connect the forestay to the alternative fitting point on the bowsprit. The advice from the marina manager was not to use the local welder as he was, I quote, "a bit agricultural and not very good with stainless" so that is another job for back in Ramsgate. As a complete aside, and absolutely nothing to do with my needing a welding job done, I hear that Russell Creighton has now officially retired and is bored already, don't know why that popped into my head, spooky eh? We have now got everything re-rigged and we are good to go. The plotter continues to do its own thing and randomly switches on and off, but each day it seems to regain another function, so I think the internals are drying out. Steve has stripped and cleaned it, and that is about all that we can do with it at present. While we were doing those jobs, Norma stripped the boat out to dry off everything and Jen sewed a chaffing patch onto our foresail, so we were all kept busy until well after lunch.

Enough of that boat stuff, my little finger has knitted back together rather nicely under Norma's ministrations and is now smaller than my thumb, which does add a certain symmetry to my left hand. We found a lovely restaurant on the back edge of the village of Lajes that provided masses of very good homemade food for ridiculously cheap prices, 60 Euros for five including drinks. Everything here is very cheap and the whole island is beautifully tended and maintained in pristine condition. My only thought is, when comparing this to the Caribbean Islands and Bermuda, there must be one hell of a lot of Euro millions pouring into the place. Willem is aboard now, so that makes six which is crowded but we will get by. His main interest is the astro-navigation and he has already cleaned and adjusted my old sextant to the Nth degree.

Yesterday was wet and windy so we hired a car to tour the island from, you guessed it, the café at the back of the village; no driving license required and 35 Euro for the day. As we headed up to the volcanoes' caldera we immediately drove into a cloud so the view from the top was spectacularly white with no sign of anything else. Not to be deterred, we headed back to sea level and found some really nice small villages huddled along the shoreline. Each one had a spectacular backdrop of high grey cliffs and cascading waterfalls. Every road, hedge row, garden and house is absolutely festooned with flowers, making a drive around the island a complete delight. At a quirky jazz bar on the beach we had a superb lunchtime meal of red grouper shared between Steve, Jen and myself. Norma, who is not a fish fan, had an omelette and, of course, as poor old Adamant is still strictly adhering to Ramadan he just watched on, although he did drool a bit at one stage and kept asking us how good it tasted. We were under the impression that Santa Cruz, the capital, was having a sardine festival but on entering the town we found out that it was closed for the public holiday and nothing was doing. Back at the marina, the café overlooking the bay was celebrating the sardine festival in style and we queued up with the locals for an amazing BBQ sardine dinner. It was delicious and, as the sun had gone down, Adamant joined us and immediately devoured two huge platefuls of sardines complete with chunks of local bread.

Later we went to the bar/restaurant at the top of the hill (again) and met up with the crew from a cat that was anchored out in the bay, who we had previously met in Bermuda. As the crew had an Irish member, Norma and Gerry were soon swapping stories and, as they say, the craic was good. One interesting discovery was that the local seagulls have a really odd call that sounds just like "Bullshit, Bullshit" being repeated over and over. The strangest thing was that as soon as I started up on a tale of my own, I was treated to a chorus of "Bullshit, Bullshit, Bullshit……. Bullshit, Bullshit, Bullshit" from the birds on the cliff, much to the amusement of the gathered masses. Damn those birds, they know too much.

On the trip around the island, I changed my mind about our route back to the UK. The lack of a refuelling facility or gas depot on Flores would mean that we would be setting off with half of our supplies already exhausted. The alternative is to go to Horta, 130 miles away, and top-up on everything there, so that is what we are going to do. The other advantage of this approach is that it will give Willem a 24-hour passage to get used to us and the boat, and for us to get used to him before we are all lumped together in a 'Tupperware box' for two weeks. Before we went to bed on the last night in Flores, Jen painted the traditional signature picture of a passing yacht on the harbour wall, alongside all of the others. Or, she committed an act of vandalism by tagging a wall, depends on your perspective I suppose.

After a bumpy night in the marina, as a vicious low-pressure front swept by, we finally set sail at 1400 yesterday and headed for Horta. Almost immediately, I felt something was wrong as *Spectra* was going nowhere near the speed that she should have been doing for the revs applied. We pulled a sail up quickly to enable us to clear the harbour and then, when in safe water, I went below to investigate. The dip stick on the gear box had worked loose with all of the bouncing about that we have been doing, and a considerable amount of fluid had escaped, resulting in the clutch slipping. I topped up the gearbox (always fun at sea laying on your back in the rear cabin with your head and one arm jammed into a cupboard, whilst your legs are sticking up in the air) and all seems to be fine now.

It is now 10am on the 26th and Faial is in sight, with Horta just around the corner. We had to motor for 5 hours from midnight, but now the wind has returned and we are zooming along at 8 knots with all sails set and we have been joined by a large group of dolphins, which, let's face it, when compared to the

London Underground, is really not a bad way to start the day...

29th Jun 2015 14:18:50
Horta...Azores
38:31.53N 28:37.30W
11,230 Miles Since leaving Ramsgate by log.

"It is raining heavens hard" as Norma would say, and we are going sailing...yey! Jen has volunteered to do the Horta blog so I will not take up too much space. As soon as we can get our refilled gas bottles back from Mid Atlantic Yacht Supplies (1500 this afternoon) we will be heading out with the next stop Good Old Blighty. The low-pressure system has given its worst and is now sitting about 70 miles to the north of us which means we should be able to hang onto its coat tails for the first couple of days and get a good start on the journey. After that there is another big system coming across on Thursday but, if my cunning plan works, we will be on the eastern fringes of that and it will also give us a push up towards Biscay. All being well, we should be back in the UK in 10-12 days and back in Ramsgate by the 18th of July. With that in mind, if anyone is in the RTYC bar on Saturday the 18th, mines a crème de menthe and Tizer, as Del boy would say. Tommy and Sue Foster, our ever-supportive support team, back in base camp

Ramsgate, will have the most up to date details of our expected arrival if you need an update on progress.

Now it's Jen's turn:

Hello to everyone!

Wow! what fantastic Islands to visit. Now we find ourselves in Horta, which is the sailing centre stop off. We have found everything we need here, gas, diesel, hot showers and a great bar!

The first day we all explored Horta.

Norma was very happy to find some shops and returned with floral trainers; I agreed they were really cute and a bargain too! Adamant, Willem and myself went on a hunt for the beach (to see if it would beat the one in Bermuda) and came across a beautiful beached cove. On one side there was the town and on the other a high volcanic mound, with only plants and a path leading to a small white church. We crossed the beach, I dipped my feet in the sea and told Adamant that it was lovely and warm, so he followed me, and he made a small grunt when he found it was freezing! The view from the mid-point of the island was so stunning (I've been teased for saying 'amazing' so I'm expanding my vocabulary now!)

The great thing about this trip, which I didn't expect, is having the opportunity to make lots of friends. I thought it would be limited to the crew on *Spectra*, but we are on a circuit and we find ourselves bumping into the same people in a variety of different locations. You end up experiencing new things together and this quickly makes you strike up strong friendships. Everyone has a story and conversation is always fun, interesting and informative. Sharing information, learning about great places in the world to visit. We made good friends with the group from the catamaran, the family from the US, and now we have a new Australian buddy, Peter. He has a very funny sense of humour, if you can understand him with his very strong accent.

The local bar has had live music every night and, honestly, all of us were won over by last night's act - an acoustic guitarist with an incredible voice. He played worldwide well-known songs, but was adding in jokes in Portuguese. Apparently, his Dad is a famous Portuguese artist. We wished we could understand the jokes!

Paul commented that he wished he could get all his family and friends to experience what we did last night, and we all agreed.

Adamant, Steve, Willem, Peter and I took the ferry to Pico yesterday which is the next island and is where the volcano is. The last eruption was 1718, which destroyed a church and half a village. We took a tour around, learning about the island, the whaling, the people, the structures and enjoyed the beauty. It was a fab day out. Unfortunately, the clouds are following us around, so we didn't get to see the top of the volcano.

Last night we had an hour of pool. Two teams, Jen and Adamant Vs Norma and Paul. Adamant had beginner's luck, plus he was sober so that was in his favour. I definitely chose the right team member and we won against "Paurma" 2:1. As you may know Paul is a bad loser, and he was still convinced he won the last game and was upset when we reminded him that wasn't the case! I might add, only 5 minutes after the game ended.

Willem has made friends with another Dutch man also called Peter and has decided to jump ship. Peter was travelling solo, but when he was hit with bad weather for three days, with no sleep and commented on hallucinating, he didn't want to continue his next leg to Southampton alone. Actually, Norma has been quite worried that Adamant would be stolen by the Australian Peter and jokes flew around that I would be taken by the catamaran. We are back to Five, all the way to Ramsgate.

HORTA TO BRIXHAM

JULY 2015

1st Jul 2015 09:41:58

Horta to Brixham 1

39:02.13N 24:09.28W

1st July 2015

11,341 Miles Since leaving Ramsgate by log.

> Day 1   96 miles 15 hours all sailing
> Day 2   137 miles All sailing
>
> The arrival in Brixham lottery stands at:
> Paul   9th AM
> Norma   9th PM
> Steve   10th AM
> Jen   11th AM
> Adamant   11th PM

Our first night out was a bit wild and windy. We departed Faial at 16:30 cut down eastwards from Horta, passed Pico to the right and then sailed between the islands of Pico and Sao Jorge. By first light we had the island of Terceira astern of us and were heading just north of east and home. A last farewell from the Azores was a savage 39 knot blast of cold air as we got caught in the wind acceleration zone, but *Spectra* lifted her skirts and we were soon crashing down waves at over 9 knots. As always, the first night out was rubbish for getting any sleep. No one is tired enough and the creaks and groans of a yacht at sea must be got used to all over again. Added to that, I have picked up a bug and spent a fairly large portion of the night speaking into the big white telephone in the aft heads, not a pleasant night sail at all.

Day two and I was in bed for most of it feeling sorry for myself as *Spectra* crashed along in a very lumpy sea. The forestay has gone slack but is still attached, so no real drama. The thought is that it must have got caught on something at the top of the mast and we tightened against that instead of its correct fitting. With the sail up and the bumpy ride it has shaken loose and slackened itself off. Once the weather settles a kind volunteer, (Steve), will go up the mast and make sure everything is secure, before we clamp it tight again and fly the big Yankee headsail.

We are finally on the last Ocean leg of our little odyssey and rushing home to see family, friends and of course, the newest arrival to the clan, Martha, when she gets here. It did seem rather fitting then, when Steve pointed out a group of stars right above us on the first night out. This small cluster of lights in the sky is known as the Northern Crown or more technically Corona Borealis. If you look inwards from the end towards the centre you can identify the brightest star in the system which is called Gemma (my daughter's name). With Gemma keeping watch from on high, I am already feeling much closer to home somehow.

See you all soon........*Spectra* and crew out

3rd Jul 2015 10:28:59
Horta to Brixham 2
41:04.52N 18:55.54W
11,630 Miles Since leaving Ramsgate by log.

RESULTS OF THE DAILY RUN CHOCOLATE BAR COMPETITION		
Day	Actual Mileage	Nearest Guess & Name
Day 1	96 miles 15 hours all sailing	88 miles Norma
Day 2	137 miles All sailing	139/135 miles Paul/Norma
Day 3	139 miles All sailing	141 miles Paul
Day 4	150 miles All sailing	140/160 Adamant/ Paul

The 'Arrival in Brixham Lottery' stands at:

Paul	9th AM
Norma	9th PM
Steve	10th AM
Jen	11th AM
Adamant	11th PM

I am sitting below, on the morning of the 2nd July, listening to the scrape, scrape, scrape, of Adamant polishing a brass porthole whilst Jen is upstairs in 30 knots of wind standing her watch and keeping us all safe. Norma is practising her Ukulele and Steve is sitting at the chart table staring myopically at the steadily falling barometer. Yes, we have bad weather again, so I will break this edition into two parts; what we got up to yesterday and then tomorrow how we faired in the gale, or near gale, let's not exaggerate shall we.

Yesterday was calm and the sea was relatively flat. With the imminent arrival of this bad weather system I decided to take advantage of the lull and sort out the forestay. If you have been paying attention, you will remember that the deck fitting sheared off on our way to Flores and that we had, we thought, fixed it. On the morning of day two of this trip, in a violently rolling sea, there was a loud bang from the direction of the mast head and the forestay went slack. Since then we have been running on staysail, main and mizzen alone with the furled foresail sheeted in tight to reduce any movement in the stay. I suspected that something had got caught at the top of the mast and we had tightened the stay against that in Flores and the subsequent rolling had shaken it free. In short, someone had to go up the mast and check things out. When I called for volunteers, Steve (being the Sterling chap he is) stepped forwards almost as quickly as the rest of the crew stepped backwards, and so we had him trussed up in the bosuns' chair and harness in no time at all. With Adamant and myself taking turns on the winch, we soon hauled him to the top of the mast which was swinging wildly from side to side as *Spectra* rolled in the swell. It is amazing how the human body reverts to an ape-like state so quickly when 60 feet up a mast, Steve was clinging on like a baby chimp to his mother's feeding station and letting out the odd squeak or two to boot. Happily, for us on deck, and for him I am sure, he was soon finished and on his return to deck level informed us that no damage had been done to the mast head fittings. This kind of confirmed our supposition that the retaining mushroom lug at the top of the stay had risen up when the deck fitting broke and got jammed when the stay came loose previously, and on freeing itself in the swell had allowed the stay to slacken.

Next problem, as Steve had managed to spin around the mast several times on his climb, the halyards were now in a right old mess and, in particular, the mainsail halyard was wrapped around the Radar reflector. Steve at this point was sitting in the cockpit drinking water and counting his new collection of bruises and I noticed his head ducking lower and lower as it became obvious that another trip up the mast was required. I didn't have the heart to ask him and so, benevolent dictator that I am, I temporarily removed my jack boots, and put on the harness and bosuns chair on for the next trip up. In order to get into the bosuns chair I did have to slacken the waistline somewhat which makes me wonder if Steve is eating enough, as the alternative is unthinkable.

Bloody hell, that was horrible! I collected a set of bruises of my own before returning to deck. Finally, all the halyards were free and we could move on. Just as an aside, Norma's running commentary from the cockpit of, "big wave, little wave, calm now, ooh really big wave, hold on!" was of absolutely no help to the poor bugger doing a conker impression half way up the mast, but it kept her busy and stopped her worrying too much, I suppose.

All that was left to do was to tighten the forestay down at the bowsprit and see how it went. This involved me lying face down on the bowsprit twisting the furling cage while Steve laid over/on top of me to hold the stay in place. I now have CQR stamped permanently into my right hip bone and, for some reason, I feel all weepy and unloved every time I look at Steve. The comments from the crew were most unbecoming and the photographs positively obscene. I will publish them later when we are in port, if I don't accidentally delete them that is. As we have added a shackle to the forestay it wouldn't tighten quite as hard as I would like but it is a darn sight better than it was and so, after 4 hours of work, we celebrated by poling out the Yankee foresail and goose winging for the rest of the day and most of the night.

At midnight the predicted low-pressure system began to make its presence known, and when Adamant came up for shift change, I decided to rearrange the sails and get the boat settled down for the night. With Adamant working the cockpit, and watching in case I went for a swim, we did the following, in this order:

1. Pulled the mizzen onto the centre line and re-rigged the preventer to Port.
2. Gybed the mainsail over and then re-rigged the main preventer to Port.
3. Furled in the foresail.
4. Dropped and stowed the spinnaker pole.
5. Eased the staysail over to Port.
6. Eased out the mizzen and rigged the preventer.
7. Boat still doing 9 knots so put another reef in main.
8. Now 00:30 hrs, had a nice cup of tea and handed the watch over to Adamant.

All this frenetic activity was watched, I am sure with great interest, from the gloriously centrally heated and luxurious bridge of a super tanker that was lying 4 miles to starboard of us at the time. I bet it gave them something to talk about later while down below playing pool on their gimballed snooker table.

We have been running all night in a force 6 to 7 and a 3-metre swell, but it has been remarkably comfortable so far. Steve is just donning his foul weather gear as he is relieving Jen in 10 minutes and all is well with the world, apart from the scrape, scrape, scrape of Adamant's polishing; I wonder if a crime of passion could be claimed in these circumstances?

It is now the morning of the 3rd of July and what a night that was. The GRIB file received earlier in the day showed that the expected low had taken a dip over the Azores and we would be in the worst of it as opposed to the bottom edge as planned. No great concern however, as the wind strength was predicted to peak at 25 knots and the swell at 2.2 metres, all easily manageable. By 6pm we had a solid F7 coming from the South East and a 2-metre swell. By 8pm it was a consistent F8 with 3 metre swell and so it went on. From 9pm through to midnight the wind did not drop below 40 knots and probably averaged nearer to 45, or a very solid F9, with a swell easily in the 4-5 metre bracket. The maximum gust recorded by the instruments, and they don't record anything that lasts for less than a minute, was 52 knots. By this time, we were reefed down to 2 in the staysail and two in the mizzen, no main and no foresail and we were still going at over 9 knots. The biggest problem was keeping the balance of steerage way on the boat and the speed down to a safe level. Earlier in the night, when we pulled all of the mainsail down, we were hitting over 10 knots of boat speed (max 10.7). Getting the beasty down in those conditions required both Steve and myself to hang onto the front edge with our feet off the deck because it was pinned so hard to the mast. At one point, with a steady 45-knot wind howling over the quarter and mountainous seas all around, a very worried Jen shouted in my ear, "are we going to be alright"? In those conditions you had to get about 2 inches away from someone's ear and shout to make yourself heard. I did my best to calm her by saying that with our sails reduced down the boat was still self-steering and we were good for at least 50 knots. Of course, as the last word was shouted into her ear the wind took on a different pitch and the needle went above 50 and stayed there. I pretended not to notice until it went away. The good thing about being in 50 + knots of wind is that when it drops to 40 you think "my that's so much better, where is breakfast?"

At 8pm I started our bad weather shift pattern. Steve was on Mummy Watch and so stayed below unless needed to change sails, he did sterling work and even provided a hearty chicken casserole for the whole crew, just when it was needed the most. I was on watch with Jen and Norma was on watch with Adamant, 2 hours on and 2 hours off, which we kept up until 2 am when the wind finally dropped below 30 knots and we reverted to the normal single shifts. The most reliable, steadfast and dependable crew member was *Spectra* herself. Even with several tons of water on deck (it was sweeping solidly across the saloon hatches, pouring into the cockpit on a regular basis and one wave even managed to fill the mainsail stack pack which is 6ft above deck level!), our good old girl just ploughed along shedding water over the bulwark rails as the hawseholes got overwhelmed. The difference between below decks and the cockpit was startling; looking down the hatch I could see Norma doodling on a note pad wedged in the corner and Steve cooking a meal, chatting away to each other, while outside it was just awful and any conversation had to be reduced to single syllables shouted directly into your crew mate's ear.

Well that was last night, this morning we have a lumpy sea, 15-20 knots of wind from the West and we are romping along at 7 knots. Everything below is wet and there are clothes hanging out to dry everywhere, whilst a very tired crew sleep the morning away accompanied by the hum of our generator which is heating water for warm showers later.

No more bad weather is predicted for several days and we should be able to push on now with our nose pointed straight at the Brixham harbour entrance.

That's it - I am going to wake up someone to keep an eye on things and then go to bed......blog again in two days...

5th Jul 2015 11:09:25
Horta to Brixham 3
44:18.84N 14:16.85W
(ETA Martha birth +1)
11,931 Miles Since leaving Ramsgate by log.

RESULTS OF THE DAILY RUN CHOCOLATE BAR COMPETITION		
Day	Actual Mileage	Nearest Guess & Name
Day 1	96 miles 15 hours all sailing	88 miles Norma
Day 2	137 miles All sailing	139/135 miles Paul/Norma
Day 3	139 miles All sailing	141 miles Paul
Day 4	150 miles All sailing	140/160 miles Adamant/Paul
Day 5	162 miles All Sailing	158 miles Norma
Day 6	139 miles All sailing	140 miles Adamant

The 'Arrival in Brixham Lottery' stands at:
Paul   9th AM

Norma	9th PM
Steve	10th AM
Jen	11th AM
Adamant	11th PM

Our Satellite linkup is not playing friendly at the moment and I am not sure if these blogs are getting through. Emails are arriving sporadically but no GRIB files which means we have no weather data at present. Our last good weather download covers up to the 5th which means we are all ok so far but, hopefully, one of the other mediums, Navtex, Weatherman, SSB will start to do its' job and give us an update soon.

Nothing much to report on the ship front; the wind has been steady meaning we are starting to put together better daily averages. In fact, we passed the halfway point to Brixham yesterday afternoon so all is well with the world. The water maker is still making and the generator still generating, what more can you ask for?

The biggest issue we have at the moment is the email connection, has Martha put in an appearance yet or not? That is the question that is slowly driving Norma and myself insane. Hopefully, when I send this, the return package of emails will come in with good news. And now Jen's bit:

Quick (ended up being long!) hello from Jen

Adamant has started to try a mixture of rulers and pencils to make a replacement sextant, after Paul kindly leant *Spectra's* sextant to Willem, who left us back in the Azores. I look at him with curiosity and think if it is possible to make one, what could we use from *Spectra's* tools and materials to make it achievable? Perhaps by the time we reach land Adamant may have come up with a new gadget.

My mum asked me what we were eating on board. Before I came on board I had no idea what we would be eating and how one can make good food for such a long passage. Norma has it all under control: She has carefully prepared meal plans, she has the ingredients printed out and then how to make it. This gives her the quantities to buy and the right amount of ingredients. We can add our own spin on the recipe with herbs and spices. We have had such a variety of meals, lasagne, curries, stews, pies, risottos, the list goes on. The first week from leaving land, we ate through all the fresh veg and fruit, using it in cooking, after this we started making our own bread and using canned veg instead.

So far, Steve is the best at making bread (but Paul closely follows), Adamant at curries (so much, he is not allowed to make anything else!) Norma's stews and crumbles, Paul's lasagne and my speciality is shortbread. I love to make food and see the team enjoy it. Food becomes a very high subject for conversation, what we are going to eat and how we are, or how we have, made it.

Yesterday the sun came out, what a wonderful change from the gale – bad weather really makes you appreciate the good. Bad weather makes you miss home more than ever, and now we are half way! Yippee!!! Come on England!

My new craving is for traditional fish and chips! This craving absorbed me so much I ended up making a poem/song up about it on one of my night shifts! And talking about it has started Paul's mouth-watering, (actually that's not hard to do!) it goes like this...

> Fish and Chips
> Fish and Chips
> All I really, really want is
> Traditional Fish and Chips
>
> Crossing the Atlantic
> On a 47 foot Vagabond
> Sailing Azores to the UK
> Need my craving to go away
>
> Shall I have Skate or Haddock?
> No, No, No, I'll have the Cod.
> I'll have salt and pepper
> Loads and loads of vinegar!!!
>
> Fish and Chips

Fish and Chips
All I really, really want is
Traditional Fish and Chips

I look at the Ocean
It's so massive
I'm just a tiny pinprick
On this huge atlas

I'm not a fan of mushy peas
So, Norma can you eat them please?
Yummy, scrummy Fish and Chips
All wrapped in paper bits

On my night shift
Writing this song
These six days
Gonna seem so long!

Fish and Chips
Fish and Chips
All I really, really want is
Traditional Fish and Chips!

There you are... sailing for days in the ocean makes you think of home, family, friends and traditional food that never seems the same anywhere else. Some things aren't replaceable, especially traditional fish and chips!!!

Paul's final comment .... ??????????????????????

7th Jul 2015 09:32:36
Horta to Brixham…..4
47:22.309N 8:58.472W
7th July 2015 (ETA Martha +3)
12,208 Miles Since leaving Ramsgate by log.

RESULTS OF THE DAILY RUN CHOCOLATE BAR COMPETITION		
Day	Actual Mileage	Nearest Guess & Name
Day 1	96 miles 15 hours all sailing	88 miles Norma
Day 2	137 miles All sailing	139/135 miles Paul/Norma
Day 3	139 miles All sailing	141 miles Paul
Day 4	150 miles All sailing	140/160 miles Adamant/Paul
Day 5	162 miles All Sailing	158 miles Norma
Day 6	139 miles All sailing	140 miles Adamant
Day 7	139 miles All sailing	140 miles Steve
Day 8	138 miles All sailing	140 miles Adamant

The 'Arrival in Brixham Lottery' stands at:

Paul	9th (favourite)	AM
Norma	9th PM	
Steve	10th AM	
Jen	11th AM	
Adamant	11th PM	

The third, and hopefully the last, low pressure system caught up with us on Sunday evening. We were, at that time, slightly north of and about three hundred miles west of La Coruna so safely outside of Biscay. This one hasn't got the bite that the last two had and, as of Monday lunchtime, the peak winds have only reached the low 30 knot mark. I can't believe I just wrote low 30 knots as being kind of ok! We are all snuggled down with three reefs in the main, no foresail, full staysail and Steve and I have just put the second reef into the mizzen. Present boat speed is 6-7 knots, all in the right direction, and we have finally managed to get through the Azorean counter current. This means that we now do not have the 0.5-1 knot current against us, which had been a constant for the last 5 days.

Last night, being Sunday, it was a full-on turkey roast with Yorkshire puddings and all of the trimmings, followed by rice pudding and mandarin oranges. It was my turn to cook and, as always, the wind seems to go up for Sunday dinner preparations, but it is a bit of a tradition on *Spectra* when on passage, so you have to try, don't you? Well it all got to the table and the gallant crew managed to eat it all without any hitting the floor, ceiling or curtains. In fact, I kind of suspect that Jen might have licked the plate if we hadn't been watching. Poor old Adamant hid in his cabin while we ate as he is still steadfastly sticking to his Ramadan rules, good on him. I did put some aside for him, with sardines substituting for the non-Halal turkey (yuk), which he heated up after dark.

You will have noticed, down there in deepest darkest Devon, that Steve has managed to win a chocolate bar in the daily run competition again, now that he has worked off his penalty points for outside assistance. So, all of you out there that think I have been picking on your little brother, well you were right! Sorry, I'm just like that. Of course, if he gets fat now, well that's all your fault.

Our email/satellite system seems to have burst into life again and the emails are pouring in/out. On the home front, I apparently have a new car, or so I have been informed by my son. No mention of make, colour or anything else mind, so for all I know I could be turning up for job interviews in a milk float next month! And of course, the burning question, the tardiness of my new granddaughter, due to arrive on the 4th and still no sign? I will have to put Norma on Valium or into restraints if she doesn't arrive soon. On that note, the ukulele practice has been noticeably lacking of late as Norma is now fully committed to knitting a dress for Martha before we arrive in Ramsgate. As for progress on that, so far there is a red square thing hanging on a metal rod in our bedroom and that is all I can say about that.

Wildlife: we seem to have run out of Portuguese Man-O-Wars since the seas got colder but dolphins and whales, we have had a plenty. Last night, a whole host of vents could be seen about a mile to port as a group of whales went by and the dolphins have been over to play several times a day. We now have seen a new breed of dolphin - slightly smaller and darker than the two-tone ones we have been getting of late. For the third time on the trip we sighted a large shark. It cruised by in the opposite direction sort of made a half turn to look us over and then continued on its way. By the way, Jen is still declining a second mid-Atlantic swim.

That's it for now as I am still on Mummy Watch, so I have toilets to clean and then lunch to make. (Note to self: wash hands after first and before second.) I will, no doubt, find something to write about tomorrow before I despatch this blog out to the reading public.

8am and I have just come off shift which was a cold and drab one. 120 miles WSW of Brest the generator is humming away putting all of those lovely wiggly amps back into our batteries and Adamant has just won today's mileage contest. Norma, Steve and Jen are all still fast asleep as *Spectra* slogs along at 7 knots into that damnable counter current that returned to plague us in the night. Today is shower day, and boy does everyone else aboard need one. Why they can't just smell of roses, "like what I does", I just don't know? So, once the batteries have charged a bit, I will be turning on the immersion heater to get some hot water or the crew could turn mutinous on me. As an aside, and as I am rambling a bit anyway, last night in the early hours I did notice that my green all round light at the top of the mast has lost its cover. I can only surmise that it was blown off in one of the 50-knot gusts during our last gale. Amazingly enough, considering the wind and rain we have been having, the exposed bulb is still shining green, so all is not lost yet. We also managed to break the connectors on both of our lazy jack lines on the main in the gale. Jen has volunteered (surprise, surprise) to go up the mast when we reach Brixham and pull some new lines through. With her usual enthusiasm, Jen is still working her way through the winch servicing, 5 down 6 to go. Due to inclement weather it has been on hold for a while but yesterday one of the big, two-speed cockpit winches was given a going over by Jen, while Adamant looked on. There was a momentary crisis of confidence when she realized just how many bits of metal she had piled into the cleaning bucket, but it all went together again apart from one spring which did what springs do and sprung out of sight. Rather guiltily, she admitted to losing the aforementioned spring and, after a thorough search, it was declared lost at sea. Luckily, I carry spares, but I wasn't about to admit that until we had searched the entire cockpit for the little blighter. Guess what? When the winch was all cleaned, put back together and tested serviceable, what should we find in the bottom of the cleaning bucket but our errant spring. So, I still have a spare, happy days.

Last night Norma made a really big pot of Irish stew for dinner which was rib fatteningly delicious. With oodles left over in the big pressure cooker, the crew have been dipping into it all night which was a real belly warmer on, what turned out to be, a rather chilly night, and I am just thinking "Irish stew for breakfast, mmmmm". After a cold night out in the elements, I think I deserve it.

And on that note, it is goodbye from me.

ETA Brixham is as of this morning 9am on the 9th July.

9th Jul 2015 12:39:27
Horta to Brixham…..5 arrived
50:23.911N 3:30.556W
8th July 2015 (ETA Martha +4)
12,497 Miles Since leaving Ramsgate by log.

RESULTS OF THE DAILY RUN CHOCOLATE BAR COMPETITION		
Day	Actual Mileage	Nearest Guess & Name

Day 1	96 miles 15 hours all sailing	88 miles Norma
Day 2	137 miles All sailing	139/135 miles Paul/Norma
Day 3	139 miles All sailing	141 miles Paul
Day 4	150 miles All sailing	140/160 miles Adamant/Paul
Day 5	162 miles All Sailing	158 miles Norma
Day 6	139 miles All sailing	140 miles Adamant
Day 7	139 miles All sailing	140 miles Steve
Day 8	138 miles All sailing	140 miles Adamant
Day 9	159 miles All sailing	160 miles Paul
Day 10	130 miles All sailing	No competition

The 'Arrival in Brixham Lottery' stands at:

Paul   9th AM (favourite)
Norma   9th PM
Steve   10th AM
Jen   11th AM
Adamant 11th PM

Arrived Brixham 0503hrs 9/7/15

The wind will just not let up on this trip! Last night was another steady force 7 with very lumpy seas. So much so that we had our biggest roll ever. Jen was on watch alone in the cockpit (strapped in of course) when a series of waves combined to roll *Spectra* right onto her beam ends. Below decks I was in bed lying across the boat, head to port feet to starboard reading, when I felt the roll and heard Jen squeal from outside. I watched my feet rise higher and higher until I did a complete backwards roll in bed, ending up wedged in the corner with my bottom on the roof. It was in this position that Norma found me after she had crawled through the galley to state the bleeding obvious, "Hi love, I think you're needed on deck". Norma and Steve had been sitting in the saloon watching films on their laptops when the wave hit, they both hung onto the electrical equipment and the saloon table and just went with the roll. This proves that the old adage from Nelsons Navy of "one hand for the ship and one for your laptop or tablet depending on your preference" still holds as true today as it did at Trafalgar. Adamant was just coming out of the forward heads and ended up laying almost flat on the wet locker door as it rapidly changed its angle to become the floor. After a couple of very long seconds *Spectra*, much to Jen's delight as she was watching solid water pour into the cockpit, shook the wave off like a shaggy dog and got back on with sailing in a straight line. All of our electrics had now gone out, along with it the auto pilot, so Steve dashed up to the cockpit to help Jen get the boat on course and start hand steering, while I took stock. Jen was, in James Bond parlance, shaken but not stirred, and once her eyes had gone from dinner plate size back to a more normal circumference she told Steve all about the 'AMAZING' wave at great length and even greater speed. Now the real tragedy of the story: I found the source of the electrical failure. When we cook our evening meal we cook without meat and then leave a portion out for Adamant for him to eat after dark (Ramadan, etc, as mentioned before). We then put the meat in and finish the preparations for us heathens. His meal and a bottle of coke were sitting on a slip proof mat on the galley top (it had stayed in this position every night for the last month including a force 9 encounter without a hint of movement). The big wave launched his meal across the boat, liberally scattering the entire chart table and surrounding area with yellow rice. Adamant's face was a picture, I honestly believe he was about to dive onto the floor and start stuffing rice into his mouth by the handful but he managed to restrain himself. It was soon all scooped up back into the bowl and put safely out of his sight. Electricity, or lack of it: the coke bottle had, with the accuracy of an Exocet missile, shot the full width of the boat and hit the domestic power switch, neatly isolating the batteries and switching off all of our power. Easy fix, and soon we were glowing in the dark again and the autopilot was pointing the way home.

We have been out of contact for a few days as the satellite phone is down, so we are all worried about those at home and in particular we are worried about them worrying about us. This constant contact malarkey is a bit of a double-edged sword to be honest, "you're damned if you do and damned if you don't". Hopefully at some point early this evening we should get into mobile coverage range and the; "We are all safe messages", can be sent out.

Likewise, this blog will not go out until we have wi-fi, and that will be late this evening (the 8th), or early tomorrow morning.

Last note: We arrived, very tired, and then received the sad news that our brother-in-law, Jim, had passed away yesterday after a long fight against cancer. He will be missed by all who knew him, loved him and came to respect him over the years.

Goodbye Jim, love Norma and Paul

BRIXHAM AND HOME

JULY 2015

12th Jul 2015 17:45:41

Brixham to Weymouth…..Martha has arrived

50:36.49N 2:26.92W

12th July 2015 (ETA Martha +10 and she's here)

12,575 Miles Since leaving Ramsgate by log.

Here we are in sunny Weymouth, or at least it will be sunny when the rain stops and the sun comes out. Our two nights in Brixham were a much-needed break and a great opportunity to get some sleep and recharge our personal batteries.

The forestay is now securely fixed, in its temporary position, if that makes any sense at all, and it is now all tightened down. When we came to adjust it, I found a crack right across the strap securing the toggle to the deck. My assumption is that the fitting must have been weakened by the stay coming loose and then fractured later. This resulted in a mad dash around Brixham looking for a new fitting which, of course, was bigger than the standard fare and no one had one in stock. My last phone call to Dan at Petersen Custom Rigging was a success. Dan duly arrived with a brand-new, shining bit of stainless steel which fitted first time, and all for a very reasonable price of £60.

Jen, as promised, went up the mast to re-run our lazy jack lines which had been damaged in the gale before last. Now all the little jobs are done *Spectra* is once again ready for sea.

We met with Debbie, Steve's sister, who is one of our most ardent 'blogateers', and enjoyed a couple of hours recounting tales of our adventures. There were, of course, no exaggerations or embellishments of the raw facts at any point. She came with a supply of chocolates and biscuits for her baby brother as she felt that it was very unfair that "poor likkel Stevie", had been unfairly penalised for receiving outside help with the daily run competition. Steve has now jumped ship (with his supply of chocolate bars I might add) to visit family and friends but will re-join us again in Dover on 17th July, for our return to Ramsgate on 18th July at 2pm.

That has left Norma, me, Adamant and Jen to complete the next leg of our journey, which was 70 miles to Weymouth and what a sail that was. We departed Brixham at 09:00 and, after a slow first hour, we were soon romping along at 8 knots with all sails set. *Spectra* was in her element and we soon passed a couple of light weight yachts that had sailed past us earlier in the day. Norma phoned Weymouth en-route as the big book of South coast harbours advised yachts of 15 metres-plus to call in advance. Karen, the very helpful lady in the office said, "No problem at all, give us a call when you are at the harbour entrance. You will be rafted about 4 out". Norma then told her, "That's not a problem for us, but we do weigh 20 tonnes". "Oh, ok", said Karen, "Give us a call 1 hour before you get here and we will shift the other boats out to get you on the inside". So that is what happened, everything went like clockwork and we are now the inside boat on a raft of 6. I'm glad I sleep in the aft cabin.

Now for the big news, the phone rang at 6am this morning and, a surprisingly calm, Duncan informed us that we are now grandparents again. Little Martha joined the clan at 5am 12th July 2015 and weighed in at a very healthy 9lbs. Mummy and baby are doing well, Nana and Grumps can't stop smiling, which, in my case, is highly unnatural and is actually causing me some localised pain behind my ears. Our son, Tony, is driving from Surrey to Weymouth to pick us up, lovely boy that he is, so the next section of this blog will, no doubt, be very gushy and Martha-centric.

Second bit: In my unbiased view Martha is the most beautiful baby ever and I have spent a happy afternoon telling her all about the family. She, no doubt, started the way she means to continue and slept right through all of my good advice. Norma, of course, was calmness itself and remained on an even keel throughout her first encounter with young Martha.

We are heading back to the boat this evening to get this final leg out of the way and then we will come back up on Monday week to see how much she has grown.

13th Jul 2015 19:33:14
Arrived Lymington
50:45.14N 1:31.525W
42 miles run
12,617 Miles since leaving Ramsgate

Arrived safe and sound in Lymington, moored on the Dan Brown Town Quay. Another wet and windy day. It really is about time we copped a break with these winds, we are getting a bit tired of everyday a new roller coaster of a soggy and cold passage. Or maybe it's just all coming to an end and I'm getting jaded.

14th Jul 2015 20:18:59
Yarmouth IOW
50:42.356N 001:30.165W
5 mile run today
12622 miles run since Ramsgate

Today we decided to stay in Lymington as Norma and I are both still really tired from the crossing and just don't seem to be able to get ourselves back into a 9 to 5 routine. Well that was the plan, the greatest plans of mice and men, etc. Lymington harbour was booked out by a fleet of Dutch barges arriving at lunchtime so we had to 'Get Out of Dodge'. We actually managed to turn the engine off for a while as we completed the 5-mile crossing to Yarmouth harbour in a brisk 20-knot South Westerly wind. Safely tucked up in Yarmouth we have just had a pleasant day sightseeing (or in Norma parlance, shopping while I carried the bags) and then slept the afternoon away.

Tomorrow we are up at 04:30 for a departure at 5 to catch the tide and head on up to Brighton for a day or two.

One little saga that I forgot to mention yesterday was our meet up with a very big racing yacht. As we were entering the Needles Channel an AIS target appeared astern approaching fast. I checked it out and it came up as *Commanche*, 100 foot long and doing 20.1 knots over the ground. It also showed it as sailing? Sure enough, a set of grey technical sails appeared behind and we were soon completely trounced by this sailing monster. I think at least 10 people were sitting on the rail, all in matching foul weather gear, as they thundered past, all very impressive. Next encounter with a yacht was a small, 27-footer that, in an otherwise empty Solent, decided to luff us up. We had the foresail poled out, plus the main and mizzen preventers on at the time and were doing about 4 knots. He was staring straight ahead, bottom lip firmly pursed, holding his course, while totally ignoring the 20-tonne cruising ketch slowly getting closer. Legally he was totally in the right; practically, "what a d:@k". I decided that, rather than gybing everything over, I would roll up the foresail, reduce speed and let him pass in front while giving him a friendly wave and a "well done, hope it was worth it, you won" comment. He sailed on, totally ignoring us, before changing course to parallel ours 50 metres further up wind. I refer to my previous assessment of the man and wish him many happy hours in traffic on the M25 where he obviously learnt to sail.

Welcome to the Solent and weekend sailors.

That's it - not a hugely interesting story and you can probably tell he got under my skin somewhat but that's all I have got for the day, if you want excitement stop reading this, go outside and do something else.

Next edition from Brighton.

15th Jul 2015 21:25:00
Sovereign Harbour Eastbourne
50:47.45N 000:19.66W
75 mile run today
12697 miles run since Ramsgate

We have crossed our outward path again and turned up at Sovereign Harbour Eastbourne, where we first took possession of our boat *Spectra* in 2010. The plan today was to leave Yarmouth at 05:00, catch the tide, and travel up as far as Brighton. Like all good plans, that didn't survive first contact with reality. Well, we had a bit of everything on the way down here. We popped out of the Solent like a cork from a bottle doing 9 knots over the ground as we passed the Spithead Forts, giving a cruising catamaran a damn good thrashing along the way, only to lose the wind and drift for an hour with the tide. Eventually I called it quits, and we motored for the next hour, then the wind came up and we soon had the spinnaker flying and the boat speed was up to respectable levels again. As we came up on Brighton, I realised that we still had a lot of the day left and put it to the vote "do we carry on to Eastbourne?" All agreed and our fate was set. Thirty minutes later, the wind went fluky and stayed that way for the rest of the day, leaving us alternately sailing or motoring as the conditions dictated, and they dictated a lot! To top it off, we ran into thick fog as we approached Beachy Head and were soon down to less than half a mile of visibility. That was it until a couple of miles outside of Eastbourne when, as if by magic, the curtains lifted and we were in clear skies and no wind. We were greeted at Eastbourne with their usual professionalism, welcoming us back by name. Obviously, they pulled all of our details from the computer, but what a good way to welcome returning visitors, we felt really at home.

That leaves us all safe and sound, snugly moored in Eastbourne at 20:00 having completed 75 miles in the last 15 hours, hardly a blistering pace but at least we have now broken the back of the return leg.

Next stop Dover on Friday and then back to good old Rammers by 14:00(ish) on Saturday for tea and medals in the club.

17th Jul 2015 18:09:51
Eastbourne to Dover and it's nearly all over
51:07.064N 1:18.607E
17th July 2015
12,742 Miles Since leaving Ramsgate by log.
Days run 45 miles

Two nights in Eastbourne and *Spectra* is beginning to look more like her old self again. We broke out the stainless-steel cleaner, nasty acidy stuff that it is, and have managed to remove most of the rust spots that the Atlantic salt scrapped into my rails and fittings. Likewise, Adamant in a mad moment of altruism, volunteered to give the rails a going over with the varnish brush whilst Norma and I went shopping. Just a quick scrub down and one coat of cheap varnish but the old girl looks 100% better already. With the insides all cleaned and tidied, our flags all sewn, and the decks scrubbed, we are now ready for Ramsgate on Saturday at about 2pm.

The trip up to Dover started at 8am when we locked out of Eastbourne and caught the North East going tide which whisked us along the coast in grand style. Without Jen aboard, we are now just three, as she, smelling the home cooking and comfortable showers jumped ship to get a good night's sleep. Can't blame her, to be honest, she will re-join us in Dover. We soon passed three Dutch boats going the same way so it was a bit of a red-letter day for *Spectra*. After a somewhat boisterous sail, we arrived in Dover after covering 45 miles in 5 ¾ hours of glorious downwind sailing.

As we travelled along this part of the country I know so well I couldn't help humming a tune that Andrew Walkling sent through to me last week. It kind of sums up how Norma and I are both feeling at the moment so here goes, an extract from the song book of Mr Andy Williams – "Home Loving' Man".....

> The harbour lights were shining,
> The moon was at its high.
> The captain said, "Thank God we're home!
> We've drunk the barrels dry."
> The mizzen mast was shaken,
> And the lanterns all burned low,
> I'd never thought we'd make it
> But we've twenty leagues to go

So, blow you southern trades
And guide me safely to the shore,

The crowd upon the quayside
Their faces long and drawn
Are suddenly awakened
As we sail in on the dawn
The wives, the sons, the lovers,
Who never gave up hope
All breathe a sigh together
As they reach to catch the rope

This afternoon Andrew B-H popped down to meet us when we came into Dover. After a few beers and a few war stories, we feel that we are back in the fold. Tomorrow I think we have eleven aboard for the final trip up to Ramsgate, which is all of the crew that have helped us on the various stages of our journey except for my son, Tony. He is meeting us in Ramsgate for the final run up to the Yacht Club bar, so everyone will be there and all in the team T-shirts, I hope. See you all in the bar later. That's it for this one I think, there will be two more blogs, one to let you know how the Ramsgate return party went, and then a final one to sum it all up and to say goodbye to you all. So not too much reading left for you 'blogateers' to get through.

Keep at it. You can go out to play after you have finished your homework.

24th Jul 2015 14:27:35

Ramsgate home again
51:19.859N 1:25.141E
18th July 2015
12,759 Miles Since leaving Ramsgate by log.
Days run 17 miles

What a home coming that was! We had previously sent out the word to all of the crew members that had helped on the various stages of our trip or, as we like to call it, "shared the dream", inviting them to come along for the final leg and they all came up in spades. With everyone decked out in the *Spectra* team T shirts we were a crew of 11 for the last leg with 2 more to join us in Ramsgate. Even with Operation Stack still slowing the traffic into Dover, everyone was on board by 11:00 and we were ready to set out on what turned out to be a beautiful sunny day for our home coming. Most arrived by car, but Jen, not to be outdone, arrived in style, chauffeured by Dan from Positive Marine Electronics at 40 knots in his fast rib all the way from Ramsgate. This turned out to everyone's advantage as Dan, acting as official photographer, buzzed around us in the Rib and captured some great shots of the homecoming parade.

The crew were, in order of appearance:

Paul Russell (whole trip)
Norma Russell (whole trip)

Steve King (UK/Biscay/N Spain,-Break-Tenerife/Puerto Rico, -Break- Wilmington/Brixham)

Andrew Beaumont-Hope (France/Biscay/Spain)

Sarah Beaumont- Hope (France/Biscay/Spain)

Peter Duke (Portugal/Barbados)

Tommy Foster (UK/Calais, Madeira/Tenerife, Barbados/Grenada, Wilmington/ICW)

Sue Foster (UK/Calais, Madeira/Tenerife, Barbados/Grenada, Wilmington/ICW)

Tony Russell (Tenerife/Barbados) (Re-joined from the fuel berth in Ramsgate)

Andrew Walkling (Grenada)

Paula Walkling (Grenada) (Re-joined us at the RTYC bar)

Jen Munns (Wilmington/Eastbourne)

Adamant Sula (Wilmington/Ramsgate)

With the exception of breaking my spinnaker pole, the trip was hassle free and we were soon in sight of Ramsgate having enjoyed some good company and great food along the way in preparation for the liquid refreshments later. On approaching Ramsgate, the first yacht that hove into sight was *Assassin* which thundered up to us turned around for a second pass and then pulled alongside to welcome us home. At this point we had a mad scramble aboard to get the flags of all nations up the masts and soon *Spectra* was resplendent, decked all over with a flag from every country that we had visited on our trip. We were soon joined by *Free Spirit*, *Luna Sea*, *Saje, Stella Maris, Eroica,*

Outlaw, Juniper, Jardice Deux and *Assumpta Anne*, there may well have been more and I sincerely apologise if I have missed you out but, unfortunately, I had something in my eye about then which stopped me seeing too clearly. Soon, we were at the entrance to Ramsgate Harbour and, as the great moment arrived, to finish the trip in style, I unfortunately had something in my throat which made it difficult to speak and so, which was actually quite fitting, Norma called them up on the VHF and asked for permission to come into the Royal Harbour.

"Permission granted and welcome home *Spectra*", came the reply.

With the sound of shouted congratulations and the odd fog horn from the quayside ringing in our ears we stopped to pick my son Tony up from the fuel berth and were soon in our new berth within the inner marina where the party could begin in earnest.

I really can't do justice to the lovely people that we know in Ramsgate and so many of you came down to the harbour or joined us later in the club that it all became a bit of a blur to be honest. To all of you from Norma and myself, "thank you so much for taking such an interest in our little adventure and I hope you have enjoyed "sharing our dream".

It was, of course, also Norma's 50th birthday and, in true style, that was not forgotten at the Club where a birthday cake, complete with candles, was produced from behind the bar. I'm not quite sure who organised that but thank you.

24th Jul 2015

The day after the night before

That's it, our journey is over and this is my last entry.

We started out on the 30th August 2014 with the simple plan to circumnavigate the North Atlantic following the trade wind route, a trip that is well trodden and many have gone before. Along the way we have been supported by a wonderful group of friends, who I hope have also enjoyed sailing with us. Back in Ramsgate our support team, Tommy and Sue Foster, have been the rock to which we have been able to anchor ourselves, every time they joined us or wrote us an email we were restocked with news and supplies from home. No request for help was ever too much of a problem, and they came up trumps every time. If you want to do a trip like this I would strongly recommend that you get yourself a Tommy and Sue, they are great!

It has not always been fun, what journey of this magnitude ever is, but we have returned with wonderful memories and as a couple we are closer than before. Credit where credit is due, Norma has made this trip the success it has been, and that is a statement that should be set in stone. There is absolutely no way that we would have met such an interesting and eclectic group of people on our travels if it wasn't for Norma's outgoing, bubbly nature. I mentioned earlier in the blogs how she always managed to collect the nice people in every harbour or anchorage and bring them back for me to talk to. She also became the radio operator of choice and the first point of contact with officialdom, which probably kept me out of prison. Most of all, she put up with me and probably has the mental scars to prove it, for that she deserves a medal. Strangely enough, before embarking, I was worried about weather, piracy, bureaucracy, and navigation; what actually caused the most grief was power production. Our original generator caused me spasmodic periods of mental anguish all of the way from the Cape Verde Islands to the Bahamas where it finally died, and I actually started enjoying the trip again. Note to self, and for your information, if you are planning a trip of this magnitude get alternative sources of power production as a priority, be it wind, solar or even a backup generator, you just can't have enough sources of power on board. Going back to a more basic lifestyle and even getting back to nature is so much easier with a cold beer in the fridge and an electric fan cooling you down. Trust me, I know. The places we visited were varied and, for the most part, both interesting, beautiful and welcoming. The people we met were almost exclusively friendly, interested in us, honest and have, as a whole, made the trip the success that it was.

In summary we travelled a total of 12,759 miles and visited the following countries in order:

France
Guernsey
Spain
Portugal
Madeira
Salvage Islands
Tenerife
Cape Verdes
Barbados
Grenada
Carriacau
Union Island
Mayreau
Canouan
Bequia
St Lucia
Martinique
Dominica
Ile de Saints
Guadaloupe
Antigua
Montserrat
St Kitts
Eustacia
St Maarten
St Martin

Anguilla
British Virgin Islands
US Virgin Islands
Spanish Virgin Islands
Puerto Rico
Turks and Caicos
Bahamas
United States, (ICW Florida, Georgia, South Carolina, North Carolina)
Bermuda
Flores, Azores
Horta, Azores
UK

If you have been paying attention and reading the blogs you will remember that blog number one was based around my daughter's wedding in Slovenia; where else would you start a sailing odyssey other than a land locked country in central Europe? It seemed fitting, somehow, to start our journey around the Atlantic with an article about Gemma and Duncan starting their journey through life together and I think that idea worked. As our adventure progressed, life back home took a sad turn, whilst we were passing down the coast of Africa we received the sad news that our dear friend Joanne had lost her battle with cancer and likewise as we arrived in Brixham we received the equally sad news that Jim, our brother-in-law, had also lost his battle with cancer. As each day ends the next starts with a new dawn and, like our journey, life moves in circles which has resulted in us finishing our circuit with a new beginning. Little Martha, our granddaughter, entered the world at 5am on the 12th July 2015 while we were sitting in Weymouth harbour. She is fit healthy and has already started her own journey in life. Who knows what adventures, triumphs, joys and sorrows lie in store for her, but one thing is for certain, Norma, myself and *Spectra* will play a part in it.

As a final note, and a final thank you, I must mention the most important member of the team and that is our lovely boat *Spectra*. It is as simple as this, we love our boat, she is wonderful, beautiful, safe and definitely has a personality all of her own. Everywhere we go she elicits comments from the very British; "Good, solid craft that, old boy" to the full on American; "Wow!! get outta here!!! "That is one good looking boat you have got yourself there Captain", to the very precious moment when a Portuguese fisherman went out of his way to paddle across a harbour entrance just to say, "I like your boat I hope you can come here again". What is more *Spectra* has carried and protected us for the last year without major fuss or drama, Peter summed up life aboard perfectly when he wrote:

"The living conditions, whilst not luxurious, are first class and it is a joy to be part of the adventure".

If you look up *Spectra* in the dictionary it means 'Everything' which sums up our relationship rather well I think. Her name is also an anagram for "carpets", as pointed out by Stuart Carter when we first arrived in Ramsgate back in 2010, and she has truly been the magic carpet that has transported us on our adventures. With all this gushy emotion about a boat it will be no surprise for you to hear that both Norma and I always give her a cuddle when she is lifted out of the water, and why not? If you don't love your boat what's the point of owning it, I say. Go buy a Winnebago or a garden shed. Caravans are an amalgamation of fibre glass, cloth, wood, plastic and metal. Boats are so much more than a simple sum of their parts, they have character, and *Spectra* has lots of character. Our lovely boat is now resting in Ramsgate inner marina and I suspect she is a lot keener and certainly more capable of heading out again, than her crew are. She is still our home and she is getting a rest whether she needs it or not, we all deserve one.

I hope you have enjoyed sharing this journey with us and we would both like to thank you all for "sharing the dream".

Until next time, *Spectra* out!

What is this life if, full of care,
We have no time to stand and stare.
No time to stand beneath the boughs
And stare as long as sheep or cows.

> *No time to see, when woods we pass,*
> *Where squirrels hide their nuts in grass.*
> *No time to see, in broad daylight,*
> *Streams full of stars, like skies at night.*
> *No time to turn at Beauty's glance,*
> *And watch her feet, how they can dance.*
> *No time to wait till her mouth can*
> *Enrich that smile her eyes began.*
> *A poor life this if, full of care,*
> *We have no time to stand and stare.*

William Henry Davies

And a final note of thanks to all of our crew who "shared the dream" at various stages of the journey. Whether you were on board for days, weeks or months you all added your selves to the mix and together we made a rather good cake, so thank you all.

In order of appearance, Steve, Andy and Sarah, Peter, Tommy and Sue, Tony, Steve (again), Tommy and Sue (again), Andrew and Paula, Mike and Kate (travelling along with us), Duncan, Gemma Lily and Martha, Sue and Tommy (again), Jen, Adamant, Steve (again), Willem.

And an extra big, big, thank you to Paula and Sue who both made valiant if sometimes unsuccessful attempts to turn my scribbles into legible prose.